Language and Meaning in the Age of Modernism

For P. W.

Language and Meaning in the Age of Modernism

C. K. Ogden and his Contemporaries

James McElvenny

EDINBURGH
University Press

Edinburgh University Press is one of the leading university presses in the UK.
We publish academic books and journals in our selected subject areas across the
humanities and social sciences, combining cutting-edge scholarship with high editorial
and production values to produce academic works of lasting importance. For more
information visit our website: edinburghuniversitypress.com

Edinburgh University Press Ltd
The Tun – Holyrood Road
12(2f) Jackson's Entry
Edinburgh EH8 8PJ

First published in hardback by Edinburgh University Press 2018

Typeset in 10/12 Ehrhardt by
Servis Filmsetting Ltd, Stockport, Cheshire
and printed and bound by CPI Group (UK) Ltd
Croydon, CR0 4YY

A CIP record for this book is available from the British Library

ISBN 978-1-4744-2503-2 (hardback)
ISBN 978-1-4744-2506-3 (paperback)
ISBN 978-1-4744-2504-9 (webready PDF)
ISBN 978-1-4744-2505-6 (epub)

Contents

Figures

Acknowledgements

Over the years in which this book has taken shape I have received instruction, support and assistance from numerous people and institutions. First among these is of course Nick Riemer, who supervised the doctoral dissertation on which this book is based. Without his guidance and, above all, the freedom he afforded me in my research, it would not have been possible for me to explore the topics and themes presented in this book.

For inducting me into the world of interlinguistics, I must thank the Gesellschaft für Interlinguistik, and Sabine Fiedler and the late Detlev Blanke, who invited me to join it. For their invaluable feedback on earlier versions of the text contained in this book, I thank Anders Ahlqvist, A. W. Carus, Arwen Cross, W. Terrence Gordon, John E. Joseph, Piers Kelly and Friedrich Stadler. The current version of the text as appears in these pages was carefully copy-edited by Geraldine Lyons, whom I also thank.

The modern-day incarnation of the Gesellschafts- und Wirtschaftsmuseum in Vienna kindly granted me permission to reproduce Figure 4.1 as well as the illustration used on the cover, both of which are drawn from their 1930 *Gesellschaft und Wirtschaft*. Figures 2.1 and 2.3 are reproduced by permission of Taylor and Francis Books UK, which asserts international copyright over C. K. Ogden and I. A. Richards' *The Meaning of Meaning*, originally published in 1923 by Kegan Paul.

Chapter 1

Introduction

> In novels, Utopias, essays, films, pamphlets, the antithesis crops up, always more or less the same. On the one side science, order, progress, internationalism, aeroplanes, steel, concrete, hygiene: on the other side war, nationalism, religion, monarchy, peasants, Greek professors, poets, horses. History as he sees it is a series of victories won by the scientific man over the romantic man. (Orwell 1968 [1941]: 142)

Written during the most hopeless days of the Second World War, this is George Orwell's (1903–1950) summary of the main themes in the writings of H. G. Wells (1866–1946). The faith in science and technology to effect progress for humanity that Orwell identified in Wells is the same sentiment that drives the efforts recounted in these pages, efforts to tame language, pin it down, bring it under the control of science and engineer it anew for the benefit of humanity. These efforts we explore from the perspective of the English scholar C. K. Ogden (1889–1957) – the C and K stand for 'Charles' and 'Kay' respectively, but he preferred to be known just as 'C. K.' – whose various projects span from the first decade of the twentieth century to the end of the Second World War, years typically identified with the age of modernism.

It is fitting that we open with Wells and Orwell. Not only did both serve, as we will see, as literary interpreters of Ogden's later work, but they also delineate our age. Each of them stands at one end of the era and of the cultural arc that begins with optimism and ends with disillusionment: Wells at the hopeful beginning and Orwell at the troubled and sober end. This is the arc of the age of modernism. 'Modernism', as every text that invokes it must observe, is a nebulous term, conjuring up various fashions and associations. The general character of modernism as a socio-historical category is well known and hardly needs to be rehearsed here. Nevertheless, the very breadth of the category necessitates some explicit attempt to delineate its contours, which are discernible also in the specific ideas and events we recount in this book.

A prominent feature of the age of modernism, and a key aspect for us, is technology. In this period, technology was often praised as the driver of progress, but the unprecedented change it brought was associated with tumult, revolution and the resulting human catastrophes that marred the age. Within a single lifetime, the transport and communication networks of the world – driven by inventions perfected in the nineteenth century: railways, steamships and the electric telegraph and telephone – were expanded and consolidated to the point that every part of the globe could be reached with unprecedented ease. With the turn of the twentieth century advances in radio technology (Guglielmo Marconi's first practical demonstrations were made in England in 1897) and powered flight (the Wright brothers' first flight was in Kitty Hawk, North Carolina, in 1903) extended this reach into the ether and air. Enumeration of these advances and the inspiration they offer is a mainstay of the rhetoric employed by the figures that appear in these pages.

Concomitant with these technological advances was rapid social change around the world. Mass political movements were formed – depending on the region – by landless lower middle classes, industrial workers and women, and through such political movements these oppressed groups asserted their rights. This brought about the expansion of voting franchises and, in some cases, full-blown revolution, such as the decisive 1917 October Revolution in Russia, and the uprisings in Germany and the Habsburg Empire after the First World War. Outside Europe – but by no means independently of events on that continent – political and social upheavals occurred in the Ottoman Empire, Persia, China and Mexico.

The major turning point within Europe, and to varying degrees beyond, was the First World War, the first war in human history to draw most of the globe into simultaneous hostilities. It saw death and destruction on a scale never before known, facilitated by technological marvels of the same kind that had so visibly accelerated humanity's progress. The events that followed in Europe and the wider western world, the Great Depression of the 1930s, the polarisation of politics in Central Europe and Russia, the rise of totalitarian dictatorships, and the eventual total war that began in 1939 and continued for six years, levelling cities and killing millions with bombers, rockets and, of course, the atomic bomb, complete the cycle. These later catastrophes, and the extremist high-flown rhetoric and actions that fuelled them, are the source of the disillusionment with which we are left at the end of our period.

Crisis and revolution were not confined to technology and the social world. Natural science – which frequently, but not invariably, both learnt from and informed technological advance – was wracked by revolutions as it annexed ever more of the world to its descriptive and explanatory sovereignty. The classic example here is of course physics. Einstein's theories of special and then general relativity – published 1905 and 1915, with full absorption into mainstream physics over the following years – not only eventually served to provide an alternative explanation that rendered the postulation of the recently conquered ether obsolete, but also broke down the old objective certainties of Newtonian physics and made them relative to the observer. Research into atoms, which proved through the possibility of their decomposition that they had been prematurely baptised, led to the development of quantum theory in the 1920s, made up of numerous attempts to capture the unpredictability of the subatomic realm.

The revolutionary advances made in the natural sciences, often intertwined with technological breakthroughs and social consequences, inspired thinkers in traditionally book-bound, human-focused fields. The frequent invocation of 'science' and 'scientific' methods that we will encounter in the treatments of language and meaning examined in this book attest to the importance attributed to the natural sciences as the source of rigorous and valid knowledge.

Similarly, in modernist art and literature old paradigms were overturned. Here we can recite the names of the numerous schools that rejected traditional measures of technique and representation: the Impressionists, the Cubists, the Dadaists. This last group of course made an art out of deliberately shocking the public out of their complacency, a task they felt compelled to undertake after witnessing the horrors of the First World War. Similar experiments with form and themes, all driven by the wish to 'make it new', as Ezra Pound famously put it, typify European literature in this period. These classical manifestations of cultural modernism appear only on the periphery of the research presented here but, as we will see, they were sparked and fanned by the same events and fashions, and exhibit the same features as the modernist approaches to language that we treat.

The central concern of Ogden and his contemporaries was the problem of 'meaning' in language, a term that eludes simple definition at least as much, if not even more, than 'modernism'. To all those engaged in fashioning 'scientific' theories of meaning in our period the problematic status of this term quickly became apparent. Opening his contribution to a debate on 'the meaning of "meaning"' in 1920, the Anglo-German philosopher Ferdinand Canning Scott Schiller (1864–1937), whom we meet properly in the coming chapters, observed how the notion is even quite peculiarly English and therefore perhaps culturally restricted:

> Greek [. . .] is so defective that it can hardly be said to have a vocabulary for the notion [of meaning] at all: it has to rely entirely on periphrases, and gets no nearer to saying 'it means nothing' than declaring that 'it *says* nothing'. Latin is a little better; it has coined the notions of '*significance*' and '*sense*' as aids to the expression of the missing word, and passes them on to the languages descended from, or influenced by, itself. But '*significatio*' is clearly a late and learned word for a special *intensity* of meaning, while '*sensus*' is a manifest misnomer. Meaning belongs to a much higher level of mental development than sense-perception. Latin notices also the volitional factor in meaning by employing periphrases with *volo* and *valeo*, and these, too, have had a prosperous career. It is only in the Teutonic languages that a specific, antique, and genuinely native vocabulary is found for the notion of 'meaning'. The root 'mean' appears to be common to all of them. In German, however, it has suffered serious degeneration. 'Meinung' has become 'opinion', though 'meinen' may still, in a context, translate 'mean'. The result is that German is nearly as badly off as the Latin tongues in expressing 'meaning'. 'Bedeutung' is 'significance' or 'interpretation' rather than meaning; 'unmeaning' is 'sinnlos', 'what does that mean?' is 'was soll das *heissen*?' or

'besagen', *i.e.* properly 'what is it *to be called?* or to *'declare'*. It would seem then that 'meaning' usually baffles language: English alone has a full and specific vocabulary for it [. . .]. (Schiller, Russell and Joachim 1920: 385–386; emphasis original)

The first step taken then in making meaning subject to science was typically either to define the word strictly, generally much more narrowly than in colloquial usage, or to abolish it altogether, replacing it with a variety of alternative technical terms. The first course was that taken by Victoria Lady Welby (1837–1912), a major influence on the young Ogden, who identified 'meaning' as just one aspect of the use of signs, the intention the creator of a sign has in producing it, which exists alongside its 'sense' and 'significance', a theory that we explore in more detail in the next chapter.

At a much later point in our story, after the main lines of contention in the debate had been established and schools of thought had become more clearly delineated, the English philosopher Alfred Jules Ayer (1910–1989) expressed the opinion that had become characteristic of logicians and logically inclined philosophers when he asserted that 'one should avoid saying that philosophy is concerned with the meaning of symbols, because the ambiguity of "meaning" leads the undiscerning critic to judge the result of a philosophical enquiry by a criterion which is not applicable to it' (Ayer 1946 [1936]: 69). Ogden, in his most comprehensive statement on the issue, the 1923 book *The Meaning of Meaning*, co-authored with his friend and colleague Ivor Armstrong Richards (1893–1979), embraced this point in even greater detail. The term 'meaning' found no technical use in their 'science of Symbolism'; they went on to treat the term using the methods they developed within their theory to reveal that no less, and possibly more, than sixteen definitions could be given for the various senses it takes on.

This book is structured around case studies of three stations in the life of Ogden. Through these we see the interwoven networks that bound him to his contemporaries, and how their ideas and practical efforts were all inevitably shaped by the broader intellectual, social and political concerns of the times. We look first, in Chapter 2, at Ogden and Richards' early philosophy of language, as presented in *The Meaning of Meaning*, and the Cambridge environment in which it was incubated. In Chapter 3, we then turn to Ogden's next major project, Basic English, which not only represented an application of Ogden's theoretical views to a practical end, but was also a contribution to the vibrant contemporary international language movement, which sought to establish a single language for international communication. Finally, in Chapter 4, we look at the later contact between Ogden and the philosophers Otto Neurath (1882–1945) and Rudolf Carnap (1891–1970) of the Vienna Circle. We see how Ogden and Neurath's views came into alignment through their resulting collaboration, and observe the characteristic conclusion of our period in the common fate of Ogden and his Viennese counterparts. Chapter 5, the Epilogue, concludes our investigation and examines the role the figures, events and ideas we describe played in shaping aspects of the treatment of meaning among linguists, the present-day pretenders to the scientific study of language.

This book is intended as a contribution to the history of ideas, a form of scholarship that is at its best when it reaches over disciplinary boundaries. Disciplinary subdivision entails a narrowing of focus onto a circumscribed subject matter, to be dealt with using a limited range of recognised conceptual tools. While this may be a desirable prerequisite for efficient co-operation between scholars working on a defined task – as in Kuhnian (1962) 'normal science' – there is also enormous value in being conscious of the bigger picture that lies beyond the limits of any one discipline. In looking at treatments of language and meaning in the early twentieth century, this book examines ideas and figures that are claimed by such present-day disciplines as analytic philosophy, semiotics, linguistics, and also the much less well established field of 'interlinguistics', the study of international auxiliary languages.

A common charge levelled at present-day analytic philosophers is a disregard, or even dislike, of history (cf. chapter 4 of Glock 2008), and the same charge could very well be levelled at many linguists. Despite this, both fields possess a vast historiography; this is also true of semiotics, and even of the much smaller field of interlinguistics. For the most part, no attempt is made in this book to overthrow existing interpretations in these historiographic traditions; rather, these traditions inform the account given here. Although numerous previously unknown or very poorly-known details come to light in the course of our exposition and discussion, the chief novelty and value of this book lies in the way it complements existing accounts to paint a broader picture of the various ideas examined. The amalgamation of different historiographic traditions and exploration of the broader social and political context offered here serve to decompartmentalise existing accounts, and to produce a more integrated historical narrative.

To establish common ground with all readers, no matter what their background, it is in places necessary to summarise key points that are well known in the historiography of some disciplines, but largely unknown in others. Analytic philosophers, for example, will already be familiar with much of the material in the exposition of the logical atomism of Russell and Wittgenstein (Chapter 2, §III), and of the protocol sentence debate within the Vienna Circle (Chapter 4, §III). Likewise, semioticians will know about Ogden and Richards' views in *The Meaning of Meaning* (Chapter 2, §I–II) and Welby's work (Chapter 2, §V). Interlinguists will recognise the main points in the history of the international language movement (Chapter 3, §II–III), and linguists, too, will know of some of the figures that appear there. The links that appear in the course of this exposition and discussion will, however, be new to most readers: up until now these topics have been isolated islands of knowledge.

It might be wondered why we have taken Ogden as the protagonist in a narrative aimed at elucidating this intellectual era: despite his best efforts and his often rather inflated rhetoric, he remained a relatively minor player in many of the events we recount. However, although Ogden may have proved to be no 'Great Man', he stood at the intersection of many of the most notable figures in the period, many of whom are still remembered today for the foundational role they played in defining the limits and parameters of investigation into language and meaning. Already in his undergraduate days at Cambridge, Ogden was in close contact with Welby, as well as Russell, and their influence is visible in *The Meaning of Meaning*. His project Basic inserted him into the international language movement, and his personal contact with Carnap and, even more so, his collaboration with Neurath, connects him with the logical positivists of the Vienna Circle. By exploring Ogden's many connections to significant players of the time, and seeing how their ideas are reflected in his work, we can acquire a broader and more representative picture of the age than would be possible through the investigation of a single prominent figure.

In looking at these connections, and positing lines of influence, preference has been given to cases where there was personal contact between individuals. This is partly a matter of evidence: the surviving published and unpublished documents – speeches, papers, personal accounts and letters – provide a record of the events and personalities of the time. Without these, the historian's work would simply be speculation. Intuitive knowledge of people and the social groups in which they live would also suggest that the people who are in the closest personal contact have the greatest influence on one other, whether that influence leads to a convergence of ideas or a repulsion to opposite poles on an issue. This is not only a theory of how ideas emerge, it is also a belief in the best way to recount this emergence: a narrative of the interaction of human characters, possessing personalities, their own histories, ideals and goals, offers a more natural and engaging, and perhaps even accurate and truthful, account than a story of disembodied discoveries.

But the personal interaction of thinkers does not exhaust the possibilities for the growth and transmission of ideas, especially in the case of someone as widely read as Ogden, whose intellectual reach was not confined to contemporary thought, but extended to ideas written down long ago, in Britain and Europe, and in lands far away. Throughout this book reference is made to insights Ogden would seem to have drawn from beyond his personal milieu. In many cases, too, there is a sense in which some ideas are simply 'in the air'. In these cases, the most prominent contemporary exponents of the ideas must be taken as their representatives. These occasional excursions into more remote regions of early twentieth century thought lend this book a slightly centrifugal character but, just as following a single established disciplinary history would be excessively constrictive, limiting ourselves to Ogden's biography alone would result in a blinkered view of the period.

Chapter 2

The Meaning of Meaning

By the turn of the nineteenth century to the twentieth, the natural sciences – which have come in the English language to enjoy almost exclusive rights over the designation 'science' – were rapidly discovering and recording the details of the natural world. Wanted was the same power over the world of the peculiarly human, populated by thoughts and ideas. But these are perceptible only through signs, such as words and sentences, which are frequently unfaithful and deceiving representatives. It is this task of subjugating signs to science and bringing order to meaning that Ogden and his main collaborator in his early career, Ivor Armstrong Richards (1893–1979), took up in their book *The Meaning of Meaning* (Ogden and Richards 1989 [1923]), an assault in equal measure on contemporary theorising about language and on the way language itself is used.[1] Their approach they dubbed the 'science of Symbolism', a label designed to declare the doctrine's scientific credentials. It was intended to provide both a suitable theory for the analysis of language and practical methods for overcoming 'word-magic', their term for the superstitious belief in the power of words.

A disaster exacerbated by word-magic looms large in *The Meaning of Meaning*: while gas and machine guns created the physical horror of the First World War, propaganda, just one manifestation of word-magic, contributed to its intellectual horror. First World War propaganda sharpened Ogden's sense for word-magic's dangers and, although the roots of the book go much deeper, it was at the end of the war, on Armistice Day, 11 November 1918, that *The Meaning of Meaning* first started to take concrete shape. The plan for the book, Richards tells us, was worked out on, and as a serendipitous result of, that day. As news of the armistice broke in Cambridge, a mob of angry rioters, incensed by the apparent pacifist stance of Ogden's *The Cambridge Magazine*, ransacked one of his bookshops, where it was sold (see Gordon 1990b: 12–20 for the history of *The Cambridge Magazine*). That evening Ogden approached Richards, whom he had seen across the square where the riot took place, to ask him if he could identify any of the perpetrators. As they spoke, the conversation turned to 'meaning' and several hours later they had outlined their future book and embarked on their collaboration:

After collecting my useless impressions of the rioters, Ogden started off, steadily talking, for Top Hole, his fantastically cluttered attic above Mac-Fisheries in Petty

> Cury. Half-way down the tightly twisting stairs, under an aged, faintly whistling, Bat's Wing gas jet, he stopped to make some remark upon a recent controversy in *Mind*. An hour or two later when we went downstairs, the main outline of *The Meaning of Meaning* was clear enough, and plans for a joint work to embody it were in being. I remember that turn of the stairway and the flickering of the Bat's Wing flame. (Richards 1977: 99)[2]

The final product, Richards (1977: 100) would later say, was a truly collaborative effort, though Ogden 'held the pen' while they jointly composed the text. *The Meaning of Meaning* is triumphant in declaring the validity and originality of the solutions it offers and – although it brims with footnotes reaching out into the web of scholarship from ancient times to the present – the treatment of all other views, whether contrary to or anticipatory of those it contains, is superficial and dismissive. The book was published in Ogden's thirty-fifth year and Richards' thirty-first: they were both, by academic standards, 'young men'. A historian of more advanced years might put the book's brashness down to youthful exuberance, an exuberance that frequently masks its place in its contemporary intellectual setting.[3] But *The Meaning of Meaning* is most certainly a product of its times, in the themes it addresses and the solutions it proposes. The Anglo-Polish anthropologist Bronisław Malinowski (1884–1942), writing in his 'supplement' to the book (Malinowski 1989 [1923]), commented:

> It is remarkable that a number of independent inquirers, Messrs Ogden and Richards, [the neurologist] Dr [Henry] Head, [the philologist] Dr [Alan Henderson] Gardiner and myself, starting from definite and concrete, yet quite different problems, should arrive, if not exactly at the same results stated in the same terminology, at least at the construction of similar Semantic theories based on psychological considerations. (Malinowski 1989 [1923]: 299)

The similar ideas these figures stumbled upon were no doubt 'in the air' – discussed in private and public forums, written down in journals and books – and served to focus attention on a common set of issues with the suggestion of similar solutions. Examining a single monument of the age, such as *The Meaning of Meaning*, however, allows us to identify its particular pedigree and the immediate environment in which it was created. This is the approach we will take in this chapter, treating *The Meaning of Meaning* and its closest relatives.

The material that finds its final form in *The Meaning of Meaning* was written in the Cambridge of the first two decades of the twentieth century. Although Ogden had already declared his devotion to the problem of meaning upon his arrival in Cambridge in 1908 – he came on a classics scholarship to study the topic of the influence of Greek language on Greek thought (see Gordon 1990b: 5) – the intellectual environment of Cambridge could only serve to further incubate this interest. This environment was dominated by Bertrand Russell (1872–1970), who – following the lead of George Edward Moore (1873–1958)

and joined soon by his student Ludwig Wittgenstein (1889–1951) – was revolutionising philosophy through a new radical realist programme centred on a
critique of language, a key step in the evolution of the tradition now known as
'analytic philosophy'.[4] Beyond the university, but still within the same milieu,
Victoria Lady Welby (1837–1912) was approaching the end of her amateur – in
the sense of non-professional – but influential career in the study of meaning,
with her theory of 'significs' which, unlike early analytic philosophy, analysed
expressions not for the meaning they contained but looked to how they were
interpreted.

Richards, too, was exposed, albeit in a slightly different measure, to these
influences: coming as an undergraduate to Cambridge in 1911, he began by
reading history but – concluding after one semester of wading through the
suffering and cruelty of the past that 'history ought not to have happened'
(Richards, quoted in Russo 1989: 35) – switched to philosophy, after being
decisively swayed by Ogden (see Russo 1989: 35–36). As we see in the following
discussion, *The Meaning of Meaning* is essentially a synthesis of the two parallel
streams flowing through Cambridge, personified by Russell and Welby.

I. The many functions of language

The Meaning of Meaning contains both a theoretical account of the nature of
language and meaning, and a practical method for taming meaning in language.
The basis of the theoretical account is a belief in language as an instrument with
many purposes. From the very outset of the book, Ogden and Richards postu-
late a multifunctional model of language, with a primary division between the
'symbolic', or referential, function, and the 'emotive' functions, a collection of
what would now be considered various pragmatic and attitudinal aspects. But
the referential use always has priority: it is not only the first to be explicated
– and the only function to receive a truly comprehensive exposition – but it is
also considered crucial for the 'reflective, intellectual use of language' (Ogden
and Richards 1989 [1923]: 10), the key to modern discourse. Reference may not
exhaust meaning, and in non-intellectual contexts or in more 'primitive' societies it may be only a subordinate function, but for the modern thinkers of the
civilised world, for whose benefit Ogden and Richards' 'science of Symbolism'
was chiefly conceived, it is of utmost importance:

> The reference of a symbol [. . .] is only one of a number of terms which are relevant
> to the form of a symbol. It is not even the dominant factor in most cases [. . .] None
> the less, since, for all our finer dealings with things not immediately present – *i.e.*, not
> in very close and simple contexts with our present experience – since for all our more
> complicated or refined reference we need supports and distinguishing marks, this
> strictly symbolic function of words easily becomes more important than any other.
> (Ogden and Richards 1989 [1923]: 233)

The model they develop for the symbolic function is introduced in the first pages of their book with the 'Triangle of Reference', shown in Figure 2.1, a diagram that has gone on to achieve iconic status in twentieth century semiotics.

Each of the points in the triangle represents an entity assumed to be involved in an act of reference; the sides in turn illustrate the relations between these entities. A 'symbol', a word or any other type of sign, evokes a 'thought or reference', an idea or 'image' in the mind of the listener or perceiver of the sign, which is then directed to a 'referent', some entity or object in the world.

Ogden and Richards do not restrict their account to the purely linguistic, but rather embed it in contemporary behaviourist approaches to psychology by describing the process in terms of 'engrams', a notion proposed by the Lamarckian evolutionary biologist Richard Semon (1859–1918) (Ogden and Richards 1989 [1923]: 52 acknowledge the source of this term in Semon 1921 [1904]). An engram is a mental impression of the relation between two entities in the world formed after repeatedly observing their co-occurrence. This can be any stimulus-response pairing in any organism, such as a person's expectation of seeing a flame after striking a match, a chicken's avoidance of yellow striped caterpillars after eating one and discovering it tastes bad, or a dog's prompt arrival at the dining table on hearing the dinner bell (Ogden and Richards 1989 [1923]: 52–53, 55–56). In the same way, repeated occurrences of a word in the

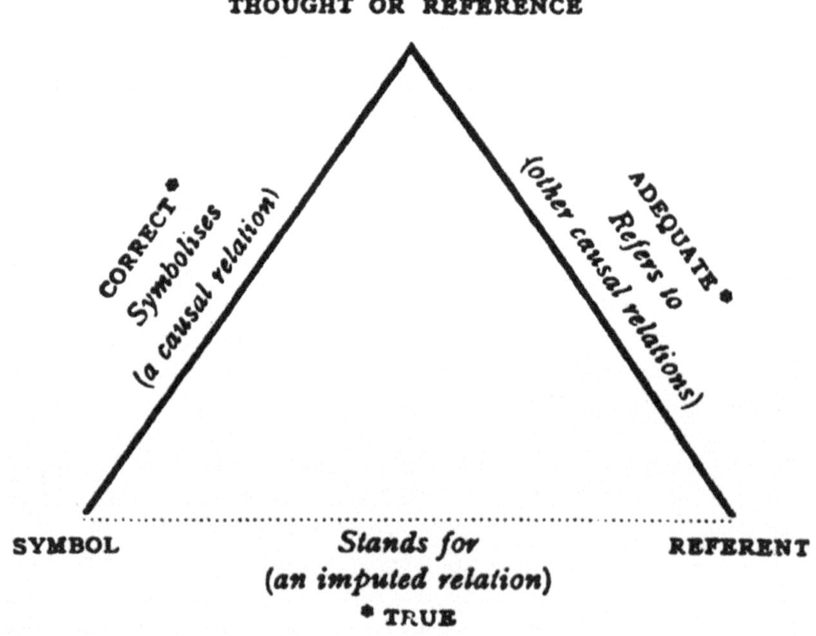

Figure 2.1 The Triangle of Reference
Ogden and Richards 1989 [1923]: 11.

presence of its referent lead to the development of a link, the 'thought or reference', that connects them. In fact, Ogden and Richards (1989 [1923]: 63) argue that all cognition is a matter of recursive inferences and interpretations that start with the impressions formed from direct sensations.

As is their fashion, Ogden and Richards do not wish to align themselves too closely with others scholars' work and seek to put some ironic distance between themselves and Semon when they introduce his term:

> Attempts to provide this account [of the process of Interpretation] have been given in many different vocabularies [. . .] The most recent form in which the account appears is that adopted by Semon, the novelty of whose vocabulary seems to have attracted attention once more to considerations which were no doubt too familiar to be thought of any importance. (Ogden and Richards 1989 [1923]: 51)

Despite this distancing, they employ 'engram' and 'mnemic causation', Semon's name for the underlying process that supposedly gives rise to engrams, throughout their book when expounding their own theory.

The moral Ogden and Richards intend to be taken away from their triangular model of reference is that there is no direct connection between the symbol and its referent. The relation between them is rather 'imputed', as the dotted base of the triangle and its caption tell us. For any act of reference to succeed, it must first pass through the intermediate step of 'thought or reference' (Ogden and Richards 1989 [1923]: 9–12). Failure to recognise this intermediate step results in 'word-magic', here the superstitious belief that for every word there is a corresponding entity in the world. This superstition, they claim, plagues modern philosophers, logicians and grammarians just as much as 'primitive' people, as the cascade of examples that makes up most of chapter 2 of *The Meaning of Meaning* demonstrates. They rhapsodise:

> [W]ords may come between us and our objects in countless subtle ways, if we do not realize the nature of their power. In logic, as we have seen, they lead to the creation of bogus entities, the universals, properties and so forth [. . .] By concentrating attention on themselves, words encourage the futile study of forms which has done so much to discredit Grammar; by the excitement which they provoke through their emotive force, discussion is for the most part rendered sterile; by the various types of Verbomania and Graphomania, the satisfaction of naming is realized, and the sense of personal power factitiously enhanced. (Ogden and Richards 1989 [1923]: 45)

The Triangle of Reference is intended to explode word-magic by highlighting the mediating role of thoughts, severing the direct link between words and objects. Ogden and Richards go on to further fortify language against word-magic through guidelines for clean references and methods for achieving clarity (which we take up below in §II).

But referring to the world does not exhaust the uses of language: symbols are also used to convey the speaker's 'attitude, mood, interest, purpose, desire, and so forth' (Ogden and Richards 1989 [1923]: 223). In addition to the 'symbol situation' of the Triangle of Reference, where a sign stands as the mark of a reference, there is the 'verbal sign-situation', where the sign reflects the internal state of the speaker (Ogden and Richards 1989 [1923]: 223–224). These two 'situations' cause the primary functional division in language, between the symbolic use and the emotive use of language (the latter they also call 'evocative', Ogden and Richards 1989 [1923]: 239 *et passim*). Providing a more finely grained breakdown of these two uses, Ogden and Richards enumerate a total of five 'functions' that language can perform:

> (i) Symbolization of reference;
> (ii) The expression of attitude to listener;
> (iii) The expression of attitude to referent;
> (iv) The promotion of effects intended;
> (v) Support of reference. (Ogden and Richards 1989 [1923]: 226–227)

Function (i), 'symbolization of reference', stands alone as the symbolic function, in which language has a solely referential use; the four remaining functions together constitute the emotive functions, where language reflects the speaker's emotional and attitudinal states and, in the case of 'promotion of effect intended', can manipulate the listener's emotions for a particular reaction (Ogden and Richards 1989 [1923]: 157–159, 223–224). All functions may play a role in shaping linguistic form, but the significance of their role varies with the type of discourse: in scientific discourse the symbolic function is primary and all other functions should be eliminated as much as possible to avoid bringing extraneous concerns into what should be an exchange of direct, referential statements. On the other side, exclamations, oaths and greetings have no symbolic content at all; they are purely emotive. Commands and threats similarly put more emphasis on the emotive than on the symbolic. Commands must at least refer to some action that can be performed properly, but threats do not have to make such references (Ogden and Richards 1989 [1923]: 234–235).

Despite Ogden and Richards' repeated assertion that all functions are important in language, only the symbolic function receives detailed examination in *The Meaning of Meaning*, through the Triangle of Reference model; the other, 'emotive' functions are largely neglected. This differential treatment continued to characterise Ogden's work: his next major linguistic project, the international language Basic English (see Chapter 3), pursued very much the goal of purifying language to its scientific, 'symbolic' essentials. But Richards followed a slightly different course. In the years following the publication of *The Meaning of Meaning*, he went on to develop fuller accounts of the emotive functions in a number of books on literary criticism (e.g. Richards 1926 [1924], 1926, 1930), and later explicitly stated that he did not want his early work to be interpreted as a defence of 'scientism' (see Richards 1948: 151, note 31), the idolisation of natural science as the sole source of knowledge. While he acknowledged both the importance of science and its intellectual autonomy, he was careful to maintain that there are provinces of knowledge and experience beyond it:

> To declare Science autonomous is very different from subordinating all our activities to it. It is merely to assert that so far as any body of references is undistorted it belongs to Science. It is not in the least to assert that no references may be distorted if advantage can thereby be gained. And just as there are innumerable human activities which require undistorted references if they are to be satisfied, so there are innumerable other human activities not less important which equally require distorted references or, more plainly, fictions. (Richards 1926 [1924]: 266)[5]

But the emotive functions continued to evade precise analysis in Richards' subsequent works. Although Ogden and Richards (1989 [1923]: 227–228) had cautiously claimed exhaustiveness for their list of functions – or at the very least that the list contains the absolute minimum of functions – Richards kept tinkering with it. In Richards (1930) he eliminated the fifth function, which was then reinstated in modified form in Richards (1936: 50); in later years he expanded the list of functions to six, seven and finally eight (see Russo 1989: 137). When asked in a lecture 'around 1970' why the number of functions had increased, he is said to have replied that there is nothing magical about the number of functions, and that there may be 'as many functions as one likes provided each is given its specific work within the context' (as reported in Russo 1989: 137). This enduring imprecision was not a failing in Richards' eyes: emotive language, he came to believe, is not amenable to the strict parameterised account that he and Ogden had developed for the symbolic function. The best way to study the emotive function is to amass examples of interpretations, the goal Richards pursued in his books on literary criticism (see Richards 1948).

In *The Meaning of Meaning*, by contrast, the only elaboration the emotive functions receive is their enumeration and brief explanation. The most clearly 'emotive' of these are (ii) and (iii), the 'expression of attitude to listener' and 'to referent' respectively, pertaining, as they do, to emotional or attitudinal aspects of an utterance: in this case, to the stance that the speaker has towards their audience or interlocutor, or to the object of their reference. Typical attitudes that a speaker may take to their listener include amity, hostility, courtesy and respect (Ogden and Richards 1989 [1923]: 224–225), a set that confirms a common-sense interpretation of this function. We are given no examples of possible attitudes to a referent, the implication perhaps being that they are parallel to those that can be held towards the listener.

With function (iv), the 'promotion of effects intended', the emotive function strays away from direct expressions of attitude and towards utterances calculated to achieve specific ends in the world. This function, they insist, is distinct from function (ii), 'the expression of attitude to a listener', since a range of very different motives may drive a speaker to seek a certain end, so the speaker's attitude may be very different from that which they appear to hold on a superficial interpretation. In their somewhat tasteless example, a speaker may encourage their interlocutor to commit suicide not, as might first be thought, out of 'dislike of his personal characteristics', but out of 'benevolent interest in his career' (Ogden and Richards 1989 [1923]: 225). These two very different attitudes to the listener could stand behind utterances aimed at the same effect.

Function (v), the 'support of reference', is perhaps the most obscure and difficult to assimilate to the whole system. About this function they say that 'references have a character which may be called, from the accompanying feelings, Ease or Difficulty' (Ogden and Richards 1989 [1923]: 225). Their illustration of this function comes through the following example:

> The two symbols, "I seem to remember ascending Mount Everest," and "I went up Everest," *may*, on occasion, *stand for* no difference in reference and thus owe their dissimilarity solely to degrees of difficulty in recalling this uncommon experience. On the other hand this may, of course, be a real symbolic difference which does not merely *indicate* difference of difficulty but *states* it. (Ogden and Richards 1989 [1923]: 225–226; emphasis original)[6]

It would seem that they take the relative complexity of the two sentences as marking a difference in the difficulty of recalling the referent, in this case the memory of climbing Mount Everest. Function (v), they insist, is not concerned with 'certainty or doubt' or 'degree of belief or disbelief' that the speaker attaches to the reference (Ogden and Richards 1989 [1923]: 226), aspects that could be assimilated to the modern conception of evidentiality, and which they would treat under function (iii), 'attitude towards the referent'. Function (v) reflects specifically the difficulty in recalling memories, a seemingly strange inclusion in the paradigm of emotive functions, which are otherwise concerned with expressions of attitude or deliberate pragmatic effects. Richards' later elimination of this function may be an indication that he was conscious of its oddness. When it briefly reappeared, in Richards (1936: 50), it became 'the confidence I have in the soundness of the remark', which sounds much more like evidentiality (cf. Hotopf 1965: 29, note 2).

Language, under Ogden and Richards' conception, is a device with many functions, grouped into the two unequal categories 'symbolic' and 'emotive', whose inequality is revealed by their uneven treatment. Although Richards alone went on to make amends in later works, in *The Meaning of Meaning*, as we have seen, it is only the symbolic function that receives proper elaboration; the emotive functions are left as a list of seemingly miscellaneous linguistic devices that express emotional attitudes, reach for certain pragmatic ends, or reflect the difficulty of mental processes. As Richards would later argue, this apparent miscellaneous character and fluidity could be an inherent property: the emotive functions do not lend themselves to the kind of rigorous analysis to which the symbolic function can be subjected.

In *The Meaning of Meaning*, however, Ogden and Richards not only suggest that the emotive functions operate in parallel fashion to the symbolic function, but also allow for them to be realised in symbolic terms, suggesting that an analysis of the emotive functions in symbolic terms ought to be possible. The referential use of language, and its abuse in word-magic, remain however the focus of *The Meaning of Meaning*. With their descriptive framework in place, they turned to combating word-magic through a combination of referential hygiene and methods for clarifying reference.

II. Definition and the canons of symbolism

'We ought to regard communication as a difficult matter', write Ogden and Richards (1989 [1923]: 123), 'and close correspondence of reference for different thinkers as a comparatively rare event'. To help safely navigate these perilous regions where word-magic dwells and secure reliable references in discourse they offered their method of definition, a technique for making references more precise and more likely to correspond for the speaker and their interlocutors. Definition rests in turn on their 'Canons of Symbolism', a set of ground rules whose observance guarantees honest and valid references.

The method of definition is a means for 'expanding' a symbol so that it reflects the 'thought or reference' it stands for more clearly and, preferably, more analytically. But a definition has no priority over the term it replaces: it is simply an alternative to the original expression, a better alternative, but not necessarily a scientifically valid decomposition that exposes the true parts and structure of the referent (cf. the later debate, in which Ogden was involved, about different forms of analysis, in Chapter 4, §II). Such definitions may be possible, they argue, but:

> [. . .] this process [of scientific classification] is only possible with complex objects which have been long studied by some science. With simple objects, or those which for lack of investigation are not known to be analysable, as well as with everything to which classificatory methods have not yet been applied, such a method is clearly not available, and here other symbols must be found as the substitutes which symbol-definition seeks to provide. (Ogden and Richards 1989 [1923]: 110)

Their definitions are merely provisional paraphrases of the original symbol negotiated between the participants in a discourse through a dialectical process. To ensure a successful definition it is necessary to have a shared starting point and a clear route to reach the reference: 'It is never safe to assume that it [correspondence of reference for different thinkers] has been secured unless both the starting-points and the routes of definition, whereby the referent of at least a majority of the symbols employed have been reached, are known' (Ogden and Richards 1989 [1923]: 123). These starting points are best sought 'outside the speech situation'; they should be 'things, that is, which we can point to or experience' (Ogden and Richards 1989 [1923]: 115). Here we see a faith in ostension and the concrete objects of the external world as anchors for meaning, a faith that was common to their philosophical contemporaries and which would develop into an emphasis on the 'pictured' in Ogden's Basic English (see below §III; Chapter 3, §V and §VI; Chapter 4, §III).

After introducing their method of definition, Ogden and Richards (chapters 7–9 of 1989 [1923]) demonstrate its application and efficacy in defining the contentious and primarily emotive term 'beauty', and the quarry of their book, 'meaning'. Both terms, they find, have a range of senses (see the tables in Ogden and Richards 1989 [1923]: 142–143, 186–187), used by different people in different contexts. This laying out of the range of interpretative possibilities Richards pursued further in his later work, developing it into 'multiple definition', a technique he used to explore the range of interpretations in cases where large differences in background between author and reader lead to potentially extreme misunderstandings. This is the technique used in Richards (1932) to explicate in English the works of the classical Chinese philosopher Mencius. Ogden, by contrast, moved away from examining the possibilities of interpretation, and instead became interested in more or less laying down fixed paraphrases to capture concepts in Basic English (see Chapter 3, §V).

The bedrock on which definition is built is made up of the 'Canons of Symbolism', which 'allow us to perform with safety those transformations and substitutions of symbols by which scientific language endeavours to reflect and record its distinctions and conclusions – those operations which [. . .] appeared to primitive man to partake of the nature of magic' (Ogden and Richards 1989 [1923]: 108). These Canons are the rules, six in number, which must be followed in constructing references to ensure that they efficiently and unambiguously take all participants in a discourse to the right referents:

> (i) One Symbol stands for one and only one Referent.
> (ii) Symbols that can be substituted one for another symbolise the same reference.
> (iii) The referent of a contracted symbol is the referent of that symbol expanded.
> (iv) A symbol refers to what it is actually used to refer to; not necessarily to what it ought in good usage, or is intended by an interpreter, or is intended by the user to refer to.
> (v) No complex symbol may contain constituent symbols which claim the same 'place.'
> (vi) All possible referents together form an order, such that every referent has one place only in that order. (Ogden and Richards 1989 [1923]: 88–106)

Canon (i) establishes the basic principle of unambiguous communication, that there should be a unique and exclusive relation between the symbol and its referent (Ogden and Richards 1989 [1923]: 88–91), the central point of their scheme on which all the following canons essentially elaborate. Two of the three 'subterfuges' that they (Ogden and Richards 1989 [1923]: 132–134) identify – common 'tricks' that people use to obfuscate references, with or without intent to deceive – are violations of this first canon. The 'Phonetic subterfuge', the abuse of homonyms, involves using two symbols with the same form but different referents, all the while claiming that the referents are the same. An alleged example of this abuse is English philosopher John Stuart Mill's (1806–1873) treatment of the *-able* in *desirable* as being the same as that in *knowable* or *visible*. In the latter two words, it carries a sense of possibility, 'able to be', argue Ogden and Richards (1989 [1923]: 133), while in *desirable* its sense is more deontic, 'ought to be'.[7] The 'Utraquistic subterfuge', the misuse of polysemous terms, occurs when a speaker moves freely among the many referents that a single symbol may have, such as when a speaker says *knowledge* and means variously, but without due recognition, that which is known and the act of knowing it.

Canon (ii) provides the foundation for the process of definition: it establishes the principle that interchangeable symbols have identical references, an essential requirement for definition, which involves the swapping out of referentially equivalent symbols (Ogden and Richards 1989 [1923]: 91–92). Canon (iii) then introduces the other requirement for definition, the notions of 'contracted symbol' and 'expanded symbol', by which they (Ogden and Richards 1989 [1923]: 92–103) mean less and more specific terms. An 'expanded symbol' goes to a more detailed 'level of interpretation' than its 'contracted' counterpart, as when the contracted term 'that animal' is substituted with the more expanded 'that lynx'. This is how definition functions: a more specific term, in the current discourse context, is substituted for a more general term. This more specific term, as in the case of 'animal' and 'lynx', need not offer an analysis but, as they make clear in their discussion, an analytic paraphrase is preferable to one that is merely more specific but perhaps equally opaque. The root of their third subterfuge, the 'Hypostatic subterfuge', lies in taking a contracted symbol as referring to individual real entities, the mistake that philosophers make in proposing the existence of classes and universal qualities (Ogden and Richards 1989 [1923]: 95, 133–134):

> In this way universal "qualities" arise, phantoms due to the refractive power of the linguistic medium; these must not be treated as part of the furniture of the universe, but are useful as symbolic accessories enabling us to economize our speech material. Universal "relations" arise in a precisely similar fashion, and offer a similar temptation. They may be regarded in the same way as symbolic conveniences. (Ogden and Richards 1989 [1923]: 96)

With Canon (iv) they give a direct warning against the creation of such entities from symbols (Ogden and Richards 1989 [1923]: 103–105). A symbol, according to Canon (iv), can refer only to what it actually refers to, regardless of whether this is the referent the speaker intended, how the interpreter understood it, or what good usage in the speech community would dictate. If the speaker mistakenly says 'My pipe is alight' when it is in fact out, there is no referent. It cannot be claimed that the symbol actually refers to the sensation the speaker had that made them mistakenly think the pipe was alight.[8]

In Canons (v) and (vi) Ogden and Richards (1989 [1923]: 105–107) extend the principle of a unique and unambiguous relation between symbol and referent to apply within 'complex' symbols, that is, symbols with multiple parts. These parts, by Canon (v), may not cover the same referent as the whole complex symbol and, by Canon (vi), each of the parts must not overlap with any of the others. Canon (vi) they see as an equivalent within the science of symbolism to Aristotle's laws of thought, the axioms that lie at the foundation of traditional scholastic logic. Each of these laws, they argue, can be reinterpreted as a kind of connection between symbol and referent covered by Canon (vi):

> For symbolism they [Aristotle's laws of thought] become a triad of minor Canons which help to keep the Cathedral of Symbolism in due order. First comes the Law of Identity – quaintly formulated as 'A is A'; a symbol is what it is; *i.e., Every symbol has a referent*. The second is the Law of Contradiction – 'A is not not-A'; no symbol refers to what it does not refer to; *i.e., No referent has more than one place in the whole order of referents*. The third is the Law of Excluded Middle – 'A is either B or not B'; a symbol must have a given referent or some other; *i.e., Every referent has a fixed place in the whole order of referents*. (Ogden and Richards 1989 [1923]: 105–106)

In the exposition of these six Canons we encounter Ogden and Richards' continual overt mention of the problems and failings of logicians and philosophers, and it is at these parties that their account, with its overarching interest in *reference*, was aimed: these are the people they saw pushing, and at times exceeding, the boundaries of our 'reflective, intellectual use of language'. But Ogden and Richards were not alone in their critique of contemporary philosophy: a new language-critical current was forming in Cambridge, led by Russell and Wittgenstein, and with these two Ogden and Richards shared a point of departure and elements of the solution to the problems they identified. But in their treatment of definition in living discourse, Ogden and Richards also brought in influences from a parallel tradition, the incipient stages of modern semiotics, as represented in the work of Welby. We now turn to these two traditions and Ogden and Richards' contact with them.

III. Logical atomism and its allies

Cambridge, in the first two decades of the twentieth century, was home to some of the most exciting developments in logic and philosophical analysis, and it was here in these years that Ogden and Richards began, as impressionable undergraduates, the studies that would induct them into contemporary debates in philosophy and logic. One of the brightest stars in the Cambridge firmament was Bertrand Russell, known not only for his work that was revolutionising the philosophy of mathematics, but also for his outspoken support of progressive political causes, in particular women's suffrage and opposition to the First World War (see Russell 1959, 1967–1969; Monk 1996, 2000). In 1911 Russell was joined by Ludwig Wittgenstein, who in the following years took Russell's philosophical programme to its uncompromising conclusion, and reigned, often unwillingly and not without dissent from his subjects, as the sovereign in a personal union between the intellectual kingdoms of Cambridge and Vienna, the two centres of the new scientific, language-critical philosophy in the 1920s and 30s (see Chapter 4, §I; McGuinness 1979; Monk 1990; Stadler 1997: 918–919).

Ogden came into association with both Russell and Wittgenstein, and under their influence. Richards, too, knew and received instruction from these thinkers, although his relationship to them never reached the degree of intimacy and mutual significance of Ogden's. Russell and Wittgenstein, as the leading proponents of the new logical methods and personal acquaintances of Ogden and Richards, played a key role in defining their position with respect to the logical tradition's treatment of meaning. *The Meaning of Meaning* can be seen to a large extent as a reflection of, and at times a reaction against, Russell and Wittgenstein's two different but closely related theories of 'logical atomism'.

That Russell and Wittgenstein should loom so large in Ogden's consciousness should be no source of surprise, given the strength of their ties. Ogden's connection to Russell was the closest, bound by many threads, both intellectual and political: as founding member and president of the 'Heretics' discussion society (see below §V; Gordon 1990b: 5–8) and editor of *The Cambridge Magazine*, Ogden constantly pursued Russell to have him talk and write in these forums. Ogden and Russell were also both active in the women's suffrage and pacifist movements. It was at a meeting between Russell and Ogden where such matters were being discussed that Wittgenstein first burst onto the stage. The scene is passed down to us as an evocative vignette, written by Russell that night in a letter to Lady Ottoline Morrell (1873–1938), his 'lady friend' at the time:

> I got home at 4.30. I had just read your letter and made my tea when Ogden (Secretary of the Heretics) came to say Chesterton is speaking the night of my P.S.F. [People's Suffrage Federation] Meeting – this raised a lot of complicated problems, which we were in the middle of when an unknown German appeared, speaking very little English but refusing to speak German. He turned out to be a man who had learnt engineering at Charlottenburg, but during his course had acquired, by himself, a passion for the philosophy of mathematics, and has now come to Cambridge on purpose to hear me. This took till 5.15; in the next few minutes I settled my business with Ogden, and then went off to my lecture, where I found my German duly established. I lectured very well, owing to excitement and insufficient preparation. I am much interested by my German, and shall hope to see a lot of him. Ogden has undertaken to do P.S.F. work for me, which is a *very* great relief. (Bertrand Russell to Ottoline Morrell, 18 October 1911; letter reproduced in full in Griffin 1992: 397–399, no. 179)[9]

Wittgenstein, an Austrian, not a German, as Russell would discover in time, had come on the advice of the German mathematician Gottlob Frege (1848–1925) (see Monk 1990: 36), inventor of a new logical formalism, the *Begriffsschrift* ('conceptual notation'; Frege 1972 [1879]), which provided much inspiration to Russell. Although his pupillage had a rocky start, by the beginning of 1912, when Wittgenstein handed Russell a manuscript he had prepared over Christmas, Russell became convinced of his genius and adopted him as his protégé (Monk 1990: 41), a role that he soon outgrew. Russell (1926 [1914]: 9) was commenting shortly after on the benefits he had received from the 'vitally important discoveries' in 'pure logic' made by 'my friend Mr Ludwig Wittgenstein'. Russell later described his 1918 lectures – which, as we will see, influenced *The Meaning of Meaning* – as being 'very largely concerned with explaining certain ideas which I have learnt from my friend and former pupil Ludwig Wittgenstein' (Russell 1918–1919: 160).

When Wittgenstein's views finally solidified into a publishable text, which eventually received the title *Tractatus Logico-Philosophicus*, Ogden was instrumental in bringing it to the world. As an editor at Kegan Paul publishers, Ogden oversaw the publication of Wittgenstein's book in 1922 in a German and English edition.[10] In the same role and in the same period, his relationship to Russell became symbiotic: Ogden needed new books to sell, and Russell, whose name had become a byword for erudition and genius, and who was a gifted and prolific writer, was in need of money (Monk 2000: 24). The result was a series of popular philosophy and science books written by Russell, edited by Ogden and published by Kegan Paul. The relationship was further solidified by Russell's romantic involvement and subsequent marriage to one of Ogden's closest friends, Dora Russell (née Black; 1894–1986). At one point Ogden was even executor of their wills (Dora Russell 1977: 82–95).

Russell began as a mathematician but turned, after his final undergraduate examinations, to philosophy (Russell 1959: 38; cf. Grattan-Guinness 2000: 269–270). The turn of the nineteenth to the twentieth century was an exciting time for a mathematician with philosophical inclinations like Russell: the debate over the foundations of mathematics, the search for the basic principles of the discipline and their justification, was gaining momentum (see Grattan-Guinness 2000). Russell, after hearing Giuseppe Peano (1858–1932), the Italian mathematician (and international language constructor; see Chapter 3, §II–III), speak at the International Congress of Philosophy in Paris 1900, was converted to the 'logicist' camp, which sought the foundations of mathematics in logic: all mathematics could be reduced to arithmetic, and this in turn to logic.[11] This led Russell to a direct engagement with logic, and the problems of meaning attached to these new logical formalisms.

By the 1920s Russell's philosophy, which he had in the meantime named 'logical atomism', had grown from purely logical concerns to address questions in metaphysics, epistemology and psychology (see Russell 1926 [1914], 1918–1919, 1921, 1924, 1959: chapter 2). Although he claimed only to have become interested in language after 1918 (Russell 1959: 145; cf. Monk 1997: 39), the formal innovations leading to logical atomism all exhibit a linguistic character, and these occurred around the turn of the century and the years immediately following (see Russell 1959: 13–14, 63–64 for a chronology). Like Ogden and Richards, Russell saw many of the central problems in philosophy as stemming from a slavish acceptance of the terms in natural language we use to describe the world, a view quite obviously akin to 'word-magic'.

One of the key innovations of the new logical notations of Frege and Peano that Russell further developed was an escape from the structure of syllogism to a logic of relations that allowed predicates with multiple arguments. This new logic Russell used against the 'monistic' varieties of idealism dominant during the time of his philosophical education in Cambridge, which maintain that the entire world is made up of a single unified entity, a view epitomised by Francis H. Bradley's (1846–1924) notion of 'the Absolute' (see Bradley 1893). This monism hangs from the doctrine of internal relations, which postulates that what appear to be relations between separate entities in the world are really just internal properties of the single whole (cf. Griffin 1991: 326–27 and §8.2, which complicates Russell's account).

Russell's rejection of the doctrine of internal relations sprang into possibility with the realisation that it was not a logical necessity, but a linguistic illusion (see Russell 1959: 54–62 for the story, and Russell 1903: 222–226, 1906–1907: 28–49 for the arguments). The form of the syllogism, the defining structure of traditional western logic, realised Russell, is merely an abstraction from the grammar of Greek and other European languages. The subject-predicate mould of sentences in these languages leads the logician to conceive of their logic in the same way: a maximum of one entity with one property predicated of it per proposition. Enslavement to language pushes the thinker into a rut; only a superior formalism that recognises a plurality of entities and the possibility of multiple relations between them can rescue the logician and bring them to a better representation of the world:

> The influence of language on philosophy has, I believe, been profound and almost unrecognized. If we are not to be misled by this influence, it is necessary to become conscious of it, and to ask ourselves deliberately how far it is legitimate. The subject-predicate logic, with the substance-attribute metaphysic, are a case in point. It is doubtful whether either would have been invented by a people speaking a non-Aryan language; certainly they do not seem to have arisen in China, except in connection with Buddhism, which brought an Indian philosophy with it. (Russell 1918–1919: 38, see also Russell 1921: 212)

The 'monistic metaphysic' is a product of Indo-European syntax; it can be cured by developing a logic of relations. The vocabulary of a language can be just as misleading: we seem to suppose that words name objects in the world and, when we find no object to correspond to a word, we have to invent it. This, claimed Russell (1918–1919: 38–39), is the origin of those entities that populate the Platonic world of forms. It is not only Russell's critique of language that is echoed in *The Meaning of Meaning*, but also the solution he proposed: to escape the influence of the ordinary language and the misconceptions it creates, we must do away with our everyday expressions and find others that say precisely what they mean. The classic example of this approach is Russell's 'theory of descriptions', which made its first public appearance in his 1905 essay 'On denoting' (Russell 1905), with further refinements and formal elaboration in the following years (Russell 1910–1911; Whitehead and Russell 1950 [1910–1913]: chapter 3).

The crux of the theory of descriptions is embodied in Russell's signature propositions 'The present King of France is bald' and 'Scott was the author of *Waverley*', each of which in its ordinary form presents a logical puzzle. In the first proposition we face the problem that there is no present King of France to which we can apply the predicate. We could argue that the proposition is simply meaningless, but Russell preferred to call it false: a fastidious logician, Russell wanted to recognise only propositions that are either true or false and nothing else. He proposed a paraphrase that lays bare the logical structure of the proposition and thereby shows why it is false.

Russell's (1905: 497) paraphrases are anchored in a distinction between 'knowledge by acquaintance' and 'knowledge by description': we are acquainted only with what we can perceive directly and everything else we know only by description. In his later elaboration of logical atomism, it is only the evidence of the senses, so-called 'sense-data' that we know by acquaintance, and all other entities are 'logical constructions' that we make from these according to the laws of logic, which we know only by our descriptions (see Russell 1926 [1914]: chapter 3). 'The present King of France', in the terms of Russell's later elaborated theory, is a logical construction, and the uttering of this expression assumes his existence. If we replace the expression with a logical analysis, the fact that it asserts the existence of the construction will be apparent; we recognise that this assertion is false and that, as a consequence, the entire proposition is false (Russell 1905: 488; for a modern exposition, see Soames 2003: chapter 5).

In the case of Russell's second proposition, 'Scott was the author of *Waverley*', the puzzle is how this sentence is informative: if 'Scott' and 'the author of *Waverley*' are simply labels that point to entities in the world and they point to the same entity, we might ask how our knowledge is furthered to be told that they are equivalent. Here again analysis provides the answer: 'Scott' is indeed simply a label, but 'the author of *Waverley*' is a complex description that both asserts the existence of an entity and points it out. The proposition therefore tells us that the label 'Scott' can be applied to the existent entity that is the author of *Waverley*.[12]

Ogden and Richards' definitions are clearly akin to Russell's descriptions. Both are aimed at the rectification of names through paraphrase. Laying bare the underlying structure of ideas, which may be concealed by the language they are habitually expressed in, was likewise a motivation for Frege in creating his *Begriffsschrift*:[13]

If it is a task of philosophy to break the power of the word over the human mind, uncovering illusions which through the use of language almost unavoidably arise concerning the relations of concepts, freeing thought from that which only the nature of the linguistic means of expression attaches to it, then my "conceptual notation", further developed for these purposes, can become a useful tool for philosophers. (Frege 1972 [1879]: 106)

While Russell may have newly popularised the need to establish correct connections between name and object in Cambridge and beyond, this issue has a long tradition in the empirically rooted philosophy of the English-speaking world. An early and influential figure in this regard is the English Enlightenment philosopher John Locke (1632–1704) (see Book III of Locke 1975 [1690]). The formulation of correct names also concerned many of Locke's contemporaries who, although they may not have agreed with his assumptions and methods, pursued a similar course. Chief among these are John Wilkins (1614–1672) and Gottfried Wilhelm Leibniz (1646–1716), whose constructed language projects aimed in part at creating philosophically sound linguistic expressions, and which may have provided inspiration to Ogden in designing Basic English (see chapters 3, 7 and 8 of Knowlson 1975 for a wider context).

Russell, too, was familiar with Leibniz's work in this area, even authoring a monograph-length exposition of Leibniz's *œuvre* (Russell 1937 [1900]). Although highly critical of Leibniz's idealistic metaphysics, which entailed a strictly syllogistic logic and a belief that all knowledge is ultimately deducible without empirical input (see Russell 1937 [1900]: 169–171, 1959: 61), Russell was clearly impressed by the autonomy Leibniz accorded to logical notation. Echoing Leibniz's faith in a notation that could reveal incontrovertible truths – when a dispute arises, Leibniz (Gerhardt 1890: 125, English translation from Maat 2004: 303) says, 'it will no longer be necessary to deal with the matter by screaming, but one can say to the other: let's calculate' (cf. Chapter 3, §I) – Russell sought a 'logically perfect language', which would sweep away the confounding form of our ordinary language and replace it with its true *logical* form (Frege 1972 [1882]: 90–91, in his *Begriffsschrift*, also looked to the example set by Leibniz).

Russell's logically perfect language would 'show at a glance the logical structure of the facts asserted or denied', and would offer the user unparalleled clarity of thought, 'for a good notation has a subtlety and suggestiveness which at times make it seem almost like a live teacher. Notational irregularities are often the first sign of philosophical errors, and a perfect notation would be a substitute for thought' (Russell in his introduction to Wittgenstein 1922: xvii–xviii). Russell saw the theory of descriptions and its later elaborations as the first step towards this language.

But whereas Russell's descriptions aimed to be a logically valid paraphrase of an expression, Ogden and Richards claimed no ontological priority for their definitions. Ogden and Richards (1989 [1923]: 253–255) were in fact highly critical of the suggestion that there could be ultimate descriptions that somehow directly correspond to facts in the world, a position explicitly taken by Wittgenstein in his own version of logical atomism (see props. 2.1–2.225 of Wittgenstein 1922). Their definitions were intended to be better than existing expressions, it is true, but only because they are more effective in the particular communicative context in which they appear. This is a guiding principle of the semiotic tradition (see §V below and Chapter 4, §II).

The psychological theory on which Russell built his logical atomism also shares a kinship with the psychological foundation Ogden and Richards sought for their 'science of Symbolism' (cf. Wolf 1988; Gordon 2006: 2584–2585). Russell's 'sense-data', as the external, observable elements of experience, emulate a line popularised at the time by behaviourist psychologists. The behaviourists claimed unassailable 'scientific' status for their doctrines with their appeals to observable, empirically verifiable data only and banishment of all supposition of mental goings-on. The scientific psychologist, according to the behaviourist, refers only to the 'stimuli' that animals and humans – which are simply 'higher' animals – receive and their 'responses'. Thoughts, memories, consciousness are considered phenomenological phantoms, unacceptable in a scientifically rigorous psychology. Russell (e.g. 1921: 26) cited favourably John B. Watson (1914), the intellectual leader of the behaviourists, but he still accorded a place for mental 'images', mental occurrences not caused by immediate sense-data, and remained critical of Watson for not permitting these in his analyses (see Russell 1919: 10–11, 22, 1921: chapter 8; cf. Russell 1914).

Ogden and Richards in turn saw the nature of their 'thought or reference' as contrasted with Russell's 'images' as the main point at which their theories differed: 'It is mainly on this point [the use of images] that the view here developed differs from Mr Russell's account of meaning' (Ogden and Richards 1989 [1923]: 62). They were targeting specifically the notion that images are 'revivals or copies of sensory experience' (Ogden and Richards 1989 [1923]: 60). Their 'thoughts or references', by contrast, need not replicate sense-data, but merely direct, in some non-specific way, the interpreter's attention to a referent (see further chapter 3 of Ogden and Richards 1989 [1923]). But this is a minor difference: 'thoughts or references' and 'images' are still fundamentally comparable in that both are some sort of acquired mental reflex of an organism generated as a response to external stimuli.

In later moving closer to orthodox behaviourism, Russell (e.g. 1988 [1926]) retreated from images as necessary methodological posits in explaining meaning, although he remained agnostic about whether or not they do in fact exist in some form. But his images were never wholly incompatible with behaviourism, in that they did not inhabit a separate mental realm. Under his metaphysical doctrine of 'neutral monism', 'mind and matter alike are [. . .] constructed out of a neutral stuff' (Russell 1921: 244): there is therefore no separate plane of mental existence, independent of the material world (see Russell 1921: chapter 15; cf. Russell 1914; cf. also the logical positivists' 'physicalism', discussed in

Chapter 4, §II).[14] Images, argued Russell, using Richard Semon's terminology, act through the process of 'mnemic causation' (Russell, in Schiller, Russell and Joachim 1920: 403; Russell 1921: 145 cites Semon 1921 [1904], 1909).

Like Ogden and Richards later (cf. §I), Russell embraced the full scope of mnemic causation. He did not limit it to linguistic signs, but extended it to all learnt behaviour. A bear made to stand on a hot floor while music is played will learn to dance whenever it hears the music, even in the absence of the heat: for the bear, the music has become the sign of the hot floor, it 'means' the hot floor (Russell in Schiller, Russell and Joachim 1920: 398). Ogden and Richards in fact emulated precisely Russell's respect for the empirical, scientific spirit of behaviourism while at the same time rejecting behaviourists' zealous enforcement of this spirit to the point of denying consciousness, a stance they took in their own assessments of Watson's work (e.g. Ogden 1926: chapter 10, 1927a; Richards 1926 [1924], 1973 [1938]: 283; cf. Gordon 2006: 2584–2585). This position finds expression again in Richards' later good-natured poem 'against' *Verbal Behavior* (1957), a book written by his friend, the leading behaviourist Burrhus Frederic Skinner (1904–1990) (see Russo 1989: 175). Since the polemical review of Chomsky (1959), this book has acquired a reputation as the incarnation of behaviourist excesses in linguistic theorising (see Chapter 5, §I).

Ogden and Richards' philosophy of language in *The Meaning of Meaning* bears, in its circumscription of the problem and its proposed solutions, the unmistakable marks of the linguistic and epistemological doctrines that grew out of Russell and Wittgenstein's logical atomism. The psychology Ogden and Richards drew on in grounding their model of reference is precisely that used by Russell in his own model. Their method of definition answered to Russell's theory of descriptions: both offer a way to sweep aside the confusions of language and reach for a reference. But Ogden and Richards' approach was pragmatic in a way that Russell and Wittgenstein's was not: their definitions did not necessarily uncover underlying structures; they were merely conveniences of communication. This emphasis on interpretation, and clarifying interpretation, is perhaps a consequence of another tradition in which they stand, the semiotic tradition, to which Ogden was personally connected through the figure of Welby. But before we come to this tradition, we will take a closer look at the inspiration Ogden and Richards drew from logicians in their Triangle of Reference.

IV. The trigonometry of reference

The positing of three terms to account for the relation of words to their referents was a commonplace of logicians' treatments of meaning in this period: between word and referent the American logician and semiotician Charles Sanders Peirce (1839–1914) (e.g. Peirce 1984 [1867]: 53–54) had his 'interpretant', Frege (1984 [1892]; see also note 13) his 'sense' and Russell his 'image' (see §III). Ogden and Richards' 'thought or reference' fulfilled a similar role in their theory. Like Russell's 'image', their 'thought or reference' could claim impeccable scientific credentials, secured as it was in the same psychological framework Russell invoked. But this three-term model is not original to any of these thinkers; it has a lineage extending back to ancient Greek thought. The specific triangular representation that Ogden and Richards postulated also has clear antecedents in contemporary scholarship.

The invocation of thoughts or impressions to mediate the relation between verbal signs and their referents is found in Aristotle (384–322 BC). He proposed a linear model with four terms – external things, impressions on the soul, spoken signs and written signs – in which each term depends on that preceding it. The Aristotelian model was rediscovered by medieval scholastic logic and, from there, carried into the modern age. Commenting specifically on Ogden and Richards' Triangle of Reference, Ullmann (1962: 56) observes: 'There is nothing fundamentally new in this analysis of meaning; the mediaeval school-men already knew that "vox significat mediantibus conceptibus" (the word signifies through the medium of concepts)' (see also John Lyons 1963:1–2; Padley 1976: 162; Gordon 2006: 2581).

In his private correspondence with Ogden in 1930, Richards himself commented: 'Rather startled to find in a Stoneyhurst [*sic*] book on theories of knowledge by Father Walker that our causal theory is very nearly the official scholastic one. Lucky we didn't know it in those days, or we'd have changed it all' (Richards to Ogden, 30 October 1930, quoted in volume 3 of Gordon 1994: xxii, note 16).[15] It would seem that Richards, at least, was not consciously aware of the scholastic theory when they wrote *The Meaning of Meaning*, although it does not tell us whether the trained classicist Ogden knew of it or not. Of course, none of this rules out the possibility that both Ogden and Richards could have simply absorbed the scholastic model during the course of their education as an unquestioned fundamental assumption.

A more recent antecedent for the precise trigonometry of Ogden and Richards' model can be found, however, in the work of the Austrian philosopher Heinrich Gomperz (1873–1943). At the centre of his *Semasiologie* – a term widely used in German at the time for sign theories, especially in their semantic aspect (see chapter 2 of Nerlich 1992) – was a semiotic model Gomperz illustrated with the *Schema* in Figure 2.2.

The resemblance of Gomperz's *Schema* to the Triangle of Reference goes beyond the merely superficial: both triangles represent very similar semiotic models. The outer triangle of Gomperz's diagram is in fact directly comparable to Ogden and Richards': Gomperz's *Aussagelaute*, the 'sprachliche Form' (linguistic form), matches Ogden and Richards' *symbol*; the *Aussageinhalt*, the 'Sinn der Aussage' (sense of the proposition), corresponds to the *thought or reference*; and the *Aussagegrundlage*, 'jene Tatsache, auf die sich die Aussage bezieht' (that actual fact that the *Aussage* relates to), is equivalent to the *referent*. The relations between each of these elements recall those between the entities in Ogden and Richards' model: the *Aussage* is the *Ausdruck* (expression) of the *Aussageinhalt*, which is in turn the *Auffassung* (interpretation) of the *Aussagegrundlage* (see

Figure 2.2 Gomperz's *Schema*
Gomperz 1908: 77.

Gomperz 1908: 61).[16] In the same way, Ogden and Richards' *symbol* causes the *thought or reference* to be brought to mind, which in turn causes the *referent* to be identified.

The 'secondary elements', those at the base of Gomperz's inner triangle, find no place in Ogden and Richards' model, however: the *Aussage* (proposition), which is a 'whole' consisting of the *Aussagelaute* and the *Aussageinhalt*, and the *Sachverhalt* (state of affairs), a 'complex' made up of the *Aussageinhalt* and the *Aussagegrundlage*. This expansion into primary and secondary elements allows for a differentiation of two semiotic levels, the primary *Bezeichnung* (signification), the relation between the *Aussagelaute* and the *Aussagegrundlage*, and the secondary *Bedeutung* (meaning), the relation between the abstract *Aussage* and the *Sachverhalt* (Gomperz 1908: 61–62, 76–77; see also Seiler 1991).

Gomperz's introduction of the *Aussage*, a complex element combining linguistic form and its accompanying concept recalls the notion of 'linguistic sign' as it is generally accepted among present day linguists and semioticians. In these circles the concept is attributed in its current formulation to the Swiss linguist Ferdinand de Saussure (1857–1913) (see Saussure 1983 [1916]: 65–67, 110–111) who, at the same time Gomperz was writing, was espousing this notion to his students in his course in general linguists in Geneva. Not part of Gomperz's account but central to Saussure's, however, is the idea of *value*, the notion that the possible range signs cover, in both their formal and semantic aspects, is mutually defined by each sign's relation to all other signs (see Saussure 1983 [1916]: 112–120).

The overarching ideas Gomperz and Saussure share in common were indubitably arrived at independently but via a common heritage: Gomperz (1908:

79–91) traced a long and complex genealogy for his ideas, going back to Aristotle and Plato, with many points of transmission and innovation in between; Joseph (2012: chapter 3) finds a similar background for Saussure's thoughts on the sign. This complex internal structure of the sign, of course, finds no place in Ogden and Richards' account, and in fact they criticised Saussure for including 'the process of interpretation [. . .] by definition in the sign!' (Ogden and Richards 1989 [1923]: 5, note 2). In defining the sign itself as a two-sided entity consisting of the signifying linguistic form and its signified meaning, they argued, Saussure posits fixed relations between words and meanings, an alleged failing that their model, with its separation of 'symbol' and 'thought', linked through experience, aimed to avoid. In his later work, Gomperz himself dispensed with his inner triangle and dealt with meaning on a single level (see Seiler 1994: 41).

Ogden and Richards were aware of Gomperz's model and its geometry: they in fact summarised it in Appendix D of *The Meaning of Meaning* (Ogden and Richards 1989 [1923]: 274–277), where they offered a survey of modern approaches to meaning. But they did not reproduce Gomperz's *Schema*, and they claimed as their source not Gomperz's original work, but a summary in Dittrich (1913). In the presentation of their own Triangle of Reference, they made no acknowledgement of any debt they might owe to Gomperz or inspiration they may have drawn from him, although later commentators have pointed it out in passing (e.g. Stern 1931: 37; Gordon 1982: 59; Seiler 1991: 102–103, 1994: 41; Nerlich 1992: 250–251). The Triangle of Reference appears much less novel than it might at first seem when it is put into its immediate context, and the broader context of the long European tradition of which it is a part.

V. Significs and sympathisers

While Russell and like-minded philosophers sought to tame meaning by extending the precise and rigorous formalisms of logic into wider domains, other thinkers approached this end by examining the functioning of signs themselves. Chief among these was Victoria Lady Welby who, through her theory of 'significs', explored the process of interpretation.[17] Despite never having any official standing in academic life, Welby maintained many informal contacts with some of the most renowned scholars of her time, some of whom promoted her work more widely. With a letter from Ogden in November 1910, his third undergraduate year, began a short but intense period of personal contact between Ogden and Welby, which continued until Welby's death in March 1912. During this time, she inducted him into her thought, and he became a champion of the significs cause. This early enthusiasm for significs leaves its mark in *The Meaning of Meaning*: though not as visible as Russell and Wittgenstein's logical atomism, Welby's theory permeates the book and lies behind its fundamentally interpretative treatment of signs.

As a woman whose life extends, at its beginning and end, just beyond the boundaries of the Victorian period, Welby was subject to the subordinate role imposed on her sex in public and her access to academic life was restricted. But through her privileged social position and perhaps as a result of her unconventional upbringing, she developed an interest in the philosophy of language that she was able to exercise through her network of scholarly contacts, an achievement she shared with only a small number of other women in that era.[18] Welby's privileged social position came by birth: like Russell, she was a member of the English high aristocracy, god-daughter of Queen Victoria, in whose honour she was named and in whose court she served as Maid of Honour. Her unconventional upbringing came through spending her formative years travelling the world with her mother between 1844, the year of her father's death, and 1855, when her mother died on the road to Beirut.

After fulfilling her womanly duties of marriage and raising children, Welby threw herself into her philosophical studies and soon built up a circle of correspondents and discussion partners (see Schmitz 1985a; Petrilli 2009). Some were enthusiastic supporters of her work and others not. Notable members of the former camp include Peirce, whose correspondence with Welby was in his later years one of his few intellectual outlets (the correspondence is published in Hardwick 1977), and the English idealist philosopher George Frederick Stout (1860–1944), who taught both Moore and Russell at Cambridge, and who not only encouraged Welby to publish her ideas in the philosophical journal *Mind*, which he edited, but also co-authored a paper with her (Welby, Stout and Baldwin 1902). In the latter camp are such scholars as the French philologist Michel Bréal (1832–1915) (see Auroux and Delasalle 1990) – coiner of the term *sémantique*, which became in English 'semantics' – and Russell himself (Schmitz 1985a: clvii–clxiii, 1995; see §V).[19] Her detractors would eventually gain the upper hand: after her death, Welby's work disappeared into relative historical obscurity. Only a small band of intellectuals in the Netherlands, the Dutch significs movement, founded by Frederick van Eeden (1860–1932), explicitly understood themselves as carrying on the tradition she established (see Schmitz 1983, 1985a, 1985b; Petrilli 2009: 748–766, 782–796, 829–885; they reappear briefly in Chapter 3, §VII and Chapter 4, §II).

When Ogden approached Welby in 1910 she was at the height of her fame and, it would seem from their correspondence, Ogden was already a keen admirer. Welby, for her part, perhaps conscious that her time was limited (she would die just over a year later), was looking for a young and energetic successor (see Schmitz 1985a: clxxviii–clxxxiv; Gordon 1990a; Petrilli 2009: 731–747, 767–782). Two months after his first letter, in January 1911, Ogden accepted an invitation from Welby to spend three days at her house, filled with conversation and perusal of her library, including her correspondence with noted scholars (Gordon 1990a: 182). Shortly after this first visit, Welby described to Peirce with evident joy her new apprentice and his interest in Peirce's work and her own theory of significs:

> Meanwhile the news that I was anxious to impart to you when I wrote my post-card
> is that I have found you, I think, a disciple at Cambridge. He has been studying with

care all I could show him of your writing on Existential Graphs, and is anxious to see your contribution to the volume of Essays which Prof. Stout is still holding back, in hopes of receiving it. The name of the recruit is C. K. Ogden, and he is at Magdalene College. He enters also with enthusiasm into the possibilities of Significs. (Welby to Peirce, 2 May 1911, in Hardwick 1977: 138–139)

Ogden soon assumed this role of protégé. Around Cambridge he spoke frequently on significs, and began, probably in 1911, to write a manuscript on it, which he may have continued to revise up until 1922, one year before the publication of *The Meaning of Meaning* (see Gordon 1990a: 185–186; Petrilli 2009: 732–736; Ogden 1994 [1911] is a reproduction of a later version of this manuscript). *The Meaning of Meaning* in turn contained what was to remain for many years the most accessible account of Peirce's theory of signs (Ogden and Richards 1989 [1923]: 279–290), based on the correspondence between Welby and Peirce, which Ogden had first seen on his visits to her house.

But in the face of the poor reception his talks encountered in Cambridge (see Gordon 1990a: 181–182), Ogden's publicly avowed enthusiasm for significs soon waned. This may have contributed to the almost complete lack of explicit mention Welby received in Ogden's later writings. Even during the period he publicly supported significs, his relationship to Welby was not without friction: Welby's unwavering Christian belief did not sit well with him, a founding member and president of the Cambridge 'Heretics', a student discussion group whose original purpose was to protest against compulsory student attendance at chapel, and which repeatedly made its opposition to all forms of institutionalised religion known. Welby specifically addressed this issue with Ogden, expressing her dislike of the name 'Heretic', '[f]or the Heretic in the last resort only differs and objects' (Welby to Ogden, 5 May 1911, Petrilli 2009: 776, and quoted p.742). She continued to proclaim the importance of her religious convictions in her correspondence with Ogden: 'As to Religion! That is where I began. I found out that none of us knew where we were or what we were battling for at the very centre of life, *that which ought to focus all our interests and powers*' (Welby to Ogden, 24 December 1910, in Petrilli 2009: 771; emphasis original). Ogden did not back down, however. In a talk on significs, he commented: 'Indeed, all who make any study of the problems of significs must find themselves in agreement with Ellen Key when she says that the most demoralizing factor in European education is Christian Religious instruction' (Ogden 1994 [1911]: 35).[20] This is hardly a conclusion Welby would have endorsed (see further Petrilli 2009: 742–743).

Welby's significs, to the study of which the young Ogden applied himself, was essentially a theory of interpretation, but it was never just that. Growing originally out of Welby's interests in theology and Biblical hermeneutics, it came, like Rusell's logical atomism, to encompass positions in metaphysics and epistemology (see Schmitz 1985a: xxix). Welby saw meaning not just as a property of language, but as part of all human experience. She drew on a broad range of contemporary scholarship, from philosophy and psychology to biology and evolutionary theory, and wove this work into a rather idiosyncratic thesis.[21]

At the centre of significs stands the act of interpretation, which consists in an interpreter assimilating what is said to their own understanding of the world, built up through previous experience and informed by the present context:

> We take his [the author's] words, we take his phrases, we fill them out with that same content as our own, we make him mean precisely what we ourselves mean. And be it noted that it is always what we mean *now*. That this in any way varies from what we meant at some time when, e.g., our attention was differently focussed, rarely enters our heads. (Welby 1985 [1893]: 512–513)

There can therefore, according to Welby, be no 'literal' meaning or 'Plain Meaning'. All language has a metaphorical quality; any expression that is not obviously metaphorical is simply so deeply ingrained that its metaphorical character is no longer noticeable.[22] 'The word "literal" itself', points out Welby (1985 [1893]: 512) cleverly, 'is indeed a case in point. It has rarely, if ever, any reference to writing.' Our inherited language necessarily contains an accumulation of these dead metaphors. Even when we use the most direct, literal language we can muster, we cannot avoid evoking the assumptions and associations fossilised, layer upon layer, in our language:

> We all "compound for sins we are inclined to, By damning those we have no mind to." Thus we are now freely banning as 'superstition' the animistic and mythical beliefs of our forefathers. Yet all the while we retain these very associations in our inherited language, the surface-sense only being altered, and the old associations being unconsciously but coercively called up in the 'subconscious' region whence come the most powerful of our impulses and tendencies, since *there* act not merely the individual but the Race whose tradition he carries. (Welby 1985 [1911]: 29–30; see also Welby 1985 [1893]: 515)

When unnoticed and unappreciated, metaphor can lead to confusion, but it is also the very lifeblood of language and the only means we have to render comprehensible levels of experience and consciousness beyond the immediate. What is required is a mastery of metaphor; we must be conscious of its existence and operation and make it our servant (see Welby 1985 [1911]: 32). The practical method for achieving this mastery is 'translation', where we seek to restate what is said in terms of another view, thereby revealing which points of similarity targeted in a metaphor or analogy are real and which are merely superficial (Welby 1983 [1903]: 287–288, 130–138; 'translation' is first used in manuscripts from 1888, see Schmitz 1985a: xxxvi):

> But there is a method both of discovering, testing, and using analogy (or in some cases homology), the value of which does not yet seem to be recognised; and this may be

> called in an extended sense Translation [. . .] The mere attempt to state one subject in terms of another, to express one set of ideas in those words which seem to belong properly to another, changing only the leading terms, could not fail, if done systematically and critically, both to enlighten us on points of connection or correspondence which have not been suspected, and also, perhaps, to reveal ignorance in some cases where we have taken knowledge for granted. It would automatically sift the superficial and partial from the deep or complex likeness; and it would lead to the recognition of a wide difference between the casual, the merely illustrative analogy, and that which indicated inter-relations not yet recognised and utilised. (Welby 1983 [1903]: 126–128)

The proper application of translation depends on an understanding of the process of interpretation, which, in Welby's final model, consisted of three stages, or levels of 'expression-value': 'sense', 'meaning' and 'significance' (Welby 1983 [1903]: 2–9 *et passim*). Triads occupied a special place in Welby's thought. She wrote her first (unpublished) essay about the triadic nature of the universe in 1886 (reproduced in Petrilli 2009: 177, 331–339), and a triadic model of meaning is found already in Part II of Welby (1985 [1896], e.g. p. 187), but this is not identical to her mature model of 1903. In this final model, 'sense' is the immediate, unreflective response an interpreter has to a sign, 'meaning' the actual sense that the creator of the sign wants to convey, and 'significance' the ultimate effect that the sign has (see Schmitz 1985a; Petrilli 2009: 264–271):

> (*a*) The first of these [levels of 'expression-value'] at the outset would naturally be associated with Sense in its most primitive reference; that is, with the organic response to environment, and with the essentially expressive element in all experience. We ostracize the senseless in speech, and also ask "in what sense" a word is used or a statement may be justified.
> (*b*) But "Sense" is not in itself purpose; whereas that is the main character of the word "Meaning," which is properly reserved for the specific sense which it is *intended to convey*.
> (*c*) As including sense and meaning but transcending them in range, and covering the far-reaching consequence, implication, ultimate result or outcome of some event or experience, the term "Significance" is usefully applied. (Welby 1985 [1911]: 103)

The feeling that Welby's definitions are impressionistic would not be misguided: whether motivated by modesty or a genuine belief that her work was only preliminary, Welby insisted that her terms were not intended to be precise, but simply a stimulus for future, more systematic studies, a point Schmitz (1985a: xciv) highlights, with reference to one of Welby's letters to Peirce:

> You have observed that I have made no attempt at formal definition of the "triad of signification". It seemed better to state it vaguely in as many ways as possible first [. . .] in order that the very inconsistencies, apparent or real, between them, may be sugges-

tive of the need of systematic study, and the rewards that this must bring. (Welby to Peirce, 18 November 1903, in Hardwick 1977: 6–7)

We see also in the framing of her terms that her theory aimed to be much more than simply an account of meaning in language, or even necessarily an account of sign systems as they are typically understood. It was instead an account of how a biological organism responds to its environment, grounded in contemporary biological theory, especially Darwinism (see Petrilli 1999).

It is at this point that her theory took on a mystical character.[23] To each level of expression-value she assigned a level of consciousness. 'Sense', the direct response of an organism to its immediate, earth-bound environment, corresponds to 'planetary' consciousness. In this category belongs all knowledge we acquire from our senses of touch, smell, taste and hearing, as well as ideas we arrive at through inductive and deductive reasoning (Welby 1983 [1903]: 94). 'Meaning' corresponds to 'solar' consciousness. This is a consciousness that comes to us through 'feeling' – we can feel the heat of the sun – and through further reflection on what we have acquired at the 'planetary' level: it 'answers to the scientific activities, made possible by the leisure and protection of civilisation, and stimulated by more and more complex demands upon brainwork' (Welby 1983 [1903]: 96). It is the ability to divine 'meaning' through our 'solar' consciousness that sets humans apart from other living organisms: 'The whole animal "kingdom" (if not also the plant order) shares the sense-world : the advent of the sense of meaning – the highest kind of sense – marks a new departure : it opens the distinctively human era' (Welby 1983 [1903]: 28). Completing the triad is 'cosmic' consciousness, corresponding to 'significance', and coming to us through sight, 'the only sense by which we respond to the sidereal universe' (Welby 1983 [1903]: 30; see also Schmitz 1985a: xciii–cviii).[24]

While the more mystical aspects of Welby's doctrines may not find expression in *The Meaning of Meaning*, her model of interpretation with its three levels of expression-value almost certainly informed Ogden and Richards' functional approach to language. Ogden and Richards' emotive function, in supplying language with what from a present-day perspective would be called a pragmatic dimension, evokes Welby's concerns with effects created by utterances. Indeed, realisation of the multifaceted uses of language and the prototypes of Ogden and Richards' later functions can be found in Ogden's (1994 [1911]) 'Progress of significs' manuscript, providing the missing link between significs and the 'science of Symbolism':

As soon as we can locate the place of words in the Hierarchy of signs – Demonstrative, Expressive, Suggestive, Substitute, Natural, Fixational, Aritificial, Social, and so on, it will be found that words and consequently Language fall into more than one of the groups. And hence we ought not to speak of Language vaguely as a whole [. . .]. (Ogden 1994 [1911]: 23)

Ogden and Richards' method of definition, their remedy for the potential confusions of language, further reveals Welby's enduring influence. Unlike Russell and Wittgenstein, who sought to legislate a new, unambiguous form for language, Welby saw significs as part of a programme of training to cultivate – through such methods as 'translation', which she also called 'definition' (see Petrilli 2009: 560) – awareness of the process of interpretation, all with the goal of improving our communication with one another:

> Significs [. . .] must therefore be considered first as a method of mental training, which, though implied in all true views of education, is not yet practically recognised or systematically applied. In a special sense, it aims at the concentration of intellectual activities on that which we tacitly assume to be the main value of all study, and vaguely call 'meaning.' Its instructive and disciplinary value must be secondary to this, as they are both ultimately dependent upon it. (Welby 1983 [1903]: 83)

Ogden and Richards' method of definition could be seen as a practical implementation of this call. It aimed to sharpen interlocutors' understanding of each other's terms by making them negotiate their meanings; there is no single ideal definition, as there is a single 'description' or 'picture' for Russell and Wittgenstein (see §III). Correspondence may be desirable and achievable in 'scientific symbol systems', but it is not found in ordinary language, which 'los[es] in accuracy but gain[s] in plasticity, facility and convenience', as Ogden and Richards say (1989 [1923]: 254–255).

This approach also has its prototype in Ogden's (1994 [1911]) 'Progress of significs' manuscript, all in terms uncannily similar to those in *The Meaning of Meaning*. In a critique of word-magic *avant la lettre*, Ogden (1994 [1911]: 21–22) discoursed at length on the power of words, using many examples that reappear in chapter 1 of *The Meaning of Meaning* – naming taboos, magical spells, and so on – and proposing the same remedies: the avoidance or complete elimination of ambiguous and confusing words (Ogden 1994 [1911]: 25–34), and some form of definition as a way of becoming clear about meanings (Ogden 1994 [1911]: 39–43). These early proposals are not specified in the kind of detail found in *The Meaning of Meaning*, however (Gordon, in his notes to Ogden 1994 [1911], indicates further parallels). Even if these ideas are not entirely part of the classical conception of significs Welby held, they were certainly present in Ogden's mind during his period of informal tutelage under Welby, and he saw them as being inspired by her work. Gordon (1990a) describes Ogden's efforts here and in *The Meaning of Meaning* as an attempt to create an 'applied significs', perhaps not precisely as Welby would have conceived it, but in her spirit.

VI. Antagonism and synthesis

The Meaning of Meaning, as we have seen, attempted to forge a synthesis between the main theses of Welby's significs and Russell's logical atomism. From Welby there is the focusing of attention on the act of interpretation, the insistence that every meaning must be negotiated in a dialectical fashion. But Welby's vague, and at times mystical, formulations are replaced in *The Meaning of Meaning* with explanations based on the latest psychological theories and outlines of concrete procedures for analysing and controlling meaning, directly inspired, as we have shown, by Russell's work. This synthesis, however, could not be taken for granted: there was a certain amount of antagonism between Welby and Russell, and the doctrines they represented.

In the first years of the twentieth century, Welby, ever keen to widen her circle of scholarly contacts, engaged Russell in dialogue over his early logicist work and theory of descriptions. Russell, however, was largely uninterested and dismissive of Welby's overtures. His antagonism may have been an extension of his fight against the idealist English philosophical establishment (see §III; Russell 1959: chapters 4–6), which drew him into a debate within the mainstream of academic philosophy in which he later had to face many queries and criticisms similar to those already raised by Welby. But in the mainstream debate, in contrast to his discussions with Welby, Russell was compelled to reply. We therefore see in Russell and Welby's correspondence a first confrontation of two very different approaches to related problems, and the opening words of a debate that would continue, with other participants, well into the twentieth century. In this subsequent debate Russell remained firm in preserving the sanctity of his formalisms. A very different route was taken by Wittgenstein, who made a radical reappraisal of his earlier views.

The Meaning of Meaning, as a synthesis of Welby's and Russell's ideas, could have been received as a mediator between these positions, but instead it was initially dismissed by leading analytic philosophers, Russell and Wittgenstein included. It would be another twenty years before it was accorded a place, and a minor one at that, in the mainstream, due mostly to the efforts of the American philosopher Charles Leslie Stevenson (1908–1979) and, by extension, the English philosopher Alfred Jules Ayer (1910–1989).[25] Stevenson saw in Ogden and Richards' book a possible precedent for the emerging philosophy of 'emotivism', analytic philosophy's answer to the problem of non-referential language. It was another twenty years again, after a rift had opened up between the Cambridge analytic camp and the Oxford 'ordinary language' camp (see chapter 3 of Baldwin 2001 for a standard account), before an acceptable synthesis similar to Ogden and Richards' – but independently formulated – appeared, which granted logicians their proposition while accounting for the problems of interpretation.

The issues that divided these two camps are visible in Welby and Russell's correspondence, which commenced in 1903, with a letter from Welby written after she read Russell's first logicist work, *Principles of Mathematics* (1903), and continued until 1910 (the correspondence is reproduced with commentary in Petrilli 2009: 294–301, 310–325; see also Schmitz 1995, 1985a: clix–clx for commentary). Most notable among the topics Welby raised in this period is a critique of Russell's theory of descriptions from the perspective of significs. The division between knowledge by acquaintance and knowledge by description neglects 'awareness', argued Welby. The theory of descriptions is too narrow: it deals only with the 'sense' (in Welby's scheme; see §V) of an utterance. The crucial aspect of an utterance like 'The present King of France is bald' is the speaker's intention to show that it is nonsense; this is its 'meaning', says Welby:

> I do not here raise the question of whether we should not gain by always using "meaning" in its immediate or central sense of intention: in which speaking of the "present King of France" as bald, we intend to convey what is sheer mistake or sheer nonsense. That is, it is not meaningless (or purposeless) *but senseless*. (Welby to Russell, 14 November 1905, in Petrilli 2009: 321; also in Schmitz 1985a: clxii; emphasis original)

Russell's response to Welby's critique is polite but dismissive. He felt that she has missed the point: his concern was simply with logical language and what can be referred to in it, and all other features of natural language are simply irrelevant. The theory of descriptions is not about '*intention*, but something logical; I do not know quite how to explain what it is that I intend, & I think perhaps I could excise the word *meaning* with advantage, as I do not intend what you intend when you use the word, & your use seems more correct than mine' (Russell to Welby, 25 November 1905, in Petrilli 2009: 322; also in Schmitz 1985a: clxii; emphasis original).

Their correspondence on this topic continued in a similar fashion until the end of the year: Welby raised further considerations and Russell politely dismissed them as irrelevant to his interests. Behind Russell's rejection of Welby is more than simply a logical point; it is also a matter of temperament. Welby's broad-ranging and discursive style and her frequent invocations of mysticism and intuition would have hardly appealed to the rational, scientific crusader Russell. Even Peirce, one of Welby's staunchest public supporters, commented in his double review of Russell (1903) and Welby (1903) – in which Welby's book received a much more favourable recommendation than Russell's – that Welby's 'is a feminine book, and a too masculine mind might think parts of it painfully weak' (Peirce 1977 [1903]: 308). Neither would have Welby's evasive style of argumentation endeared her to Russell: harnessing the convictions that motivate significs, she would often insist that an argument was the result of misunderstanding rather than a genuine difference of opinion (an observation that Chipchase 1990: 50 makes on her style of argumentation).

Russell's reception of Welby was, however, not completely negative. On the cover sheet to his collection of letters from Welby, he wrote: 'From Lady Welby who helped to turn my attention to linguistic problems' (reported in Petrilli 1988: 80). But these concessions and Russell's unimpeachable politeness towards her may merely be due to the dictates of gallantry. In his other correspondence Russell was much more candid about his feelings towards her. To the English mathematician Philip Jourdain (1879–1919) he wrote:

> Many thanks for your amusing letter about Lady Welby [. . .] I have in the past been very nearly rude to her, in refusing to go there [her home], because I found it was quite impossible to be sincere if I saw her. I think it is very wrong of all these philosophers to encourage her as they do, and I don't want to be a party to it; at the same time, when one is with her, one can't be as rude as truth requires. (Russell to Jourdain, between March and October 1908, quoted in Grattan-Guinness 1977: 111)

Russell's reception of *The Meaning of Meaning* followed the same lines as his treatment of Welby's overtures: he was quick to dismiss it, without engaging with it in any great depth. In his review of the first edition Russell described it as 'undoubtedly important and valuable' (Russell 1988 [1923]: 137), and in his review of the second edition as 'of considerable importance' (Russell 1988 [1926]: 138), but he still concluded:

> Whether it achieves all it professes to achieve, I have found it impossible to decide. If it does so, it is of first-class philosophical importance. The authors, however, seem a trifle too prone to believe that every question would be easy if the wilful obscurities of metaphysicians were swept aside, and this makes their discussion sometimes seem a little perfunctory. It is to be hoped that future elaborations of the theory will enable us to judge whether this is a defect in their thought or only an impatience in their manner of exposition. (Russell 1988 [1923]: 137)

Russell's assessment of *The Meaning of Meaning* applied also to the person of Ogden, it would seem. Five years after Ogden's death, Russell commented in 1962 that he was 'the cleverest man that had been at Magdalene since Pepys', but added: 'To be the cleverest man at Magdalene since Pepys is no very great praise, because it was not a college that went in for intellect, particularly – it was a sporting college' (see Anderson 1977: 235).

Russell's assessment of *The Meaning of Meaning* and Ogden came after almost two decades of defending his doctrines against objections similar to Welby's and those of her supporters within the English philosophical establishment. In connection with the publication of his original 1905 paper on the theory of descriptions, Russell (1959: 83) tells us: 'This doctrine [the theory of descriptions] struck the then editor [of *Mind*] as so preposterous that he begged me to reconsider it and not to demand its publication as it stood.' This editor was G. F. Stout, who in preceding years had encouraged Welby to publish in *Mind* and co-authored a paper with her (see §V). Russell does not tell us why the doctrine struck Stout as 'preposterous' but it is possible that his reasons were related to Welby's.

A decade and a half later Russell had to face further objections, which he met with detailed and reasoned rebuttals. In 1920 *Mind* organised a 'symposium' on the 'meaning of *meaning*', involving Russell, the pragmatic philosopher and Welby supporter F. C. S. Schiller, and Harold Henry Joachim (1868–1938), an adherent of British idealism (Schiller, Russell and Joachim 1920). Schiller charged, in terms reminiscent of Welby, that there must be some interpretive force that creates meaning, for which Russell gave no account. Meaning, says Schiller (Schiller, Russell and Joachim 1920: 389), is 'essentially an *activity* or *attitude* taken up towards objects by a subject or energetically projected into them like an α particle, until they, too, grow active and begin to radiate with "meaning"'. Russell countered that he never claimed that meaning is 'an intrinsic property inherent in objects' but rather the 'causal efficacy of that which has meaning', by which he meant the response that a particular stimulus brings forth (Schiller, Russell and Joachim 1920: 398). Here Russell introduced his pseudo-behaviourist model, which still left a place for 'images' (see §III).

Russell's 'causal efficacy' is not intrinsically incompatible with significs and allied doctrines. As the direct response of an organism to its environment, it is essentially equivalent to Welby's 'sense'. Ogden and Richards' use of 'engrams' as the psychological element creating references (see §I) can similarly be assimilated to this group of ideas. The irreconcilable difference between Russell and Welby's approaches arises with Russell's introduction of descriptions, which seek to be unique and unambiguous, to eschew interpretation and capture what Welby would call 'Plain Meaning'. In attempting to eliminate interpretation by legislating linguistic form, Russell – and for that matter the early Wittgenstein – made a return to Cratylan linguistic naturalism. Russell not only believed that it is possible to create unambiguous forms, he also believed that words originally matched what they name and have become obscured over time. He put his faith in philology, which may yet be able to undo the changes and reconstruct the original forms:

> If we trace any Indo-European language back far enough, we arrive hypothetically (at any rate according to some authorities) at the stage when language consisted only of the roots out of which subsequent words have grown. How these roots acquired their meanings is not known, but a conventional origin is clearly just as mythical as the social contract by which Hobbes and Rousseau supposed civil government to have been established. We can hardly suppose a parliament of hitherto speechless elders meeting together and agreeing to call a cow a cow and a wolf a wolf. The association of words with their meaning must have grown up by some natural process, though at present the nature of the process is unknown. (Russell 1921: 189–190)

Despite his naturalism, Russell respected the ambiguity of ordinary language; it is an essential feature that makes communication possible:

> When one person uses a word, he does not mean by it the same thing as another person means by it. I have often heard it said that this is a misfortune. That is a mistake. It would be absolutely fatal if people meant the same things by their words. It would make all intercourse impossible, and language the most hopeless and useless thing

imaginable [. . .] We should have to talk only about logic – a not wholly undesirable
result. (Russell 1918–1919: 174, see also p. 176; Russell 1923)

The difference between Russell and Welby, and one of the reasons why he
would reject the kind of synthesis Ogden and Richards attempted, is that he saw
his 'logically perfect language' as distinct from ordinary natural language. The
words of the logically perfect language Russell strove for could only describe
each individual's sense-data; it would be an entirely private language through
which we could communicate nothing to other people (Russell 1918–1919: 176;
cf. Russell 1988 [1923]). This is a complex stance on language and meaning.
Although he believed in a naturalistic origin of language, Russell saw the historical departure of language from this naturalism as an inevitable result of
how it functions. In his logical work he hoped to restore this naturalism by
establishing isomorphy of form and meaning, but his logically perfect language
was intended only for scientific and philosophical purposes; the ambiguity of
ordinary language is an essential property. In the theory of descriptions Russell
was concerned, as he insisted in his correspondence with Welby, specifically
with 'something logical', not with language altogether. 'Logicians', pointed out
Russell (1919: 7), 'so far as I know, have done very little towards explaining the
nature of this relation called "meaning," nor are they to blame in this, since
the problem is essentially one for psychology'. Whether it is in fact possible
to construct a notation that escapes from the vagaries of natural languages and
approaches 'Plain Meaning' is, however, still a valid question.
    Even though Russell strove for a logically perfect language and found it
'impossible to decide' whether *The Meaning of Meaning* in fact answered the
questions it raised, he was at least impressed by those questions, whether or not
he was consciously aware of it. In later years, his rhetoric came ever more to
resemble Ogden and Richards' description of word-magic:

> Words have been objects of superstitious awe. The man who knew his enemy's name
> could, by means of it, acquire magic powers over him. We still use such phrases as 'in
> the name of the Law'. It is easy to assent to the statement 'in the beginning was the
> Word'. (Russell 1940: 23)

In chapter 2 of *The Meaning of Meaning*, a twenty-page catalogue of instances
of word-magic, we find examples comparable to those Russell raised (see in particular Ogden and Richards 1989 [1923]: 26–30). Russell's words above recall
the opening lines of this chapter:

> From the earliest time the Symbols which men have used to aid the process of think-
> ing and to record their achievements have been a continuous source of wonder and
> illusion. The whole human race has been impressed by the properties of words as
> instruments for the control of objects, that in every age it has attributed to them occult
> powers [. . .]. (Ogden and Richards 1989 [1923]: 24)

Russell's absorption of the approach Ogden and Richards cultivated extended to accepting a multifunctional model of natural language in his later work, but he never allowed ordinary language to encroach on his logical formalisms. Russell (1940: 204, cf. 53–55, 1988 [1926]) endorsed a functional model of language with three purposes: '(1) to *indicate* facts, (2) to *express* the state of the speaker, (3) to *alter* the state of the hearer', each of which may be more or less present in sentences of different types. But the problem remained always for Russell 'something logical': 'The question of truth and falsehood', insisted Russell (1940: 212), 'has to do with what words and sentences indicate, not with what they express'.

But Russell had to answer once again criticisms of his theory of descriptions from a pragmatic perspective, this time coming from Peter F. Strawson (1919–2006), a proponent of Oxford ordinary language philosophy. With arguments reminiscent of those Welby used half a century before (a similarity noticed also by Schmitz 1995: 301–303), Strawson (1950), addressing Russell's theory of descriptions, insisted that it is necessary to consider how an expression is used to make a reference rather than the formal properties of the expression itself. Russell's (1959 [1957]) rebuttal recalls his reply to Welby in all but tone; it is more polemical than polite. He contended that Strawson has confused the problem of descriptions with 'egocentricity', that is, the variation in basic ostension through language because of differences in experience. Russell believed that the two problems are separate and that in fact descriptions provide us with a way to overcome the variation due to egocentricity by giving us access to data beyond our immediate senses. He reiterated, a final time, his goal of the logically perfect language, a language divorced from the ambiguity and vagueness of ordinary language, two features indispensable in 'daily life' but not suitable to the purposes of science:

> This brings me to a fundamental divergence between myself and many philosophers with whom Mr Strawson appears to be in general agreement. They are persuaded that common speech is good enough, not only for daily life, but also for philosophy. I, on the contrary, am persuaded that common speech is full of vagueness and inaccuracy, and that any attempt to be precise and accurate requires modification as regards vocabulary and as regards syntax. Everybody admits that physics and chemistry and medicine each require a language which is not that of everyday life. I fail to see why philosophy, alone, should be forbidden to make a similar approach towards precision and accuracy. (Russell 1959 [1957]: 241–242)

The Oxford ordinary language philosophy that Russell found so objectionable had its origins in the later teachings of Wittgenstein. Although, as we have seen, initially aligned with Russell and also engaged, as Russell (in his introduction to Wittgenstein 1922: 7–19) claimed, in the search for the 'logically perfect language',[26] he began to question the possibility of such a language and turned to investigations of language in use in the later 1920s and 1930s (see Wittgenstein

1958; Waismann 1979). When *The Meaning of Meaning* appeared, one year after the *Tractatus*, Wittgenstein was unimpressed. To Wittgenstein Ogden sent a complimentary copy of the book, which prompted the following response:

> I have not been able to read your book thoroughly. I have however read in it and I think I ought to confess to you frankly that I believe you have not quite *caught the problems* which – for instance – I was at in my book (whether or not I have given the correct solution). (Wittgenstein to Ogden, March 1923, in Wright 1973: 69; emphasis original)

In a letter to Russell, Wittgenstein was even more candid: 'Is it [*The Meaning of Meaning*] not a miserable book?! Philosophy is not as easy as that! From this one sees how easy it is to write a thick book' (Wittgenstein to Russell, 7 April 1923, quoted in Monk 1990: 214).[27] Frank P. Ramsey (1903–1930) tried to console Wittgenstein, who was greatly irritated by Russell's apparent support for *The Meaning of Meaning*: Russell, Ramsey claimed, 'does not really think *The Meaning of Meaning* important, but he wants to help Ogden by encouraging the sale of it' (Ramsey to Wittgenstein, 20 February 1924, in Wright 1973: 84). Ramsey's (1924) own short review of *The Meaning of Meaning* was not particularly flattering.

Wittgenstein's final statement on language, contained in the posthumous Wittgenstein (1953), no longer treats language as a mirror for reflecting the world, but as an activity, a 'game', in which people participate (Wittgenstein 1953: §7), and not a single game, but a series of games, each related to the other but not sharing a single common property that unites them all (Wittgenstein 1953: §67). There is no longer a complete analysis of an expression that shows its meaning (Wittgenstein 1953: §46–49, §60, §91), but 'the meaning of a word is its use in the language' (Wittgenstein 1953: §43). The possibility of a logically perfect language is denied and examination of interpretation in ordinary language is raised to the utmost significance:[28]

> [L]ogic does not deal with language – or thought – in the sense that science deals with a natural phenomenon, and the most one can say is that we construct ideal languages. But here the word "ideal" would be misleading, because it sounds as if this language would be better, more perfect, than our everyday language; and as if it were needed for the logician to finally show people what a correct proposition looks like. (Wittgenstein 1953: §81)

Russell was not swayed by Wittgenstein's later views in any way. Russell (1959: 216) claimed that Wittgenstein's later doctrines 'remain to me completely unintelligible' (although he did find use for some aspects of them, e.g. Russell 1940: 330).

In mainstream analytic philosophy, reconciliation between what became the two poles of a semantic and a pragmatic approach to language emerged only in the 1960s through the work of the English philosopher Herbert Paul Grice (1913–1988). His breakthrough was to distinguish between the logicians' literal meaning and 'implicatures', the meaning intended and taken away by participants in a discourse, determined by a mixture of cultural conventions and factors specific to the context. This granted the logicians their literal meaning but then modulated it through pragmatics, all the while appealing to logicians' sense of rigour by positing 'maxims' that constrained pragmatics (see Grice 1961, 1989: chapter 2, based on material from 1967; cf. Baldwin 2001: chapter 3). In Grice's maxims – which are intended to be descriptive, but which have a normative character in being expressed as imperatives – we can perhaps hear the faint echo of Ogden and Richards' canons of symbolism, which similarly sought to specify the conditions under which references are to be made.

The only explicit recognition *The Meaning of Meaning* found in mainstream contemporary analytic philosophy came for the distinction it makes between symbolic and emotive language. Stevenson (1944: 33), in identifying what he called the 'descriptive' and 'emotive' aspects of meaning in language, cited Ogden and Richards' distinction between the symbolic and emotive functions, a distinction that became a central pillar of his theory of ethics: he even quotes Ogden and Richards (1989 [1923]) in the opening leaf of his book. Disagreements over moral and ethical questions, according to Stevenson, generally involve both difference in beliefs and differences in attitudes: the former are matters of fact expressed in 'descriptive' terms, while the latter are matters of feeling expressed in 'emotive' terms. Although Stevenson (1944: 8–11) criticised Richards (1926 [1924]) for later collapsing the distinction between belief and attitude, making both a matter of belief amenable to empirical psychological investigation, he praised Ogden and Richards (1989 [1923]) for first establishing it.

Stevenson (1944: 265–268 *et passim*) counted Ogden and Richards among those who would now be considered early analytic philosophers, citing them alongside Russell (1925, 1935), Rudolf Carnap (1935) and Ayer (1946 [1936]) as a source of inspiration. Ayer (1946 [1936]) – specifically chapter 6, 'critique of ethics and theology' – has in turn acquired the reputation of a foundational text in the 'emotive theory of value', as Ayer (1946 [1936]: 20) retrospectively called it in the second edition. He acknowledged Stevenson's (1944) achievement in giving 'a more detailed analysis of specimen ethical judgements' (Ayer 1946 [1936]: 20), but nowhere mentioned Ogden and Richards.

The Meaning of Meaning represents an early effort at forming a synthesis of the logical and semiotic approaches to meaning, although the effort was little appreciated by the leaders of the logical school at the time. Russell, who was already engaged in defending his doctrines against the encroachment of interpretative concerns raised by Welby and her supporters, saw little value in Ogden and Richards' attempts. Wittgenstein, too, was unimpressed. Although he acknowledged many of the points raised by his opponents, and came to talk in terms uncannily reminiscent of *The Meaning of Meaning*, Russell maintained his hard line in searching for the logically perfect language, commenting that 'it is not impossible to whittle away the element of interpretation, or to invent an artificial language involving a minimum of theory. By these methods we can approach asymptotically to the pure datum' (Russell 1940: 124).

Wittgenstein, however, departed from his initial views and arrived at the opposite extreme, providing inspiration to the 'ordinary language' camp, which Russell continued to rebuff with similar arguments. It was only in the 1960s that the two sides were brought together again within mainstream analytic philosophy, due to the efforts of Grice, whose maxims of conversation may remind us of Ogden and Richards' canons of symbolism. The only explicit recognition that *The Meaning of Meaning* achieved within the mainstream came from Stevenson, who accorded them a place in the development of emotivism.

VII. Philologists, psychologists and anthropologists

Welby and her theory of significs may form the personal link between Ogden and the beginnings of the modern semiotic tradition, but she was not alone in developing doctrines of this type. Among others – philologists, psychologists and anthropologists – similar ideas about the interpretation of signs, communication as action and the role of emotions were finding expression, and Ogden and Richards were not deaf to these voices.

The Meaning of Meaning is today remembered not only for Ogden and Richards' text, but also for the platform it provided to the Anglo-Polish anthropologist Bronisław Malinowski, whose contribution to the book (Malinowski 1989 [1923]), one of two 'supplements' appended to the end, presents his own functional model of language and ties it into Ogden and Richards'. Malinowski's supplement took shape alongside Ogden and Richards' final text: in the lead-up to the publication of *The Meaning of Meaning*, shortly after his return from a half-decade field trip to the Trobriand Islands of New Guinea, Malinowski was a regular visitor to Ogden's apartment (see Richards 1977: 104). The convergence that we see between his views and Ogden and Richards' no doubt owed much to their discussions during these visits.

Malinowski (1989 [1923]: 206–209) endorsed Ogden and Richards' concept of 'sign-situation' and widened it in his own 'context of situation' to encompass not only the immediate discourse context, but also the entire culture of the speech community, a necessary extension for an anthropologist trying to make sense of an alien people. Malinowski then embraced Ogden and Richards' functional model, identifying three uses of language in which various functions predominate to greater and lesser degrees. In the first of these, 'speech in action', language is used to the direct pragmatic end of co-ordinating an activity, such as a hunting or fishing expedition, and here reference predominates. In the next, 'narrative discourse', the referents are displaced and, even though the narrative depends on there being a possibly existing situation that it recounts, the 'emotive' effect of the tale on the listeners is more important than any reference to the world. Finally, language becomes wholly detached from reference in the

'phatic communion', the meaningless trivialities and gossip exchanged to break
the silence and establish amicable relations, such as greetings, enquiries about
one another's health, discussion of the weather, and so on (Malinowski 1989
[1923]: 309–316; see also Malinowski 1935; Schmidt 1984).

These are the fundamental uses of language, most visible in 'primitive' communities, but serving still as the basis of speech in 'civilised' societies. The
decontextualised, purely referential use of language characterised by Ogden
and Richards' 'symbolic function', Malinowski (1989 [1923]: 321–323 *et passim*)
argued, is derivative of the three fundamental uses and occurs only at the more
advanced levels of linguistic and intellectual development found in the Indo-
European languages, and even then only among the more educated members
of a society. 'The illiterate members of civilized communities treat and regard
words very much as savages do', observed Malinowski (1989 [1923]: 323). Here
he treats 'Indo-European' as a more advanced phylogenetic stage, somewhere
beyond the 'primitive', rather than as a developmentally value-free linguistic
grouping. Malinowksi (e.g. 1935) softened this implication in his later work,
but in 1923 it is unmistakable (see Schmidt 1984: 127, 170–175 for discussion).

The developmental character of language Malinowski saw as being reca-
pitulated in each generation through language acquisition. Taking Ogden and
Richards' Triangle of Reference, Malinowski (1989 [1923]: 316–326) showed
how it is built up through the successive development of each of the uses of language in the individual (see Figure 2.3). A baby begins by babbling; these sounds
are 'expressive, significant and correlated with the situation, but not involving
any act of thought' (Malinowski 1989 [1923]: 323). The baby's babbling is
merely a natural, reflex reaction to its environment and internal desires. In the
second stage of development the child begins to form actual articulate sounds
and simultaneously to pick out parts of the environment. It comes to correlate
particular sounds with their referents, forming symbols, and these symbols
become tools to manipulate their referents: when the child utters 'mama', the
mother appears (Malinowski 1989 [1923]: 319–320).

Only in the third stage of development does reference acquire its triadic
character and Ogden and Richards' triangle begins to take on visible shape.
'Speech in action' continues the childlike understanding of meaning – words
remain tools to act on their referents – but in 'narrative speech' the referents
are not immediately present and a third term, the 'act of imagery', must stand
in for them. Malinowski (1989 [1923]: 322–323) then introduced a new use of
language, 'language of ritual magic', which has the same displaced character as
narrative speech, but where the speaker tries to achieve the pragmatic ends of
speech in action. This is literally word-magic: spells and incantations become
for speakers tools that they assume act directly on the world.

Malinowski's reworking of Ogden and Richards' triangle represents both
the acceptance of its underlying tenets and, as Gordon (1982: 49, 1990c: 825)
argues, a quiet restriction of its applicability, since 'language in its primitive
function and original form has an essentially pragmatic character [... and] to

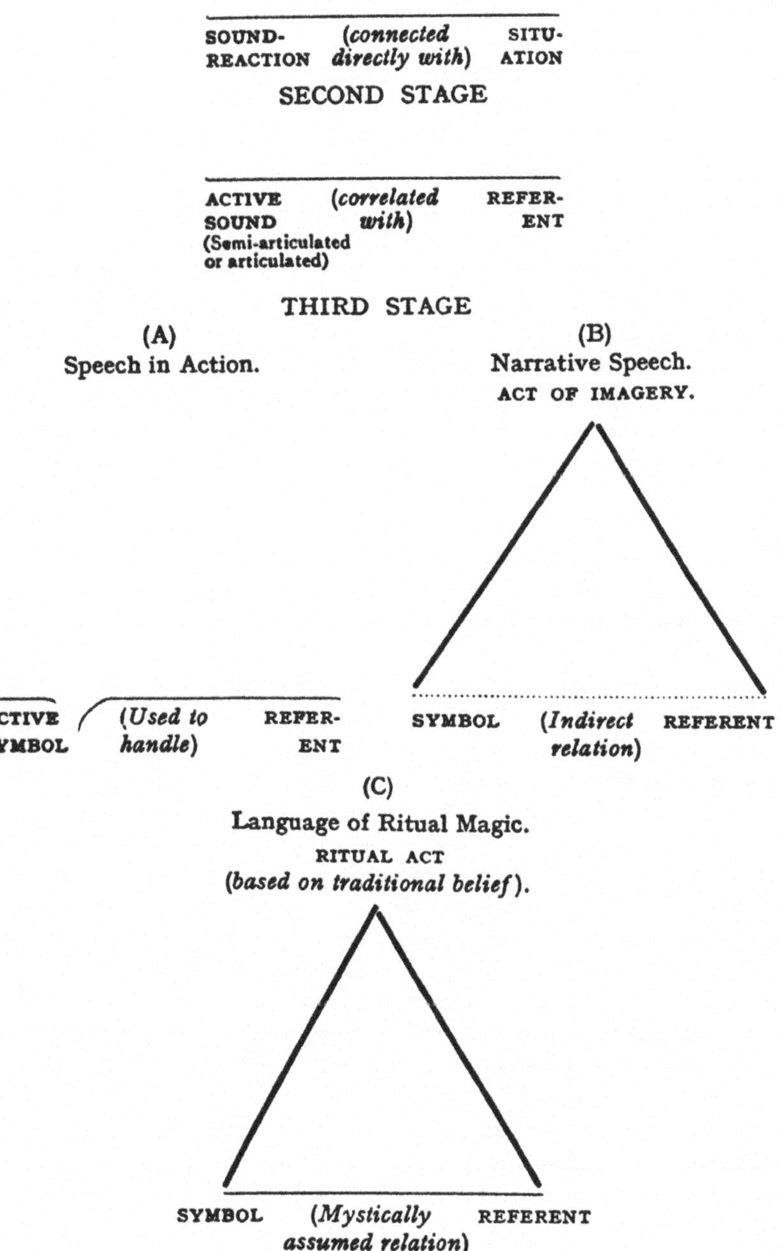

Figure 2.3 Malinowski's adaptation of the Triangle of Reference
Malinowski 1989 [1923]: 324.

regard it as a means for the embodiment of thought is to take a one-sided view of one of its most derivative and specialized functions' (Malinowski 1989 [1923]: 316).

This emphasis that Malinowski placed on the 'essentially pragmatic character' of language was becoming a commonplace in contemporary European linguistic theory. The English Egyptologist and philologist Alan Henderson Gardiner (1879–1963), whose 1922 paper Ogden and Richards (1989 [1923]: 192–193, 230) quoted, recognised a 'volitional attitude' of the speaker to the listener, a desire to cause some effect on the listener through their words, an idea already expressed by Gardiner (1919), which was 'extracted [. . .] from a letter to Dr. B. Malinowski'. Ogden and Richards assimilated Gardiner's 'volitional attitude' to their function (iv), 'the promotion of effects intended' (see also Firth 1935; Nerlich 1992: 258–266).

On the continent in the following years similar ideas gained traction: Nerlich (1992: 166–171) highlights the French psychologist Frédéric Paulhan's (1856–1931) notion of the 'double function of language' (Paulhan 1927), where on the one hand language reports thoughts and facts in the world, and on the other hand creates them.[29] The German psychologist Karl Bühler (1879–1963), a colleague of Heinrich Gomperz at the University of Vienna (introduced in §IV), elaborated his *Organon* model of language, in which language 'represents' objects or states of affairs in the world as well as making an 'appeal' to the listener and providing a means of 'expression' for the speaker (Bühler 1990 [1934]; see also Innis 1982; Eschbach 1988). Later, Gomperz (1941) adopted the notion of 'appeal' as the defining property of 'linguistic signs' in his taxonomy of sign types. By 'appeal' he meant the use of a sign 'for the purpose of modifying $P2$'s [the listener's] future behavior in some particular way' (Gomperz 1941: 164).[30]

Gardiner and Bühler – who were aware of one another's work and acknowledged the similarities, although not uncritically (see Gardiner 1951 [1932]: 4, 7; Bühler 1990 [1934]: 28; see also Nerlich 1992: 261) – both named Philipp Wegener (1848–1916), a German gymnasial teacher and independent scholar frequently cited by the Neogrammarians, as a major inspiration (see Gardiner 1951 [1932]: 12 *et passim*; Bühler 1990 [1934]: 27, 38 *et passim*). Wegener (1991 [1885]: 68) held that speech is primarily a means for the speaker to excite the 'Sympathie oder Interesse' (sympathy or interest) of the listener towards themselves or the object of discourse. Wegener's view, like Malinowski's, grew out of observation of child language acquisition: speech begins with a child's cries for its mother's attention. Firth (1957 [1950]: 181–182), surveying the study of meaning in British linguistics up to that time, made the connection between Wegener, Gardiner and Malinowski (cf. Nerlich 1992: 81–87).

In this wider circle of language scholars beyond Ogden and Richards' personal acquaintances we find precedents also for their distinction between purely referential use of language and the emotional and attitudinal aspects that emerge in the emotive functions (ii) and (iii) (see §I). The independent German scholar Karl Otto Erdmann (1858–1932) – whose 1900 *Die Bedeutung des Wortes* Ogden and Richards (1989 [1923]: xvii) list among the studies from which they have 'derived instruction and occasionally amusement' – drew a distinction between the *begriffliche Inhalt* (conceptual content) of a word and two other kinds of value it contains, the *Nebensinn* (connotation), all the ideas beyond the immediate conceptual content associated with a word, and *Gefühlswert* or *Stimmungsgehalt* (emotional value or content), all the feelings the word evokes (Erdmann 1900: 80–82). The linguists Charles Bally (1865–1947) and Hans Sperber (1885–1963), the former Swiss (and a prominent promoter of Saussure) and the latter German, produced simultaneously and independently studies of the role affect plays in semantic change, in the process identifying the 'emotive' in the sense of 'attitudinal' as a component of meaning in language, on a par with reference (see Sperber 1914; Bally 1965 [1913]; Nerlich 1992: 250 also comments on the similarity of these three approaches to Ogden and Richards'; cf. McElvenny 2017).

The concerns about language in use that Ogden and Richards raised – the problem of interpretation in context, the pragmatic uses of language to create effects in listeners and the world, and the expression of emotions and attitudes – did not all stem from Welby, although in her position as mentor to the young Ogden her influence was no doubt great. We see among contemporary anthropologists, psychologists and language scholars discussion of many of the same themes, in similar terms. Ogden and Richards were acquainted with the participants in the contemporary discussion, in some cases personally and in others only through their works. The philosophy of language that comes through *The Meaning of Meaning* can equally be placed in this tradition.

After *The Meaning of Meaning*, Ogden and Richards increasingly worked independently of one another and emphasised different aspects of the theory of language they had developed together in the book. Richards principally pursued the semiotic course, while Ogden drew himself closer to the logicians. Richards explored the emotive function and in his hands the method of definition became 'multiple definition', used to explicate the range of interpretations available for a linguistic expression. By contrast, Ogden, in his next major project, Basic English, which we take up in the next chapter, sought to neutralise the emotive as much as possible and make definition a means for prescribing precise, unambiguous linguistic forms. Definition became a means of reduction, elimination and minimisation of language and its effects, as Richards would later recall:

The chapter on Definition in "The Beadig of Beadig", as we came to call it in memory of a frustrating cold in the head, led us into long discussions of the number of radically different ways there may be of telling anyone what any word may mean. This inquiry was the germ of Basic English. Ogden had long been deep in the history and theory of universal languages, and it was no long step from our account of Definition to notions of a minimal English capable of serving all purposes. (Richards 1977: 108; repeated in Brower, Vendler and Hollander 1973: 34, and Richards 1943: xliii, 22–23)

Notes

1. There were ten editions of *The Meaning of Meaning* published in Ogden and Richards' lifetime, the first from 1923 and the last from 1949. Although Ogden and Richards later discussed the desirability of making revisions to the 1949 edition (see volume 3 of Gordon 1994: xxii–xxv), this never occurred. The first edition is significantly longer than all subsequent editions: under pressure from their publisher, who wanted to reduce production costs, chapter 2, 'The power of words', was shortened in the second edition of 1927 to a quarter of its original size (Gordon 1994: xxi). Ogden had intended to publish the cut material as a separate work on 'word-magic'; this never appeared as an independent book, although portions were published as articles (Ogden 1934b and Ogden 1938–1952). The revisions made from the second to the tenth edition are all minor (see Gordon 1990b: 67–68). The discussion in this chapter is based on a 1989 reprinting of the 1949 edition, which represents the book in the final state that Ogden and Richards left it. There is a more recent critical edition (volume 3 of Gordon 1994), but this is an idealised version of the book that combines later revisions with the material cut from the first edition. There are various in-depth critiques of the theory of meaning presented in *The Meaning of Meaning*. Some of the most significant of these are collected in volume 5 of Gordon (1994). See also Hotopf (1965: 10–32) and chapter 7 of Russo (1989). Gordon (2006) presents a comprehensive, up-to-date and very compact assessment of *The Meaning of Meaning* and its subsequent influence in linguistics and semiotics.

2. Richards tells another version of the story, with only inconsequential differences in details, in Brower, Vendler and Hollander (1973: 19, 22). Russo (1989: 704, note 5) catalogues Richards' different versions of the story. See also Joseph (1999: 51–53).

3. Hotopf (1965: 10) remarks: 'Perhaps the best way of describing it [*The Meaning of Meaning*] is as a book written by two young men who pretend to be angry. It is an immensely high-spirited book. They attack almost everybody, and claim to solve a host of fundamental problems in philosophy, psychology, linguistics, and aesthetics, or, if not to solve them, at least to indicate the general lines upon which others might now proceed to their solution. Some of the brash positivism associated with youth reveals itself in their attitudes. It shows itself in great hopefulness, in impatience with uncertainties, in a belief in the practical importance of their mission.' Carington (1994 [1949]: 168) says of *The Meaning of Meaning*: 'I, personally, find it most gratuitously written, and in places quite gratuitously obscure; it gives me the impression, perhaps quite unjustly, that the authors are more interested in making the reader feel small and ignorant than in explaining pellucidly to him just what they want to say – but this may be my fault [. . .] But despite these animadversions I regard it as a work of the utmost importance; in fact, I do not think it too much to say that it is one of the key books of the century, and one that should not only be read but closely studied by anyone who is anxious to think clearly on any but the most concrete subject-matter.'

4. As a major sub-discipline in English-speaking philosophy, analytic philosophy has a vast literature. A recent but very traditional introduction to the history of this

approach is Soames (2003). Glock (2008) presents a more critical discussion that looks at analytic philosophy from a number of different perspectives, including the historical.

5. In saying 'fictions' Richards most probably intended to invoke the theory of fictions of the eighteenth-century English utilitarian philosopher Jeremy Bentham, whom Ogden was rediscovering and reinterpreting around the time Richards wrote these words (see Chapter 3, §VII). A 'fiction' under this conception is essentially an abstract entity with no real existence in the world that we create and use in our thinking.

6. The obscurity of function (v) is only enhanced by Ogden and Richards' apparent terminological confusion in their exposition; or perhaps their terminological confusion is indicative of the function's obscurity. *Stand for* has already been established in the Triangle of Reference model as the imputed relation between a symbol and referent (see Figure 2.1) – and Ogden and Richards' italics would suggest that they intend this technical sense – but here they appear to be talking about a relation between 'symbols' and their 'reference', an interpretation encouraged by the wider textual context. This relation should, under their model, be *symbolise*. But perhaps by 'reference' they mean an act of referring to a *referent*, in which case they have identified the correct relation according to their own model. In any case, the passage is by no means clear, and this lack of clarity would seem to come from their confusing and inconsistent use of terms, a charge that they faced from other quarters (see Gordon 2006: 2579–2581 for discussion). The other words that Ogden and Richards typographically raise to technical status in the quoted passage, *indicate* and *state*, they go on to explain as being either the realisation of a function directly in a linguistic sign (*indicate*) or through the symbolic function (*state*). That is, the emotive functions can either shape the linguistic form or they can describe in referential terms the end to be realised: 'Each of these non-symbolic functions', Ogden and Richards (1989 [1923]: 226) say, 'may employ words either in a symbolic capacity, to attain the required end through the references produced in the listener, or in a non-symbolic capacity when the end is gained through the direct effects of the words'.

7. The example of Mill's treatment of *-able* was first raised by G. E. Moore in his critique of Mill's utilitarian ethics (Moore 1993 [1903]: 118–119). Ogden and Richards do not cite Moore, presumably on the assumption that their readers will recognise the example and its pedigree. Ogden (1994 [1911]: 27), however, also uses this example, with reference to Moore.

8. The principle embodied in Canon (iv) Ogden and Richards (1989 [1923]: 291–295) apply to the problem of 'negative facts', which exercised logicians, Russell among them, in this period. There are no negative facts, they conclude, just symbols that have no referents, like any other non-referring expression.

9. The People's Suffrage Federation was an organisation which campaigned for universal adult suffrage, which Russell helped to found and in which he was active. The episode Russell describes in his letter is also recounted in Monk (1990: 38–39), with an excerpt from the letter.

10. The German text of Wittgenstein's *Tractatus* had already been published in

Germany the year before in Wilhelm Ostwald's *Annalen der Naturphilosophie* (the chemist Ostwald had broad-ranging interests in philosophy and internationalisation; he reappears in Chapter 3, §II–III, in the context of the international language movement). Wittgenstein disowned this first edition, however; he was not satisfied with the final copy and complained that his revisions had been ignored. The *Entstehungsgeschichte* of Ogden's edition of the *Tractatus* is told most comprehensively in Wright (1973). The book contains letters from Wittgenstein to Ogden in which Wittgenstein comments on draft English translations and the original German text, as well as an introduction by Wright where a narrative of the translation, informed by primary research not contained in the letters, is given. The most significant aspect of the narrative told here is that it appears Frank Plumpton Ramsey (1903–1930), who is introduced into the main discussion in §VI, was responsible for the first draft of the English translation (Wright 1973: 8–9).

11. Peano placed a crucial piece in the logicist puzzle with his axioms of arithmetic, although much of the theoretical framework and formalism that lay behind them (the foundations of what is now referred to as first-order logic) had in fact already been developed by Frege. Russell only discovered this later, but Peano may have known about Frege's prior work. See Grattan-Guinness (2000: 247–249) for discussion of Peano's and Frege's most important intellectual interaction in this period, and Russell (1959: 66) for his retrospective account of Peano and Frege.

12. With the further development of his epistemological doctrines in the years following the initial presentation of his theory of descriptions, Russell also turned the proper names of natural language into descriptions; only truly logical proper names, which refer to the sense-data with which we are directly acquainted, remained unanalysable labels (see Russell 1910–1911: 114, 1921: 193, 1959: 167).

13. Frege (1984 [1892]) of course proposed his own solution to these logical puzzles with his well-known notions of *Sinn* (usually translated as 'sense') and *Bedeutung* ('reference'), which Russell (1905: 482–483) cited. In short, the 'sense' of an expression is what guides us to make a particular 'reference' to a thing in the world. Russell saw his theory of descriptions as superior to Frege's solution, since, as Russell contended, it does not account for the falsity of 'The present King of France is bald'. Surely 'is bald' is a predicate of the object referred to by 'the present King of France', and if the sense fails to produce a reference to an object then there is no subject for the predicate. Although Russell did not explicitly say so, Frege's account would have presumably been unappealing to him on other grounds: Frege's 'sense' is a thoroughly Platonic conception, timeless and abstract, that would be difficult to reconcile with Russell's realism (see, in particular, Frege 1984 [1918–1919]). Another solution to problems of this sort that Russell cited is that of the Austrian idealist philosopher Alexius Meinong (1853–1920) (Russell 1905: 482–483 cites Meinong 1904; Russell 1910–1911 cites Meinong 1910 [1902]). Meinong proposed that every grammatically correct expression denotes an entity that exists, but that there are different ways in which entities can exist (the chief distinction here being between 'existence' and 'subsistence'). 'The present King of France' is therefore a kind of existent entity, but an abstract one whose existence is not part of the

time-bound physical world. Quite apart from doctrinal objections, Russell (1905: 482–483, 1910–1911: 122–123) claimed that this is a contradiction: we would have to accept that 'the present King of France' both exists and does not exist.

14. Note that Russell's neutral monism is different from the idealist forms of monism he earlier refuted: neutral monism is not a general theory of metaphysics, but is rather restricted to the problem of mind-matter dualism.

15. The 'Stoneyhurst [*sic*] book on theories of knowledge by Father Walker' that Richards refers to is probably Walker (1910).

16. 'Interpretation' is the English translation Ogden and Richards (1989 [1923]: 275) use for Gomperz's term *Auffassung*.

17. Welby seems to have only started using the term 'significs' to refer to her approach around 1900. In Welby (1985 [1896]) she still used the earlier term 'sensifics'. See Schmitz (1985a: l–lii) for an account of the coining of the name 'significs'.

18. Some other 'ladies of the time who worked in logic and philosophy' mentioned by Grattan-Guinness (1977: 111) include Mary Everest Boole (a friend of Welby and wife of the logician George Boole), Sophie Bryant, Emily Elizabeth Constance Jones (who engaged in academic debate with Russell over meaning and reference, see Jones 1910, 1910–1911; Russell 1910–1911), Eleanor Jourdain (sister of Philip Jourdain, see §VI), and Christine Ladd-Franklin (a student of Peirce).

19. Although no great enthusiast of her work, Bréal was superficially tolerant in his dealings with Welby (see Auroux and Delasalle 1990; Petrilli 2009: 285–287, 302–307). His tolerance was most probably motivated largely by self-interest: his chief work on semantics, *Essai de sémantique* (Bréal 1900 [1897]), was translated into English on Welby's initiative, by her daughter, Nina Cust.

20. Ogden was presumably referring to Ellen Key (1849–1926), the Swedish feminist and educational reformer.

21. For the uninitiated, Welby's papers (such as Welby 1893, 1896, 1911) offer the best introduction to her work. Her papers are more restrained than her books, generally treating a more clearly defined topic in a succinct fashion, and do not drift off into the wider metaphysical, epistemological and mystical concerns. Her two most important books are Welby (1983 [1903]) and Welby (1985 [1911]). Exegeses of Welby's works have multiplied in recent years, with her adoption by semioticians exploring the historical roots of their discipline (e.g. Schmitz 1985a; Petrilli 2009).

22. The parallel between Welby's notion of ingrained metaphors and modern studies of conceptual metaphor in the wake of Lakoff and Johnson (1980) is obvious.

23. A further mystical aspect to Welby's thought, which lies at its base, hidden and unpublished, is her notion of the 'mother-sense' or 'primal sense', the force that drives interpretation, that causes us to pick out 'sense', 'meaning' and 'significance' from our environment. Although the term 'mother-sense' never appeared in her published work, Welby elaborated it in manuscripts from 1904 and 1907, with suggestions of the concept going back to 1890 (see Schmitz 1985a: ccxxxvii–cclxvii, cccxxxvii; Petrilli 1999: 53–61, 2009: chapter 6 for reproductions of the manuscripts with commentary). The mother-sense is the complement of the intellect; it makes an interpretation of experience while the intellect constructs rational, logical schemes.

This term remained a point of unresolved disagreement between Welby and her academic supporters – in particular the pragmatic philosopher Ferdinand Canning Scott Schiller and the founder of the Dutch significs movement Frederik van Eeden – which may explain why it never found its way into her published writings. They objected to the overt femininity of the term, which Welby strenuously defended, claiming: '[T]he dominant Man with his imperious intellect has for uncounted ages stamped down their [women's] original gift: all the activities beyond the nursery (and, alas, there also, now) are masculinised [. . .] the whole social order is laid down, prescribed for the woman on masculine lines only' (Welby to Schiller, October 1907, in Schmitz 1985a: ccxlix–ccl and Petrilli 2009: 634). Although she was by no means a conventional feminist – like her namesake Queen Victoria, she had no sympathy for the suffragettes, the contemporary vanguard of political feminism (see Chipchase 1990: 39) – Welby clearly possessed her own feminist sensibilities.

24. Peirce, who in later years shared a similar mystical bent (see, for example, chapter 9 of Hookway 1985), saw in Welby's division of 'sense', 'meaning' and 'significance' his own scheme of 'immediate interpretant', 'dynamical interpretant' and 'final interpretant'. He commented: '[. . .] I had not realized, before reading it [Welby (1985 [1911])], how fundamental your trichotomy of Sense, Meaning and Significance really is. It is not to be expected that concepts of such importance should get perfectly defined for a long time [. . .] I now find that my division [of the three kinds of Interpretant] nearly coincides with yours, as it ought to do exactly, if both are correct' (Peirce to Welby, 14 March 1909, in Hardwick 1977: 109; cited by Ogden and Richards 1989 [1923]: 287–288; see also Schmitz 1983: 126). The only major point of difference Peirce could see is that he conceived of his 'dynamical interpretant' as the effect actually produced on the listener, which is not necessarily the effect intended by the speaker, as in Welby's 'meaning'.

25. Charles W. Morris (1901–1979), an American philosopher who developed a hybrid approach combining American pragmatism with logical positivism (and who also inhabits the notes to Chapter 4), was a keen reader of *The Meaning of Meaning* and cited it extensively in his semiotic works (e.g. Morris 1938, 1946). While Morris' work has not gone entirely unnoticed – his division of 'semiotic' into 'syntax', 'semantics' and 'pragmatics' has, for example, provided labels that live on to this day in closely related senses – he never became a hugely influential figure among analytic philosophers. For this reason, we do not include his enthusiasm for *The Meaning of Meaning* among our evidence of the book's impact on mainstream analytic philosophy.

26. F. P. Ramsey – the principal translator of the *Tractatus* into English and friend to Wittgenstein – in fact even denied that finding the 'logically perfect language' was Wittgenstein's aim in the *Tractatus*, claiming instead that he was concerned with the functioning of all languages (Ramsey 1923: 465). This view is possibly buttressed by Wittgenstein's reactions against constructed international languages a few years later (see Chapter 4, §IV).

27. Ogden and Richards would seem to have taken this rebuff to heart. Over fifty years later, Richards (1977: 102; see also Brower, Vendler and Hollander 1973: 26)

claimed that the only value he and Ogden could see in Wittgenstein's *Tractatus* was as a 'plainly [. . .] magnificent specimen of the unintelligible, certain to be the occasion of rich misunderstandings of the sort we were studying'. This assessment ignores the common elements in *The Meaning of Meaning* and the *Tractatus* that we have observed, as well as other common points that emerged between Richards' and Wittgenstein's theorising. Richards (1926: 45), for instance, went on to adopt Wittgenstein's (1922: prop. 6.54) distinction between 'saying' and 'showing' as a way of characterising the distinction between symbolic and emotive language, although even here he tried to distance himself from Wittgenstein somewhat (cf. Richards 1926: 53–54, note 2).

28. Some recent scholarship, such as Nolan (1990) and Pietarinen (2009), postulates the influence of Welby's work and her followers on Wittgenstein's later views. Unfortunately, due to a lack of explicit documentary evidence in this area, such suggestions remain rather speculative, although highly compelling.

29. Ogden was certainly familiar with Paulhan's work: he translated Paulhan's (1930 [1887]) *The Laws of Feeling*, a treatise on the psychology of emotions (which is not related to Ogden and Richards' distinction between symbolic and emotive language).

30. There is a temptation to hear the distant echo of Ogden and Richards (1989 [1923]) in Gomperz's (1941) essay. Its title, 'The meanings of "meaning"', and its observation that meaning 'is used in quite a number of senses' (Gomperz 1941: 157) would encourage this. But Gomperz's answer, which is to identify the common element of all senses of 'meaning' and then provide a taxonomy of sign types by their mode of signification, does not necessarily follow Ogden and Richards' example.

Chapter 3

Basic English

'What the world needs most', Ogden (1931: 13) tells us, 'is about 1,000 more dead languages – and one more alive'. By the 1930s the unprecedented technological advances delivered through modern engineering, the practical-minded sibling of science, had shrunk the world: railways, radio, telephones and aeroplanes made it possible to send messages instantly to the furthest parts of the globe; people and goods could reach them in a fraction of the time it took only a generation before. But despite European civilisation's conquest of the natural world, the barbarism and base national jealousy buried at its foundations had not been overcome. In Ogden's mind, and the minds of many others, the root of the problem was the curse of Babel, and the solution was the adoption of an international language. Only a common medium would secure scientific intercourse, progress and efficiency, and peace. But just as the modern technology that had already brought us so far was not of nature – wheels and rails, fixed wings and propellers, speakers, microphones and the transmission apparatus in between are wholly artificial products – so, Ogden was not alone in thinking, no existing natural language could solve the problem of international communication. What was needed was a new, artificial language, better than those that already existed; it would be the product of a new form of linguistic engineering informed by the scientific study of language and meaning already underway.

Ogden's solution was his project Basic English, a specially modified form of Standard English.[1] By the time his first publications about it appear in 1927, interest in the international language problem had reached its height, having been in the general public consciousness for almost fifty years, with myriad proposals for a common international tongue.[2] The historian who wants to quote dates to delineate one age from another will place their stake at the year 1879, the year in which the first publications on the language project Volapük appeared, the first of the international languages to actually win a community of speakers. Following closely behind, in 1887, is Esperanto, the most successful of the international languages, both in terms of the number of speakers it was able to acquire and the longevity it was able to achieve. Today there is still a small but active worldwide community of Esperanto speakers.

Although interest in international languages persists in pockets around the world, the time has passed when the issue was of mainstream concern. The end of the period could be dated to 1951, the year in which IALA Interlingua, the last of the major international language projects, was published: the subdued welcome it received was a sign that the problem of international language was no longer a pressing issue.

Beginning with Volapük, but becoming increasingly marked with the emergence of a self-consciously 'scientific' approach to language construction, there developed a 'common solution' to the international language problem that embodied the practical considerations as well as the aesthetics of the age. Most major projects proposed a constructed language, based on the existing European national languages, but 'improved', generally in the same direction as the new systems of mathematical logic of the kind that Russell and Wittgenstein were developing, and which we saw reflected in Ogden's own philosophy of language in *The Meaning of Meaning* (see Chapter 2, §III). Irregularity and illogicality would be banished; these were minimalist languages, with a minimum of grammar (understood primarily as morphology), a minimum of ambiguity, and maximal efficiency in the bond of form and function. To avoid national jealousies and advantage, no single existing language should be privileged in the design.

Basic English reflected many of the design and aesthetic concerns current in this environment: Ogden (1931: 27) described Basic as 'a language that is as simple, as regular, and as economical as possible; a language which starts with a minimum of demands on the learning capacity of the humblest individual and can yet do the maximum amount of work'. But at the same time, in its adherence to the national language English, Basic offered some unusual, even perverse, conclusions to the questions raised by the challenge of international language construction.

I. The Enlightenment and modernity

The international language movement began with enthusiastic amateurs, but as it reached maturity around the turn of the century it came to be increasingly dominated by scholars who sought to seize the issue and treat it in what they considered a properly scientific manner. For these scholars it became a burning priority to save the movement from what they saw as cranks, fanatics and Bolsheviks, whose undesirable political views and dilettantish attempts at linguistic engineering were doing so much to discredit it. They looked back to the Enlightenment, which they saw as the most recently preceding period of intellectual upheaval. They cast their Enlightenment forebears as conscious fighters against medieval superstition, exalting in its place science and universally shared human rationality. A pillar of Enlightenment linguistic thinking was the search for the philosophical basis of language and the fashioning of improved languages for international communication on this basis. Many modern language constructors styled themselves as the heirs to this tradition.

The turning point that marks the official intervention of scholars in the international language movement is the calling into being of the *Délégation pour l'adoption d'une langue auxiliaire internationale* (Delegation for the adoption of an international auxiliary language) in Paris in 1900. In this year, Paris played host to several international scholarly conferences, including the International Congress of Mathematics and the inaugural International Congress of Philosophy, organised to coincide with the *Exposition Universelle*. Left to us are stories, often told in mythical tones, of scientists and scholars from all corners of the 'civilised' world assembled at these conferences, standing on the cusp of the twentieth century, which promised to multiply exponentially the successes of the outgoing nineteenth, trying to exchange news of their discoveries but constantly hindered and frustrated by the Babylonian confusion of their speech. Through universal recognition of these problems, and by the individual suggestion of the French mathematician Léopold Leau (1868–1943), the Délégation was called into being. It was to be a committee that would examine the international language problem and recommend a solution to the International Association of the Academies, the worldwide union of national learned societies, which would definitively decide on the issue.

The forming of the Délégation was not the first time that a learned society officially investigated the international language problem – that honour goes to the American Philosophical Society's examination and resulting rejection of Volapük – but it was the first time that such an investigation led to practical action. The American Philosophical Society's call for a conference to work out an alternative to Volapük 'suited to the needs of modern thought' (see Brinton, Phillips and Snyder 1888: 12) was answered only by the London Philological Society, which came out in support of Volapük and rejected the need for a conference (see Ellis 1891). The establishment of the Délégation finally raised the international language problem to the level of academic respectability, after twenty years of its being the domain of 'scientifically untrained persons', the worst of whom were 'fanatics and Utopians', as the Austrian chemist Richard Lorenz (1863–1929) (1910 [1909]: 24), a leading member of the Délégation, described them.

The driving force of the Délégation after its establishment was the logicist mathematician Louis Couturat (1868–1914), who was also a leading Leibniz scholar of his day (see Couturat 1901, 1903) and initiator of research into the history of constructed languages (see Couturat and Leau 1903, 1907). Clearly seeing an analogy with his own time, Couturat portrayed the Enlightenment projects, in particular those of his own hero Leibniz, as products made possible by the ideals of the adjoining Renaissance, which, 'in the renewal of all the sciences and philosophy, had revealed the fundamental unity of the human spirit and had given birth to the idea of the international union of all scholars, as is well put in the expression "Republic of Letters"' (Couturat 1901: 55–56). The 'emancipation of thought from ancient authority and the yoke of Aristotle' in the Renaissance led to modern scientific research and a 'desire for a logic more modern, most appropriate to the needs of the new science'. As a result, '[r]eason became aware of its strength and independence, and tended to overcome all barriers of tradition and routine, and we began to see that we could surpass antiquity in our knowledge of the universe, and to envisage an infinite progress' (Couturat 1901: 55–56).[3]

Couturat's portrayal may be more a projection than an analogy (indeed Maat 2004: 7–10 specifically takes issue with some details of Couturat's account), but the period of the late Renaissance and Enlightenment and the modernist era are undoubtedly kindred in their belief in new, previously inconceivable possibilities, including that of 'infinite progress'. But the Enlightenment would seem to be characterised more by musing than the direct pragmatic action of the early twentieth century. Enlightenment projects were more experimental than their modern counterparts: theoretical questions were given more time than the practicalities of implementation (although Maat 2004 shows many concessions on the part of Dalgarno and Wilkins to practicality). René Descartes (1596–1650) summed up the Enlightenment language constructors' aspirations, problems and their eventual resolution right at the beginning of the period:[4]

> If someone were to explain correctly what are the simple ideas in the human imagination out of which all human thoughts are compounded, and if his explanation were generally received, I would dare to hope for a universal language very easy to learn, to speak, and to write [. . .] I think it is possible to invent such a language and to discover the science on which it depends: it would make peasants better judges of the truth about the world than philosophers are now. But do not hope ever to see such a language in use. For that, the order of nature would have to change so that the world turned into a terrestrial paradise; and that is too much to suggest outside of fairyland. (Descartes to Marin Mersenne, 20 November 1629, reproduced in translation in Kenny 1970: 6)

Notable among the Enlightenment projects, especially for the potential inspiration they provided Ogden (as we see in §VII), are those of the British philosophers – in the broadest sense of the term, befitting Enlightenment figures – George Dalgarno (see Maat and Cram 2000) and John Wilkins (1968 [1668]), which originally began as a collaboration but soon split into separate projects as a result of their irreconcilable differences. We see in these projects a faith in the improvement deliberate human work can deliver over the accidents of nature: existing languages, Wilkins (1968 [1668]: 19) tells us, 'must needs be liable to manifold defects and imperfections, that in a Language at once invented and according to the *rules of Art* might be easily avoided'.

The centrepiece of both projects – although to a greater extent in Wilkins' – were vocabularies organised around classificatory tables that look back to the Aristotelian categories, established in antiquity and refined through scholastic logic. Slaughter (1982) sees this approach as an attempt to create taxonomic nomenclatures, a final outing for the traditional Aristotelian epistemic scheme in the face of the explosion of knowledge resulting from the new science. Maat (2004: 171–172, 257–258 *et passim*), by contrast, sees no simple relationship between tradition and the new science in either Dalgarno's or Wilkins' projects, but rather tangled networks of tradition and innovation, further complicated by concessions in design that reveal their frequent betrayal of principle to practical convenience (see, for example, the commentary in Maat 2004: 54–59; see also Cram 1980, 1985; Maat and Cram 2000: 32–62).

Completing what is often seen as a trinity of the most famous Enlightenment projects was Leibniz's contribution (see chapter 5 of Maat 2004), which served in equal measure as an inspiration to the new mathematical logic and the modern constructed languages (see Chapter 2, §III).[5] Leibniz's various ideas, many of them recorded only in draft form in unpublished fragments, eschewed preconceived classificatory schemes and instead aimed to elucidate the composition of thoughts expressed in the language, right down to the constitutive primitive concepts. This would not only offer a universal language, which, because of the shared basis of human rationality, would be understandable to all people, but would also provide a calculus of thought that could automatically deliver proofs and expose fallacies. It promised escape from the confines of language boundaries and from linguistic confusion and the pointless disputes that arise from it. Couturat, in his dual roles of Leibniz expositor and language constructor, can be credited with bringing much of Leibniz's thought on this issue into the modern movement.

At the turn of the nineteenth century to the twentieth, scholars eyed the new international language movement, which by this time had been an issue of widespread public concern for around twenty years. Conscious of the precedent set in the Enlightenment, but living in a time when *philosophe* was no longer a pastime but a profession, the scholars set out to seize the international language problem and make it the object of proper 'scientific' study. To this end, the Délégation was founded, to resolve the problem with official academic sanction. This new technocratic current in the international language movement is the one later joined by Ogden with his Basic.

II. Peace and progress

The modern international language movement into which the technocratic language constructors sought to manoeuvre was marked from its early days by tensions between those who looked to the international language as a humanitarian project, directed at international reconciliation and preserving peace, and those whose interest was mainly in efficiency in international communication, for securing the continued scientific progress of humanity. Volapük, the first of the major modern international languages, was surrounded mostly by the rhetoric of progress. By contrast, Esperanto, its main rival, was associated much more with humanitarian goals.

As European politics moved to extremes and boiled over into revolution and war in the early twentieth century, many technocratic language constructors distanced themselves from overtly humanitarian rhetoric, in the fear that their careful plans would fall victim to political intrigues. But many figures resisted retreat to extremes, Ogden among them: as a pacifist (see Chapter 2, §III), he was committed to international language as an instrument of peace, but he also embraced the technocratic hopes of furthering science through an improved language. His appeal for a single international language, which opened this chapter, continues:

> The absence of a common medium of communication is the chief obstacle to international understanding, and therefore the chief underlying cause of War. It is also the most formidable obstacle to the progress of international Science, and to the development of international Commerce. (Ogden 1931: 13)

In order to gain an understanding of the now little-known social and intellectual background to Basic and kindred efforts of the time, we will now take an extended excursion into the social and political history of the modern international language movement. We begin with Volapük and Esperanto, the two language projects that set the tone and established a pattern for much of what followed. Esperanto, in particular, played an incomparable role in defining the international language movement. Most major projects which came after it were either reforms or challenges to it: the philosophical proposals of Couturat and his collaborators were intended as reforms, and other projects generally expended considerable effort demonstrating their differences. Ogden, for one, worked hard to trumpet the superiority of Basic to Esperanto (see, in particular, Ogden 1935). Our historical survey closes with IALA Interlingua, the last of the major projects.

Appearing first in 1879, Volapük was the creation of a Swabian priest, Johann Martin Schleyer (1831–1912), a man who saw modernity as the great uniter of humanity (see Haupenthal 2005a for a biography). He sought a catholic, in the sense of universal, language to add one further piece to the unification of the world. In his characteristically rhapsodic style, where even the typography is compelled to enthusiasm through bold text and *Sperrung*, he discoursed on how modern technology brings us daily closer together, and how steps towards world union are already being taken at a political level. The natural next step, he insisted, is union through language:

> Through railways, steamships, the telegraph and telephone the globe has shrunk both temporally and spatially. The countries of the earth have, so to speak, become significantly closer. For this reason the times for petty, narrow-minded national pride are forever finished. Mankind becomes daily more cosmopolitan, and longs for **Union**. With the **World-post** a major step forward to this magnificent goal has already been made. The brotherhood of man should also unite more and more in terms of money, measures, weights, units of time, laws and **language**. This current work hopes to give the first push towards this **language-unification** in great measure [. . .] After mankind has united in the World-post, it must also unite in a **world-script**,

language and grammar! This is indubitably a great, intellectual gain and advance. (Schleyer 1982 [1880]: 1; emphasis very much in the original)[6]

Schleyer's call was heard across Europe, and in the following years Volapük societies and journals sprang up all over the continent. In 1885 the *Kadem Bevünetik Volapüka*, the Volapük Academy, was established to direct the further growth and development of the language, and by 1889, ten years after the first Volapük publications, there were 1.5 to 2 million users of the language in the world (as estimated by Schmidt 1988 [1963]: 13–14).

1889 is the year in which the Volapük movement reached its peak, and the year of its spectacular downfall, precipitated, it would seem, not so much by any features of the language itself, but by Schleyer's proprietorial attitude to his creation. He saw himself as the infallible pope of the Volapük movement, with zero tolerance for heretics.[7] But the success of the Volapük movement depended on many people. Most prominent among them was Auguste Kerckhoffs (1835–1903), a Parisian professor of languages, whose *Cours complet de Volapük* (first edition 1885, but with many subsequent editions) provided the main introduction to the language for French speakers and the speakers of other Romance languages. Kerckhoffs' status within the Volapük movement was institutionalised when he was elected the director of the Academy in 1889, a position that he exploited to submit his proposed reforms to the language to Schleyer. Schleyer's not unexpected rejection of the reforms led to a schism in the movement between those loyal to Schleyer and those loyal to Kerckhoffs, a schism that was solidified in 1890 when Schleyer disowned the Volapük Academy and founded a new, rival organisation. In the following year, 1891, Schleyer struck Kerckhoffs off his register of officially recognised Volapük speakers. The language never recovered from the split, although the Academy lived on for several decades.[8]

While Volapük in its own right may have failed in its first decade, it had proved that a constructed language as a solution to the international language problem was feasible and had succeeded in whetting the appetites of enthusiasts for such a system. The Volapük void was soon filled by the new project Esperanto, which first appeared in 1887 in a series of self-published brochures in Russian, Polish, French and German by Dr Ludwig Lazarus Zamenhof (1859–1917; see Zamenhof 1889 [1887]), an eye doctor from Białystok, in what was then the westernmost regions of the Russian Empire and now eastern Poland.[9] Haupenthal (2005b) argues that the rapid spread of Esperanto was in fact enabled by the collapse of the Volapük movement: disillusioned Volapükists, who already possessed the infrastructure of societies and journals, converted *en masse* to the Esperanto cause.

From the very beginning Esperanto displayed a different character from Volapük: Schleyer's soaring rhetoric of the Progress of Man was replaced with more muted hopes of achieving inter-ethnic understanding. Whereas Volapük was the 'world-language', Esperanto was 'the hoping one', the pseudonym

Zamenhof used when he introduced his *lingvo internacia* (international language). As a Jew from a highly assimilated Russian-speaking family in a region where Poles were ethnically dominant, Zamenhof experienced at first hand the friction and mutual hatred that can exist between the subgroups of humanity. His goal was to fashion a bond that would unite all people, a bond that does not seek to supersede existing linguistic cultures but is rather superimposed upon them. In response to an enquiry from the Russian Esperantist Nikolaj Afrikanoviĉ Borovko in 1896, Zamenhof offered the following story about his motivations for creating the language:

> I was born in Białystok, district of Grodno. This place of my birth and my childhood gave the direction to my future aims. In Białystok the population consisted of four diverse elements: Russians, Poles, Germans and Jews; each of these elements spoke a different language and was hostile to the other elements. In this city more than anywhere else one felt the heavy unhappiness of linguistic diversity and was convinced at every step that this diversity of languages is the only, or at least the chief, cause that separates the human family and divides it into hostile parties. I was brought up as an idealist. I was taught that all men are brothers, while on the street and in the yard, everything at every step made me feel that men did not exist: only Russians, Poles, Germans, Jews, etc exist. This tormented my young spirit, although many would laugh at this 'sorrow for the world' of a child. Because it appeared to me then that the 'elders' possessed an omnipotent strength, I repeated to myself that when I was older I would definitely do away with this evil. (Zamenhof 1929 [1896]: 417–418)[10]

Zamenhof's hopes for the unification of humanity did not remain restricted to the linguistic. Almost a quarter of a century after his publication on Esperanto, he began in the 1900s to publish his design for a new religion, which he first called 'Hillelism' after the ancient rabbi Hillel, whom Zamenhof took as his inspiration, but later renamed *Homaranismo* (generally rendered in English as 'Humanitism'). Homaranismo is to religions what Esperanto is to languages: it is a superimposed set of principles that seeks to draw out the commonalities in religions. The adherent of any religion can adopt Homaranismo, without having to deny their existing religion (Zamenhof 1929: 312–345 contains a selection of Homaranismo materials; see also Forster 1982: 91–94). At the Universal Races Congress in London, Zamenhof (1911) presented to a general audience his thesis that differences in language and religion alone are the causes of division and antipathy in humanity.[11]

Although the use of Esperanto was a feature of Homaranismo, Zamenhof was careful not to associate his language project too closely with religion. The overtly humanitarian message of Esperanto, which blended into Zamenhof's religious interests, was well received among the language's early supporters, but with the spreading of the project across Europe, its purely humanitarian aspects came under pressure. Matters came to a head at the first Esperanto World Congress at the French seaside town of Boulogne-sur-Mer in 1905 (see

Forster 1982: chapter 3; Lins 1988: 26–27). Here Esperanto acquired for the first time its official trappings: the reference grammar *Fundamento de Esperanto* (Foundation of Esperanto; Zamenhof 1905) was adopted as the official statement of Esperanto's linguistic system and the *Lingva Komitato* (linguistic committee) was established to defend the *Fundamento* and regulate the further linguistic growth of the language. But the congress did not restrict itself to purely linguistic matters: contained in the *Fundamento* is the *Deklaracio pri la esenco de la Esperantismo* (declaration of the essence of Esperantism), five points that seek to normatively define what the Esperanto movement is. Point 4 confirms the language as the property of its speaker community, not the property of any single person (Zamenhof 1905: 37), as was the case with Volapük, to that project's detriment. This is a point that Zamenhof sought to establish from the very beginning: inside the front cover of Zamenhof (1889 [1887]), he writes, 'For a language to be universal, it is not enough to call it that. / An international language, like every national one, is the property of society, and the author renounces all personal rights in it forever.' The comment 'it is not enough to call it that' may be a jibe at Volapük, the 'world-language'. Point 5 of the declaration then goes on to state the absolute neutrality of Esperanto: an Esperantist is simply someone who uses the Esperanto language, regardless of what they use it to do (Zamenhof 1905: 37).

The legislated apolitical and irreligious nature of Esperanto was a result that Zamenhof permitted but did not endorse. His speech to the congress reiterated his hope that Esperanto would specifically aid humanity in living in peace and harmony, a message that did not sit well with the congress organisers, who feared the potential of exposing the movement to charges of pacifism and communism, widely considered the symptoms of a chronic lack of patriotism in this nationalistic age. Even more alarming was Zamenhof's plan to close his speech with a prayer, a plan from which the organisers could not dissuade him, although they managed to convince him to drop its final stanza, which contains its overtly religious and pacifistic conclusion (see Forster 1982: 84–87 and Lins 1988: 28; the speech and prayer, complete with final stanza, are contained in Zamenhof 1929: 360–365, 589–590).

Conscious of the tensions revealed at the congress, and hoping to maintain the success of Esperanto, Zamenhof stood down as official head of the movement and devoted himself instead to the promotion of Homaranismo. Despite relinquishing his official status, Zamenhof continued to be hailed as the *Majstro* (master) and spoke in this unofficial capacity at subsequent world congresses. Neither did he give up his activism: at the 1906 congress – held in the year in which the anti-Jewish pogroms in Russia came to Białystok and touched Zamenhof personally – he spoke about the *interna ideo* (internal idea) of Esperanto, the goal of which is to achieve 'fraternity and justice between all peoples'. This formulation might seem sufficiently bland and vague to be inoffensive to most, but in the nationalistically charged atmosphere of the first decade of the twentieth century it was still considered dangerous by many in the Esperanto movement (see Forster

1982: 95–99 and Lins 1988: 35–36; Zamenhof 1929: 368–374 contains the text of the 1906 speech).

It was in this highly charged atmosphere, at the very beginning of the twentieth century, before the issue had played out publicly in the Esperanto movement, that the *Délégation pour l'adoption d'une langage auxiliaire internationale* was called into being, by scientists and scholars who wanted to facilitate international co-operation in their fields, but wanted to stay far from political and religious entanglements. We see here a return from the humanistic rhetoric of the Esperanto movement, to the rhetoric of progress that heralded the arrival of Volapük, as in the words of the Délégation's secretaries, Couturat and Leau (introduced in §I):

> It is a commonplace that there is extraordinary progress in the means of communication: soon we will be able to travel around the world in forty days; we can send a message by telegraph (or by wireless) from one shore of the Atlantic to the other; we can telephone from Paris to London, to Berlin, to Turin. With these communication facilities comes a corresponding extension in economic relations: the European market extends over the whole earth, and the principal producing countries compete at all points of the globe. The great nations possess colonies all the way to the Antipodes and have interests in the most distant countries. Their politics is not confined to the European stage; it has become colonial and 'global'. Always for the same reason, they are obliged to agree and unite, for commercial interests (Brussels Sugar Convention), and for moral interests (International Convention on the White Slave Trade). (Couturat and Leau 1903: vii)[12]

Couturat and Leau together dominated the Délégation from its founding in 1901 to its conclusion in 1907. In this year, after the tensions in the Esperanto movement had already played out, the Délégation moved to make a final decision on the international language problem. As a result, a committee was formed, made up of fourteen eminent scientific men (not all of whom could attend the committee's meetings), representing all parts of the 'civilised' world – Europe, North and South America – and all modern fields of endeavour (see Lorenz 1910 [1909]: 15; Kotzin 1915 [1913]: 5; Guérard 1922: 146–147; Jespersen 1960 [1921]). Prominent among them, apart from Couturat and Leau, were the linguists Jan Baudouin de Courtenay (1845–1929), Otto Jespersen (1860–1943) and Hugo Schuchardt (1842–1927), all already known as defenders of constructed languages within linguistics (see §III below); Giuseppe Peano, pioneer of logicism in mathematics and inventor of Latino sine Flexione, which he spoke on occasion at the committee meetings;[13] and German professor of chemistry Wilhelm Ostwald (1853–1932).[14]

The committee's final decision fell in favour of Esperanto, providing a few revisions were made to the language, revisions that were outlined in a mysterious pamphlet submitted to committee under the pseudonym 'Ido' (an Esperanto suffix meaning 'offspring', here used as an independent word). The reforms (which we address in §III) were designed to simplify the language – that is, make its grammar more natural to speakers of less inflected western European languages – but also to impose a 'logical' structure on it. Esperanto, according to the committee, needed to meet the requirements of modern science. The philosophical concerns of the Enlightenment language projects once again took over the humanitarian aspects. The Ido advocate Richard Lorenz put it so:

> The fact is that science, philosophy and technology are constantly waging a fierce battle with existing languages. What they want is a language that is as simple and clear as the fundamental laws of nature, as logical as the precision of experiment, and as many-sided as the complexity of the facts which it has to describe. (Lorenz 1910 [1909]: 12)

The Esperanto *Lingva Komitato*, not unsurprisingly, rejected the Ido reforms. The tension between the founding amateurs and their academic usurpers is palpable in contemporary accounts of the Délégation (positive accounts include Lorenz 1910 [1909], and negative accounts Kotzin 1915 [1913] and Guérard 1922: 135–160; Blanke 1985: 185–188 provides a more neutral modern view). The ensuing dispute plunged to new depths of acrimony when Louis de Beaufront (1855–1935), who had been chief patron of the Esperanto First World Congress and was Zamenhof's hand-picked advocate of Esperanto to the committee, claimed authorship of the Ido pamphlet. In later years it emerged that Couturat and the prominent French Esperantist and confidant of Zamenhof Alfred Michaux (1859–1937) also had a hand in authoring the Ido reforms (see Forster 1982: 128–130; Blanke 1985: 187). Esperanto and its offspring Ido went their separate ways: Ido continued to change under following waves of reforms, which were proposed and implemented in the splinter group's main journal, the aptly named *Progreso* (Progress).

Only a few years after the Ido schism, the catastrophe of the First World War realised the dangers of European nationalism, and highlighted the urgency of the international language problem for the pacifist camp. It is from this time that we find Ogden's first hints at the need for an international language. After the typed pages in the chapter 'Universal language' of his 'significs' manuscript, which went through various drafts from 1911 to 1922 (see Chapter 2, §V), Ogden the pacifist has scrawled, in an 'uncharacteristically large hand', as Gordon (1990a: 187) puts it: 'Symbolic language would unite sense and meaning', 'Differences in language make war possible', and 'To cause the spread of English is to extinguish the possibility of war.'

It was also in these years that the Esperanto movement became more radical, or at least it appeared more radical in the polarised light. During the war, the *Universala Esperanto Asocio* (Universal Esperanto Association, UEA), founded in 1908 as an expressly pacifist and internationalist Esperanto body in the wake of the Ido schism, supported its causes in such material ways as operating a mail and package forwarding service between the warring countries via Switzerland (see Forster 1982: 159 and Lins 1988: 52). After the war, in 1921, the *Sennacia Asocio Tutmonda* (Worldwide Anational Association), a group dominated by Marxists until the end of the 1920s, was established as a splinter group from the UEA. In the 1930s both organisations went on to be banned and their members persecuted under the new totalitarian regimes of Nazi Germany and, perhaps ironically, given the blanket designation 'communist' in western countries, in the Stalinist Soviet Union (Forster 1982 and Lins 1988 cover this history in some depth).

In the 1920s, as Ogden began to work out the details of his Basic English, the failure of projects like Ido to find wide-scale adoption and the political unpalatability of Esperanto due to its apparent radicalisation kept the final resolution of the international language problem far away. In 1924 Alice Vanderbilt Morris (1874–1950), heiress of the New York Vanderbilt family, whose fortune derived from a private transport empire built in the nineteenth century, established the International Auxiliary Language Association (IALA). Although her interest in the problem may have dated back to as early as 1918 (see Falk 1999: 38–39), it was almost certainly piqued in 1921 through conversations with Frederick Gardner Cottrell (1877–1948), professor of physical chemistry at the University of California, Berkeley, and former doctoral student of Ostwald in Leipzig. Cottrell was chairman of the Committee on International Auxiliary Language, founded in 1919 under the auspices of the International Research Council in Washington DC (see IALA 1945; Esterhill 2000: 1–2), and he came to talk to Morris on the topic after she and his wife became friends while they were both resident at the Pompton Lakes Sanitarium, New Jersey, where they were recovering from illnesses (Falk 1999: 41).

The IALA implemented the approach of the American private research foundation, sponsoring programmes into the three aspects of the international language problem that it identified: linguistics, education and sociology (see chapter 9 of Falk 1999). Each of these programmes was led by an expert in the field: linguistics initially by the anthropological linguist Edward Sapir (1884–1939), education by the psychologist Edward L. Thorndike (1874–1949) and sociology by the sociologist Herbert N. Shenton (1884–1937) (see Falk 1999: 48). Over the following years each programme brought forth studies into similarities and differences across existing languages (Sapir 1930, 1949 [1944]; Sapir and Swadesh 1932; Swadesh and Morris 1934), optimal second-language pedagogy (Eaton 1927, 1934a, 1934b, 1940; Thorndike and Kennon 1927), and problems of communication in international settings (Shenton 1933). IALA scholars also produced some popular propaganda for the international language cause, such as Sapir (1931, 1933) and Shenton (1930). The last of these was published in Ogden's journal *Psyche* and offers a fascinating visionary statement of the role of the IALA and 'social engineers' in solving the international language problem. Ogden was among the many 'consultants' asked by the IALA in this period to offer their thoughts on and propose solutions to the international language problem (see Falk 1999: 54–55; Esterhill 2000: 5).

Although the IALA provided some support to Esperanto activities – the complete works of Zamenhof (1929), Stojan's (1929) *Bibliografio* of international language, which is written in Esperanto, and Eaton's (1934b) 'general language course', based around Esperanto, were prepared and published with grants from the IALA – it is clear that Esperanto's political associations alone made the language undesirable within the IALA. Like the Délégation before it, the leaders of the IALA sought to rescue the international language movement from radicals and utopians, to make it the servant of decent scientific enterprise. In his 1922 'program-circular of the Committee on International Auxiliary Language of the International Research Council', we see the words that Cottrell undoubtedly uttered in Morris' ear the year before, as he urged her to set up her foundation, the only hope for snatching the international language movement from the fingers of the Bolsheviks:

> From a sociological standpoint one of the most important features of the whole subject of international language development is the surprising interest and fidelity to the cause shown by the proletariat. It has really been from this class that there has come to the movement not only the great bulk of personal effort, but of financial support as well. It has been truly the multiplication of the "widow's mite" which has supported the word thus far ... If this interest of the masses can be carefully studied and sympathetically grasped by competent sociologists, it may be given constructive guidance for the benefit of all; but if neglected and left entirely to be developed by radicals, it may serve to merely fan the flame of bolshevism. (Cottrell, quoted in Guérard 1922: 185–187)

This is a message that resonated with Morris: in her directions to Sapir she dismissed certain types of language projects, which, she casually added, '[l]ike communism [... have] been tried and failed' (Morris in a letter to Sapir, 1925, quoted in Esterhill 2000: 5).

The story of the IALA after 1930 mimics in its outlines that of the Délégation. At its first international meeting in Geneva in 1930, the IALA moved to select an international language. None of the projects reviewed by the subsequent Committee for Agreement in 1935 was found to be satisfactory, and in 1937 the IALA began to design its own language project under the direction of the English Germanist William Edward Collinson (1889–1969) (see Falk 1995: 250–252; Esterhill 2000: 7–8). This project was concluded under the direction of Alexander Gode (1906–1970) in 1951, with the name 'Interlingua'. Although there were several directors of the IALA language project from its inception in 1937 – Collinson, then E. Clark Stillman (1907–1995) from 1939, and then André Martinet (1908–1999) for the brief period 1946–1948 – it is Gode's name that appears on the final works: the dictionary, Gode (1971 [1951]), and the grammar, Gode and Blair (1971 [1951]). He is widely considered to have had the greatest influence on the shaping of the final product (see, for example, Blanke 1985: 173; cf. Falk 1999: chapter 12). Gode, it should perhaps be noted, was actively anti-communist in the later Cold War period; he translated into English Gerhard Szczesny's (1969 [1966]) attack on Bertolt Brecht's socialism.

We see then the international language movement as a part of the social and political environment of late nineteenth and earlier twentieth century Euro-America, the expression of widespread hopes for easing international communication, but for very different, and increasingly antagonistic, reasons. On the one side were the humanitarians, hoping to bring about the brotherhood of man through a common language, which in some minds became associated with communist aspirations; on the other side were the technocrats, looking for a medium for international scientific intercourse to secure and accelerate the progress of civilisation, but keeping their distance from the apparent left-wing politics of the humanitarians. This split mirrored a division between amateur enthusiasts, who tended towards the humanitarian side, and scholarly language constructors, who were more interested in international language as a tool of science.

But whatever their politics and despite their mutual denunciations, the forms of the major language projects proposed in this period looked ever similar, as they moved towards a 'common solution'. It was as these tensions were at their height and with no resolution in sight that Ogden put forward his Basic. Ogden was publicly involved in broadly 'progressive' causes, but there are no hints of the 'communist' sympathies that so alarmed the technocratic camp in the international language movement. It was with this technocratic camp that Ogden principally aligned himself, as we will now see, with his rhetoric and design proposals for Basic. But his adherence to a single living national language, namely English, presents an unusual, perhaps characteristically British, solution to the problem, which in many ways stood in opposition to the cherished ideals of neutrality that the technocrats held.

III. The common solution

'[J]ust as bicycles and typewriters are now nearly all of the same type, which was not the case with the early makes', commented the Danish linguist and language constructor Otto Jespersen (1860–1943) (1928: 52), 'we are now in the matter of interlanguage approaching the time when one standard type can be fixed authoritatively in such a way that the general structure will remain stable, though new words will, of course, be constantly added when need requires'. Even though the large number of new projects that appeared in this period inevitably displayed a high degree of diversity, the major projects – that is, the projects that actually found supporters beyond their creators – all 'show[ed] an unmistakable family likeness', as Jespersen continued, 'and may be termed dialects of one and the same international language'. The common solution of this period follows a pattern largely established by Esperanto: the result was invariably a language lexified by the major European languages and offering a grammar based on them, but simplified and regularised.

Superficially, Basic seemed to go against this trend. It was based solely on the English national language: its vocabulary and grammar were simply a subset of those offered by Standard English, not modified according to any scheme at all. But Basic did answer to the broader design considerations that lay behind contemporary international language projects. Ogden believed that the English language already offered many of the features the artificial language constructors worked so hard to incorporate into their languages.

The traditional classification of constructed languages comes from the French Esperantist Gaston Moch (1859–1935) (1897), and was popularised by Couturat and Leau's (1903, 1907) surveys of language projects. This classification offers a primary division into *a priori* and *a posteriori* languages: an *a priori* language is constructed *de novo*, usually according to a particular 'logical' or philosophical scheme, while an *a posteriori* language makes use of lexical material and the grammatical organisation of existing, usually European, languages (Moch 1897: 44; Couturat and Leau 1903: xxvii–xxviii). This classification into the *a priori* and *a posteriori* is, however, by no means absolute; it is rather a continuum, and there is a clear trend from the advent of Volapük to the publication of IALA Interlingua in which constructed languages shed *a priori* properties and became increasingly *a posteriori*.

Alongside the contrast between *a priori* and *a posteriori* is a tension between the 'analytic' and 'synthetic' in language. In the linguistic sense, the terms 'analytic' and 'synthetic' originate in the language typology of August Wilhelm von Schlegel (1767–1845) (cf. Koerner 1989b; Morpurgo Davies 1998: 71–76) and went on to enjoy a genericised existence in subsequent language study. Drawing on existing morphology-based language classifications – Schlegel (1818: 85) cited those of his brother Friedrich von Schlegel (1772–1829) and the Scottish Enlightenment figure Adam Smith (1723–1790) – Schlegel posited a three-way primary division into *les langues sans aucune structure grammaticale* (later dubbed 'isolating languages' in English), *les langues qui emploient des affixes* (agglutinative languages) and *les langues à inflexions* (inflecting languages). The Indo-European languages belong to the final, inflecting group, which Schlegel subdivided into *les langues synthétiques* (synthetic languages) – Latin, Ancient Greek and Sanskrit – and *les langues analytiques* (analytic languages), exemplified to varying degrees by modern Romance and Germanic varieties.

These analytic languages, Schlegel (1818: 16) tells us, have developed in historical times out of their synthetic ancestors through a process of decomposition, while the origins of the synthetic parents, as with the other incommensurable primary typological classes, remain 'lost in the night of time'. In making this classification Schlegel, and his contemporaries, were concerned with inflectional morphology alone, but the later language constructors, in adopting this contrast, applied it also to vocabulary, where multimorphemic compound words were understood as analytic in contrast to the synthetic forms of monomorphemic words.

For the language constructors, there was an increasingly strong preference for all that was analytic and a shunning of the synthetic (cf. Falk 1995: 254,

1999: 57–58, 61–66; Joseph 1999: 55–56). In the context of nineteenth-century language study, this represents a new fashion, contrary to European language scholars' traditional love for the subtle complexities of inflection embodied in the classical languages. This judgement would seem to have been first explicitly expressed by Friedrich von Schlegel, who famously admired the 'organic' Indo-European languages, in which the inflections grew from the *lebendiger Keim* (living germ) of the root, while all other languages merely combine roots and affixes 'mechanically' (Schlegel 1808: 50–52). Following this assessment, August Schlegel himself assigned *le premier rang* (first place) to the inflecting languages (Schlegel 1818: 15).

Wilhelm von Humboldt (1767–1835), although recognising and valuing the diversity of grammatical processes exhibited by the world's languages, similarly admired inflection, and provided a detailed justification for his judgement in terms of the philosophy of Immanuel Kant (1724–1804). According to Humboldt, language is the locus of the Kantian *Einbildungskraft* (faculty of imagination), which effects a synthesis of 'sensuality' and 'understanding'. A word in language combines a physically perceptible sound with a concept, and through this combination the two sides, the sound and the concept, take on definite form. Only in inflected forms is this process of Kantian synthesis properly achieved. The inflected word combines the concept and its relation to the rest of the proposition – expressed by the root and inflection respectively – into a single package where the concept retains its identity. This is in contrast to isolating and agglutinating structures, where the relation is only in loose association to the concept or not expressed at all, and to 'incorporating' structures – an additional type recognised by Humboldt, exemplified by the Mexican language Nahuatl – where one concept swallows up another (see Humboldt 1836: 169; Trabant 2012: 103).

In an intellectual environment in which the synthetic inflecting languages represent the height of linguistic development, the loss of inflection in their modern analytic descendants could only be a sign of degeneration. This attitude found its most extreme expression in the work of August Schleicher (1821–1868), the leading comparative grammarian of the mid-century (see Morpurgo Davies 1975: 652–682, 1998: 196–200; Koerner 1989c). Discussing the 'evolution' of the older synthetic Germanic languages, represented by Gothic, into the modern, analytic Germanic languages, Schleicher wrote:

> Our words, as contrasted with Gothic words, are like a statue that has been rolling for a long time in a bed of a river till its beautiful limbs have been worn off, so that now scarcely anything remains but a polished stone with faint indications of what it once was. (Schleicher 1860: 34)[15]

Although many rebutted what they saw as excesses in his theorising – prominent here is the American linguist William Dwight Whitney (1827–1894) (see Alter 2005) – Schleicher's thought shaped much of the linguistic landscape in the middle of the nineteenth century. This is no doubt the reason why Jespersen made an example of Schleicher in combating this attitude to language. In his doctoral dissertation, published in 1894 in English translation, with the frank title *Progress in Language*, Jespersen argued against the exaltation of the synthetic, which he attributed squarely to Schleicher. On Jespersen's account, Schleicher wanted to force existing typologies into a Hegelian scheme of development and decline where, with the progress of civilisation in prehistory, languages climb from isolating origins to the heights of flexional synthesis, and then collapse into analytic forms in historical times (see Jespersen 1960 [1920]: 698–701; and Schleicher 1860: 35; cf. Schleicher 1865: 28–29).

By contrast, Jespersen (1894: 25–26) saw analyticity as an advance: 'In language, analysis means suppleness, and synthesis means rigidity.' Analysis hands the speaker the means to express themselves naturally, as they wish; synthesis, on the other hand, forces the speaker to fit their expression to complex inherited arbitrary forms. This is a view that Jespersen maintained throughout his career: his last publication, Jespersen (1960 [1941]), revisits the topic. It is also a view that would resonate with Ogden's later work, especially in its admiration of English as one of the best present-day representatives of the analytic tendency. Schleicher's scheme, asserted Jespersen (1894: 9–10), is simply the product of unfounded prejudice, 'a grammar-school admiration, a Renaissance love of the two classical languages and their literatures'. He concluded: 'The so-called full and rich forms of the ancient languages are not a beauty but a deformity' (Jespersen 1894: 14).

The reaction against Schleicher, Jespersen (1894: 14–16) believed, was the beginning of a shifting tide: he cited scattered statements from a handful of his contemporaries who were drawn to the new analytic aesthetics. We also observe that the committee of the American Philosophical Society, in rejecting Volapük, commented:

> Volapük is synthetic and complex; all modern dialects become more and more analytic and grammatically simple; the formal elements of Volapük are those long since discarded and outgrown by Aryan speech [… Volapük] seems to us a distinct retrogression in linguistic progress. (Brinton, Phillips and Snyder 1888: 12)

In a supplement to the report, in which they responded to criticisms of their conclusions, the committee continued:

> The crucial test of the development of language is that the sentence shall express the thought intended to be conveyed, and *nothing more*. When this can be attained simply by the order of words in the sentence, without changes in those words, such changes are not merely useless, they are burdensome, and impede the mind. (Brinton, Phillips and Snyder 1888: 14)

'Analyticity', in a related sense, was in these years a key desideratum of the new logical notations. This sense of analyticity was similarly anchored in Kantian philosophy: in his epistemology, Kant classified knowledge along the dimensions of the *a priori* versus the *a posteriori*, and the *synthetic* versus the *analytic*. Analytic judgements, said Kant (1998 [1781]: 141), 'do not add anything to the concept of the subject, but only break it up by means of analysis into its component concepts, which were already thought in it (though confusedly)'. Synthetic judgements, by contrast, 'add to the concept of the subject a predicate that was not thought in it at all, and could not have been extracted from it through any analysis' (Kant 1998 [1781]: 141).[16] The additional input required to form synthetic judgements comes from human intuition.

The history of logical developments from Frege onwards is to no small extent one of trying to expand the analytic domain by broadening the applicability of logical analysis. This is the impetus behind logicism in mathematics, of which Frege and Peano were pioneers (see Chapter 2, §III). Although in later years he engaged much less with the distinction between synthetic and analytic, Frege (1959 [1884]: §88) sought to demonstrate that mathematical truths are analytic, in that they can be reduced to and proved in logic, and not synthetic, as Kant (1998 [1781]: 144) had claimed. 'The truth is that they [mathematical truths] are contained in the definitions', argued Frege (1959 [1884]: 101), 'but as plants are contained in their seeds, not as beams are contained in a house'. It is to reveal this analytic character and set it out in visible form that Frege was driven to invent his *Begriffsschrift* (Frege 1959 [1884]: §91). Through his enhanced notion of analytic judgements Frege sought a means for perspicuously capturing the creative insights that allow us to grasp such truths, all in a form that can be mechanically verified (see chapters 3 and 4 of Dummett 1991).

While Peano did not address Kant directly, Russell certainly saw his developments in logical notation and the accompanying axiomatisation of arithmetic (see Chapter 2, §III) as helping to demonstrate the underlying analytic nature of mathematical judgements, against Kant's erroneous insistence on their synthetic character:

> [T]he Kantian view [. . .] asserted that mathematical reasoning is not strictly formal [i.e. analytic], but always uses intuitions [... i.e. synthetic]. Thanks to the progress of Symbolic Logic, especially as treated by Professor Peano, this part of the Kantian philosophy is now capable of a final and irrevocable refutation. (Russell 1903: 4)

Russell's later technical and theoretical efforts, in particular his theory of descriptions, were aimed at broadening this facility for analysis to expressions beyond mathematics. This was perhaps also the motivation behind Wittgenstein's characterisation of the structure of logic as the structure of the world (Wittgenstein 1922: prop. 5.6–5.61).

In the same tradition, Rudolf Carnap, a former student of Frege's (introduced into this book properly in Chapter 4), explicitly embraced Kant's distinction in his general epistemology and identified the *a priori* with the analytic and the *a posteriori* with the synthetic, eliminating Kant's category of the 'synthetic *a priori*', knowledge prior to experience that is not contained in the terms themselves, the category to which Kant assigned mathematical truths (Carnap 1967 [1928]: §106). Carnap's example, followed notably by the British exponent of Viennese logical positivism Alfred Jules Ayer (1910–1989) (1946 [1936]: 77–83), became one of the two 'dogmas of empiricism' that the American philosopher Willard Van Orman Quine (1908–2000) identified in his later critique of logical positivism (Quine 1953 [1951]), a dogma that Quine and others found problematic (other critiques include White 1950; Hempel 1965: chapter 4, based on material dating back to 1950–1951; and the much later Kripke 1980 [1972]). Beginning with Frege and Peano, and coming to a close with Quine, there is an undeniable preference among logicians for analysis, which leads to efforts to expand the domain of what can be analysed by fashioning formalisms that lay analytic structures bare.

The new logical notations may have in fact contributed to changing aesthetic preferences in linguistics. Certainly links between linguistics and the new language-critical analytic philosophy are attested later in this period. Joseph (1996) convincingly demonstrates that Sapir's well-known views on the connection of linguistic form to speakers' habitual patterns of thought owe much to new developments in philosophy, and in particular to *The Meaning of Meaning* (cf. Koerner 2000 for a simultaneous reinforcing and tempering of these arguments). In his role as director of linguistic research at the IALA, Sapir was also an advocate of an analytic structure for the international language (Sapir 1925; cf. Falk 1999: 61–63). Leonard Bloomfield (1887–1949), another leading pioneer of American structural linguistics, was deeply impressed by the later logical positivists' work in logic and epistemology (see Chapter 5, §I), and incorporated many of their tenets and methods into his approach to linguistics (see Bloomfield 1936, 1938; Hiz and Swiggers 1990; Tomalin 2004). Although no great supporter of the international language movement (see Falk 1999: 61), he saw 'simplification' towards the analytic pole as an inevitable, if not desirable, process in language change (see Joseph and Newmeyer 2012: 347; see also McElvenny 2017: 430–432).

Fashions in the international language movement accord with those in mainstream philology and linguistics: the earlier international language projects, such as Volapük and Esperanto, tended more towards synthesis, while later projects turned increasingly to analytic structures. Basic stands at the end of this trend, with Ogden arguing that English presents the most suitable basis for the international language precisely because of its naturally analytic structure, even more analytic than most of the constructed languages.

In the earlier projects grammatical simplification over natural languages was achieved through regularising the morphology and removing the most obviously arbitrary grammatical categories, such as grammatical gender. Inflection in Volapük admits no irregularities or exceptions, and common but often redundant categories such as adjective-noun agreement and grammatical gender are absent. But Volapük nouns still inflect for four cases – nominative, accusative, dative and genitive, as in German – and singular and plural number. Verbs agree with their subjects for person, number and natural gender, and exhibit a number of voice, aspect and tense inflections; Carlevaro (cited in Blanke 1985: 209) calculates 2,688 distinct forms of each transitive verb in Volapük (for guides to Volapük grammar, see Kerckhoffs 1885; Schleyer 1888, 1982 [1880]; Blanke 1985). Schleyer believed that his reforms to the general European grammatical pattern made the language clearer: 'All artifice, unclarity and bizarreness are proscribed in it [the language]!! [. . .] The language is not for hiding one's thoughts, but for sharing them!' (Schleyer 1982 [1880]: 5).[17] He did not seem to have any overarching scheme dictating how that clarity should be achieved, however.

Esperanto represents in many respects an extension of the Volapük pattern. There is the same absolute paradigmatic regularity and movement away from grammatical gender and agreement, in this case subject-verb concord, but morphology remains an integral part of the nominal and verbal system of the language. Central to the language is a system in which the parts of speech that traditionally inflect and are mutually derivable in the European languages are explicitly marked with certain endings: nouns with *-o*, adjectives with *-a*, adverbs with *-e*, and verbs in the infinitive with *-i*. Verbs have five additional endings, covering several tenses and moods – present, past, future, conditional and imperative – and can be derived to create active and passive participles in each of the tenses. Nouns and adjectives inflect for two cases, nominative and accusative, plus singular and plural number, and they exhibit agreement in this inflection (see Zamenhof 1889 [1887] and Zamenhof 1905 for outlines of Esperanto grammar).

With the growing technocratic current in the international language movement, logicians came to play an increasingly important role and the juggernaut of analytic syntax made its progress. The elimination of morphology was the leitmotiv of such languages as Peano's Latino sine Flexione, literally, 'Latin without inflections'. Indeed, Peano, in his two capacities of pioneering logicist and language constructor, provides an illustrative example of the convergence of fashions between these groups. In both his logical notation and his international language project he aimed for unadorned, linear analytic forms. Even in the case of Latino sine Flexione, however, the commitment to analytic forms came into conflict with naturalising *a posteriori* design considerations: in his original proposals for the language, Peano (1903) did indeed eliminate all inflection, but in subsequent revisions number inflection on nouns crept back into the language (see Barandovská-Frank 2003: 20).

Similar conflicts arise in the history of Ido and IALA Interlingua. The Ido reforms saw a dismantling of much of the morphological apparatus of Esperanto: adjective-noun agreement was eliminated and the accusative case was made optional. This represented the '[s]uppression of certain useless grammatical rules, which are troublesome to many nations, and *especially to persons possessing only an elementary education*' (Couturat *et al.* 1910: 75; emphasis original).

That is, the elimination of the arbitrary insofar as it is superfluous and the naturalisation of the grammar for speakers of languages without these features (most notably English, and most modern Romance languages, at least as far as the accusative is concerned). Further naturalising reforms in Ido are scattered throughout the grammar. In many cases, these actually make the language less 'analytic', in that isomorphy between form and meaning in Esperanto is collapsed in some Ido forms; for example, the Esperanto plural noun ending *-oj*, where *-o* marks noun and *-j* plural, is collapsed in Ido to the monomorphemic *-i* (see Beaufront 2004 [1925]; Couturat *et al.* 1910: 75–85; Blanke 1985:189–192 for Ido grammar and contrasts to Esperanto).

IALA Interlingua, released around fifty years later, represents the almost complete surrender of the analytic in grammar to the *a posteriori* (cf. chapter 8 of Blanke 2006). Grammatically, it is essentially English: nouns inflect for number, pronouns for case and verbs for tense. By this time, the *a posteriori* had grown so much in importance that the frequent and quasi-grammatical verbs *haber* 'have', *esser* 'be' and *vader* 'go' were granted irregular past tense forms, mimicking their behaviour in the major European languages (see Gode and Blair 1971 [1951]). Despite his preference for analytic structures, Sapir, as director of research at the IALA, recognised the overriding importance of harmonising the international language with existing languages (cf. Falk 1999: 65). He presaged the IALA's surrender of analyticity to the *a posteriori* as he observed:

> [S]o far as the logical structure of a language is concerned, we are perhaps not at the end of our researches [... W]e, who are fashioning Occidental culture[,] have been using certain useful linguistic tools. These tools vary from place to place, but by and large are remarkably similar [... W]hy not use the common bond of experience which is implicit in the use of all these tools in a simplified and regularized form? (Sapir 1929: 17–18)

In fact Gode, the principal designer of Interlingua, later spoke frequently of 'Standard Average European', a term coined by Sapir's student Benjamin Lee Whorf (1897–1941) to designate precisely the commonalities in linguistic structure that Sapir describes (see Whorf 1956; Gode 1959: 30). Basic also surrenders logical structure to the *a posteriori*: being essentially a subset of the natural language English, its grammar exhibits all the exceptions and irregularities of English that are represented in the subset. English was sufficiently superior in other respects, argued Ogden, that such unfortunate lapses could be tolerated (see §VI).

The same tension between *a posteriori* considerations and the desire to achieve an 'analytic' structure played out in the design of vocabularies. Volapük, in both its grammar and vocabulary, so claimed Schleyer (1982 [1880]: 3, 7), was derived from the major European languages, with special attention given to English. But Schleyer's desire to improve the languages, in this case to force words into a better phonological scheme, frequently rendered the borrowed roots unrecognisable: *vol* and *pük*, for example, are derived from the English words 'world' and 'speak' respectively (the intervening *a* is a genitive ending on *vol*). Schleyer (1888) provided lists of the rules he said he used in constructing the vocabulary, but the rules have a rather miscellaneous and arbitrary character: nouns must not end in sibilants, words must not be longer than six syllables, clusters of three consonants or vowels were not allowed, the letters *s*, *k*, *o*, *ä*, *ö*, *ü*, *p*, *h*, *r*, *l* should be avoided as much as possible, and syllables that do not contribute directly to the clarity of a word can be dropped. Schleyer never felt the need to justify these rules, and in fact gave himself licence to ignore them in any particular case if he felt they would be inappropriate, which only served to increase their arbitrariness.

In Esperanto the source of Zamenhof's borrowed lexical forms is more transparent, but he imposed an *a priori* agglutinative affix system on the vocabulary, mainly as a means of reducing the amount of material a learner would need to assimilate to use the language: he claimed that the learner would need to memorise only 900 roots and affixes (Zamenhof 1889 [1887]). For example, in Esperanto the prefix *mal-* marks 'opposite', so from *bona* 'good' it is possible to derive *malbona* 'bad'; from *sana* 'healthy', *malsana* 'sick'. The suffix *-il* indicates an instrument; from the verb *tranĉi* 'to cut' can be derived *tranĉilo* 'knife'. Zamenhof's stated motivation for using recognisable borrowed roots is also mnemonic; he had experimented with wholly invented forms, but found them too difficult to remember. In any case, he noticed, there is already a huge store of shared words in the major languages, words that are already international, with an origin mainly in the Romance and Germanic languages (Zamenhof 1929 [1896]: 419–420).

The rigorous statistical identification and selection of 'international words' became a hallmark of the later technocratic international language projects, such as Ido and IALA Interlingua. Jespersen (1910 [1909]: 30–34) devoted himself to the technical task of measuring the internationality of forms in Ido against Esperanto, and credits the idea of rigorously evaluating the international credentials of existing words to Rosenberger (1902) in his Idiom Neutral (see Guérard 1922: 157–158 for some refinements on Jespersen's observations). Jespersen (1928) later applied the international metrics he developed to the vocabulary of his own language, Novial. In IALA Interlingua, the design of the vocabulary became simply a 'standardization project' (a term used in IALA 1945, among other places) of the divergent yet fundamentally similar European languages, in keeping with the direction Sapir had already suggested. Schleyer never accepted international recognisability as the leading criterion in word selection. Long after Esperanto with its familiar roots had already eclipsed Volapük, Schleyer commented bitterly:

> [T]o simply adopt purely Latin words in a charlatan's language [a term Schleyer used to refer to Esperanto], like *homo, sed,* and similar – any language-charlatan, who wants to make the matter easy and only wants to make a bit of money, can do that. And that

is something that many other imitators of Vp. [Volapük] before S. [Zamenhof] have already done, but also without success. (Schleyer 2001 [1900]: 7)[18]

With the *a posteriori* principle that word roots should be 'international' firmly entrenched in Esperanto, *a priori* 'analytic' concerns further directed principles of word formation in many subsequent projects. Leading the analytic charge in the Esperanto versus Ido debate was Couturat, first and foremost a mathematician and logician. Every morpheme, Couturat (1910 [1909]: 43–44; see also Couturat 1907, 1910) said, attributing the insight to Wilhelm Ostwald but also reprising his idol Leibniz, should correspond exclusively to a single idea: there should be no homonymy or synonymy. Words with related meanings should display their semantic relationship in their forms; the meanings of the derived words should always be predictable and reversible. Agglutination, which for Zamenhof was mainly an aid to learning the language, became the servant of logic:

> [T]he [international] language will become the exact and faithful expression of our thoughts, and will conform to that indwelling and instinctive logic which, in spite of all sorts of irregularities and exceptions, animates our languages [. . .] Not only does it [the international language] offer to them [philosophers], as it does to all men, a medium of communication between all countries, but it furnishes them also with an instrument of precision for the analysis and exact expression of the forms of thought, which is very superior, from the point of view of logic, to our traditional languages, encumbered as these are with confused and ambiguous expressions. (Couturat 1910 [1909]: 51–52)

These principles led to strict, logically motivated rules of word derivation in Ido (for comparisons of Ido and Esperanto word derivation, see Couturat 1910 [1909]: 46; Jespersen 1910 [1909]: 40; Blanke 1985: 193).[19] The IALA continued the tradition of striving for form-meaning isomorphy and relentless consistency, a goal that frequently lost out to *a posteriori* requirements: Interlingua *per-mitt-er* should mean 'send, put through', but instead means 'permit, allow'; *con-clud-er* means 'conclude', not 'close along with' (these examples are adapted from Blanke 1985: 180; see Gode 1971 [1951]: xlvi–xlvii for a description of the system of Interlingua word composition). Basic, by contrast, did not subscribe to the logicians' ideal of form-meaning isomorphy: Ogden embraced metaphor as a means to extending the semantic range of words in his language, drawing on the theory of interpretation and definition outlined in *The Meaning of Meaning*, and possibly inspired by features of preceding projects from the Enlightenment (see §V).

Over the course of the modern international language movement we see a growing commitment to the *a posteriori* in designing the international language, which often conflicted with the desire to make the international language 'analytic', as that term was understood in both logical and linguistic circles. The solution settled on towards the end of the period was generally to ensure that the lexical substance of the international language was *a posteriori* – largely for the ease this provided in learning the language – but that the grammar and rules of word formation answered to logical, 'analytic' dictates. Ogden essentially shared these aesthetic concerns in Basic, although he had no time for the painstaking striving for international neutrality that was so central to most of these projects.

IV. Basic English and the common solution

The common aesthetic considerations in vocabulary and grammar, the striving for a logical structure in language, Ogden took on board in Basic, but the endless agonising over the most inclusive *a posteriori* forms for the international language he simply threw overboard. 'Make everybody speak English', Ogden (1931: 13) said, quoting the contemporary American capitalist Henry Ford. Ford in fact permeates Ogden's project: the ubiquity of his name, rendered a trademark, led Ogden to admit it into Basic as a permissible word for 'automobile' (see §V below; Ogden 1943: 25 repeats the Ford anecdote with a more tolerant moral). The advanced 'analytic tendency' of English, argued Ogden, already offers the perfect basis for logical language; the job of the language constructor is merely to exploit this tendency and make the language accessible to the foreigner. While it is true that other language constructors looked favourably on English – Schleyer (1982 [1880]: 3) said that 'Volapük is based on English, since it is the easiest and most widespread of all the civilised languages',[20] Zamenhof (1929: 418) drew inspiration from 'the simplicity of English grammar', and Sapir (1925: 248) saw English moving towards the analytic ideal, already reached by Chinese – the conclusion that English alone, and not some carefully composed pot-pourri of the major languages, provided all that was needed to solve the international language problem was, to most in the international language movement, nothing short of scandalous.

Although there were proposals to officially sanction some national languages, such as English and French, in particular geographical 'zones', such proposals remained far from the mainstream (see Stojan 1929). Some constructed languages, such as Peano's Latino sine Flexione, took existing languages as their basis, in this case Latin, but this is emphatically a dead language and one that already has a long history as a medium of international communication. The only directly comparable projects, which attempted to refashion one living national language for international purposes, were widely denounced as chauvinistic. One notable and somewhat inexplicable episode involved Wilhelm Ostwald (1915), who in the early phases of the First World War called for the creation of *Weltdeutsch* to help protect German interests. Baumann (1915) represents an effort to implement this proposal, and the earlier Salzmann (1913) was a similarly conceived project for the already faltering multi-ethnic and multilingual Austro-Hungarian Empire (see Stojan 1929 and Krajewski 2006 for further details).

In the face of such denunciations, however, Ogden argued that the *a posteriori* constructed languages, with their Romano-Germanic vocabularies and grammar, offer an unfair advantage to native speakers of languages from those families and discriminate against others, a state of affairs that would not be tolerated if the Romance and Germanic languages were not already dominant. 'If orientals were to agree to promote some modification of Cantonese or Hakka, similar in many respects to Chinese and Japanese, as an international language for Europe', Ogden (1935: 8) pointed out, 'its claims to "neutrality" would hardly be taken seriously'.[21] Ogden's gaze beyond Europe to the world is perhaps peculiarly British, the perspective of a nation whose territories and trade lay mostly beyond that continent; although, it must be noted, the charge of Euro-centrism against constructed languages had already been made by the German linguists Gustav Meyer (1850–1900) (1976 [1891]: 41), Karl Brugman (1839–1919) and August Leskien (1840–1916) (Brugman and Leskien 1907: 22), among many other objections they raised.

Further pressing the claims for English, Ogden (1933 [1930]: 1) observed that, quite apart from its naturally superior structure to the constructed languages, English was already more widespread than any of them, including Esperanto: 'English is the expanding administrative (or auxiliary) language of over 600,000,000 people and financial reasons alone should convince even those who take statistics seriously that it is bound to expand more rapidly in the near future.' In any case, the arousal of national jealousies should be no argument against English; foreigners must simply put aside their petty interests in the face of the best solution:

> The objection that many Frenchmen and Indians would not be in favour of the adoption of any form of English as an auxiliary language is not more serious than the objection that many diplomats and military men are not in favour of peace – as an argument against international arbitration. (Ogden 1931: 107)

As we have seen, Ogden's first recorded thoughts on fashioning English for international purposes were written at the outset of the First World War (see §II). In Ogden's mind, securing peace and progress relied on exporting the English tongue, and the English mind it serves. This is essentially a colonial project, where those to be colonised are no less than the entire non-English speaking population of the world. This view was no peculiarity of Ogden's: his collaborator I. A. Richards spent a significant part of the 1930s and 1940s in China, bringing, with the support of the American Rockefeller Foundation, the Chinese into the modern world, where they would, according to Richards (1935: 45), 'need an understanding of an enormous number of ideas, feelings, desires and attitudes that they can only gain through some form of Western Language. In practice this means some form of English.' Richards' attitude was not one of cultural genocide – he loved traditional Chinese culture and worked to aid its further transmission – but at the same time he saw the expansionist march of the colonial west and felt he had to give the Chinese the intellectual tools they would need to remain their own masters (see Russo 1989: 405; cf. Joseph 1999: 69–70). Present-day mores would brand Richards' attitude paternalistic, not without reason.

Richards, like Ogden, also endorsed Basic as a technologically advanced tool of pacifism because, in breaking down language barriers and forcing people to work at thinking through their ideas, it would foster mutual understanding and contemplation. 'Without canned food, modern metallurgy, and oil, there could be no global war', Richards (1943: vi) writes. What is needed are corresponding 'developments in the means of mental transport – and thereby in the spreading of common truths which would make antagonism and disloyalty harder to cultivate'. Basic would provide this 'means of mental transport', and in so doing ensure that speakers have properly formulated ideas to transmit, preventing pointless and hollow arguments, which can spill over into attempted resolutions through physical force:

> Basic as a tool in training thought discourages dispute. It curbs our eternal temptation to argue before we know what we are arguing about. It is a restraint upon the habit of verbal warfare which may be connected more closely than we suppose with actual warfare as a key institution of our traditional culture. We shall never have a reasonable world until we are more reasonable within ourselves. (Richards 1943: 101)

The faith in the English language as the ultimate medium of reason and resolution took the first steps to becoming British government policy in 1943, as British Prime Minister Winston Churchill (1874–1965) laid out his vision for the world after an Allied victory in the war:

> I like to think of British and Americans moving about freely over each other's wide estates with hardly a sense of being foreigners to one another. But I do not see why we should not try to spread our common language even more widely throughout the globe, and without seeking selfish advantage over any, possess ourselves of this invaluable amenity and birthright [. . .] Such plans offer far better prizes than taking away other people's provinces or land, or grinding them down in exploitation. The empires of the future are the empires of the mind. (Churchill 1944 [1943]: 97–99)

The white man's burden had become the Anglo-American burden of post-war reconstruction; the spoils were no longer natural resources and limitless labour, but the fertile territories of people's minds; and the gifts of civilisation were no longer products of industry, but words and thoughts.

Churchill acted on these words immediately and ordered an enquiry into Basic, with a view to adopting it as government policy. The machinations of public servants and the hostility of the British Council – which had its own vision of the reconstructed, Anglicised world – meant, however, that the project withered on the bureaucratic vine (see Graham 1977: 159–160; Lauwerys 1977:

163–166; Gordon 1990b: 50–53; cf. the account of British and American language policy in Phillipson's 1992 study of 'linguistic imperialism'). A lack of co-ordination between Ogden and Richards in this period may have also played a role: by this time Richards had become the main representative of Basic in the United States, a status resented by Ogden, a language creator perhaps no less jealous than Schleyer. With confusion on either side of the Atlantic over what support was forthcoming from what institutions, and with Ogden and Richards unwilling to mount a joint campaign, official support and funding for Basic evaporated (see Russo 1989: 438–441; Joseph 1999: 61–64).

But in 1943, riding on the swell of Churchill's endorsement, Ogden – drawing a straight line through Schleyer, the technocrat language constructors, Churchill and the science fiction author H. G. Wells (whose contribution we examine in §VIII below) – allowed himself to imagine the reconstructed, technological Anglo-American future, supported by Basic (and described here in Basic):

> [I]t has long been clear that the divisions between countries have become far less natural than the rivers and mountains which have kept men shut up, as if in boxes, for thousands of years. Our present-day boxes are the systems of ideas by which, through education, the mind is limited to the words of one "nation" – walled in, as the prisoner of language. But in the past 20 years science has at last taken the roof off, and through the air come the voices and the machines, which, as was noted by the Prime Minister at Harvard, have overcome the distances of the past and made the earth suddenly seem so much smaller. That is why an International Air Force, policing land and sea, and a second or International Language, working with Radio, are the two chief instruments by which the future may be guided to Peace [. . .]. (Ogden 1943: 23–24)

Not everyone saw the benevolent role of the English-speaking nations in leading the world to peace and progress, however. Albert Guérard (1880–1959), in his survey of the mature international language movement, saw little difference between English-speaking exceptionality and the belligerent nationalism fostered by fascism (see also Drezen 1931: 138 for a similar critique):

> [T]he adoption of any national language for international purposes is not to be desired even if it were feasible. It is well to insist upon this point, for in every man there slumbers a Hitler, eager to force his will and to assert the supremacy of his own tribe. Many Americans, not consciously imperialistic, take it for granted that when the world comes to its senses it will adopt the language as well as the fashions of Hollywood. Among English radicals there survives an enormous insularity which would be ludicrous if it were not appalling. H. G. Wells chides mankind for not creating the World State – but the Wellsian World State must be of English speech [see §VIII]. A subtle logican like Mr. Ogden is on this point as obtuse as any realtor from Zenith [. . .].[22] What most advocates of International English fail to realize is that the materialistic arguments they adduce really militate against the language. Wealth, numbers, "dominion over palm and pine," "mastery of the seven seas" – all that

blatant Kiplingesque self-assertion is a bid for universal supremacy; and against such supremacy the world will eternally revolt. (Guérard 1944 [1941]: 134)

Of course, in today's world the international language problem is rarely mentioned, at least not in the terms we have seen here. A solution has been found: English – Standard English, or at least varieties that approach the codified ideal – is at this moment the international language – in science and technology, travel, the media – a status it has won not through the careful plans of any scholar, but through the sheer weight of British and then, especially in the decades following the Second World War, American economic, military and cultural hegemony. Whether this state of affairs vindicates Ogden or whether it is the realisation of his opponents' fears is a difficult question. As the simple victory of might over mind, it is probably fair to say that it is not precisely what Ogden and his supporters envisaged.

From time to time simplified versions of English are propounded and even implemented, but these are almost always intended for special purposes or as stepping stones to the standard language. A representative selection would include such projects as 'Special English', used by the Voice of America since the end of the 1950s for broadcasts targeted at English learners (see Voice of America 2009); 'Caterpillar Fundamental English', developed by the Caterpillar Tractor Company in the 1970s for international manuals (Verbeke 1973; Kamprath *et al.* 1998); and the recent 'Globish' of Nerrière (2006), which is conceived principally as a medium for international business communication. Each project has its individual features – slow speaking rate, avoidance of idiom, incorporation of gesture, and so on – but a common thread running through all of them is the adherence to a restricted core vocabulary, the key feature of Ogden's Basic, as we see in the following sections.

Unlike the projects espoused by Ogden and his generation, however, latter-day simplified Englishes are generally conceived with specific practical goals in mind and do not rest on grand theories and sentiments. Increasingly, too, these reduced Englishes do not seek to establish or serve Anglo-American hegemony, but are a reaction against it. Globish, for example, is marketed as a remedy to the *fait accompli* of international English: it seeks to provide a compromise variety that eliminates any expressive advantages native English speakers might have over second-language learners.

Basic occupied a curious place in relation to the 'common solution' to the international language problem. While in his preference for 'analytic' structure with minimal morphology Ogden conformed to the established design aesthetics of the mainstream international language movement, in his abandonment of the ideal 'international' compromise in discovering *a posteriori* forms he abnegated one of their dearest principles. Ogden's attitude was perhaps typically British, the attitude of a nation whose unparalleled power was built, first and foremost, on its global trading empire, whose exports included not only material goods but also its language and culture. British conquest and expansion, in the received narrative, was effected more through peaceful and mutually beneficial economic exchange than by military means.

V. Panoptic conjugation

Whereas most earlier language constructors concerned themselves in equal measure with grammar and vocabulary – even if only to eliminate grammar, understood as morphology, in approaching the analytic ideal – Ogden concentrated solely on vocabulary. The key to a successful international language, according to Ogden, was to have a minimal vocabulary consisting of words 'scientifically selected' for their reliability in reference, a claim Ogden repeated frequently (but probably first mentioned in Ogden 1929a: 1, repeated word for word in Ogden 1933 [1930]: 1). This is a conviction deeply rooted in his thought. In *The Meaning of Meaning*, the malady he and Richards identified was 'word-magic', the superstitious subjugation of sense to the lexicon (see Chapter 2). Their remedy there was the unpacking of references to find what each word actually means, if anything.

Basic pursued the principles set out in *The Meaning of Meaning* to their conclusion. The language offered a restricted core vocabulary of what were claimed to be the most necessary and reliable words, 850 in number, and thereby forced users of the language to spell out what they mean. This had the additional advantage of reducing the amount of material the learner had to assimilate. The solution to 'the problem of a Universal language', asserted Ogden (1929a: 1), lies in shrinking the entire language down to 'no more than can be made easily legible to the naked eye, in column form, on the back of a sheet of notepaper'. His ideal was a 'panoptic' language, a language 'seen at a glance'.

To arrive at the 850 words of the Basic core vocabulary, Ogden developed the method of 'panoptic conjugation', essentially a procedure for revealing the semantic relations between words. From a central 'root word', the semantic 'conjugates', as Ogden called them, can be discovered by following various 'radial definition routes'; that is, semantic dimensions along which the 'conjugates' differ from the root word. From the root word 'man' we find such words as 'Southerner' (a man from a certain place), 'octogenarian' (of a certain age), 'dwarf' (of a certain size) (Ogden 1930: 13–14). This is 'conjugation' since Ogden imagined these words forming a semantic paradigm – like the inflectional paradigm, or conjugation, of a verb – where each of the peripheral words is derived from the root word. He described the technique in the following terms (see also Ogden 1930: 9–17; Lockhart 1931a: 73–75):

To conjugate a verb is to put it through its tricks. Conjugates, in another connexion, are words related to the same root. If we apply the terms to words in general so that any word can have its conjugation and conjugates, it will be convenient to exhibit these so that they can be appreciated at a glance – panoptically. The most convenient panoptic method is to place the word under consideration at the centre of a circle, whose radii can then represent the directions in which the conjugates may be sought. For example, in the case of 'House', cottage, bungalow, hotel, sanatorium, palace, hut, hovel, home, city, room, chimney, etc. (Ogden 1928c: 2)

This method is 'panoptic', as Ogden put it, because the words should be laid out in such a way that their relationships are all visible 'at a glance' (echoing a hope Russell held out for his 'logically perfect language'; see Chapter 2, §III). To this end Ogden further indulged his penchant for visualisation and offered the diagram in Figure 3.1, which has a place for a root word, twenty 'radial definition routes' – clearly the definition routes of *The Meaning of Meaning* catalogued and enumerated (see Chapter 2, §II) – plus conjugates related by opposition, marked and unmarked derivation.

The semantic roots discovered through panoptic conjugation become the words adopted into the Basic core vocabulary, while their peripheral conjugates are eliminated, a procedure Ogden (1930: 14) codified in his 'elimination formula': 'Given the word at the centre [of the panoptic conjugation diagram], and the means of covering the radial definition route in not more than nine words, then the conjugate at the periphery can be eliminated.' The eliminated words are replaced by paraphrases based on the root word and the radial definition route: 'Southerner' becomes 'a man from the South'; 'dwarf' becomes 'a man much smaller than normal size', and so on. The paraphrases are enshrined in the Basic dictionary as 'dictionary clichés', the standard translation of the eliminated words into Basic (see Ogden 1929b: 20, 1930a: 14; Ogden 1932c is the actual Basic dictionary).

But several practical restrictions on word elimination complicate this picture. As Ogden stated in his 'elimination formula', if the paraphrase is more than nine words long or otherwise 'awkward', the original word should be retained. Peripheral words can also obtain a reprieve from elimination if they help avoid homophony, are very frequent, or are useful in forming derivatives and metaphors (Ogden 1929a: 5, 1930a: 14). With further exposition, Ogden's 'scientific' method is increasingly taking on the character of an art, dependent on his intuition and ineffable judgement. The radial definition routes, for instance, are never described rigorously; we have to divine them from the examples Ogden provides. Likewise, we are never given a way to assess the 'awkwardness' of paraphrases. Determination and elimination of homophony, on the other hand, can be performed mechanically, but this principle clearly has subordinate status in forming the core vocabulary: *I* and *eye* are both among the 850. Word frequency similarly requires no special talent – it is simply a matter of counting – but Ogden was highly critical of learning vocabularies based on word frequency, of which there were many compiled at the time (see §II), commenting:

[T]he real statistical task of linguistic [*sic*] is not so much the determination of the number of words actually used by any particular person or class of persons as the study of how a reduction may be effected in the number of words which need be used; i.e.

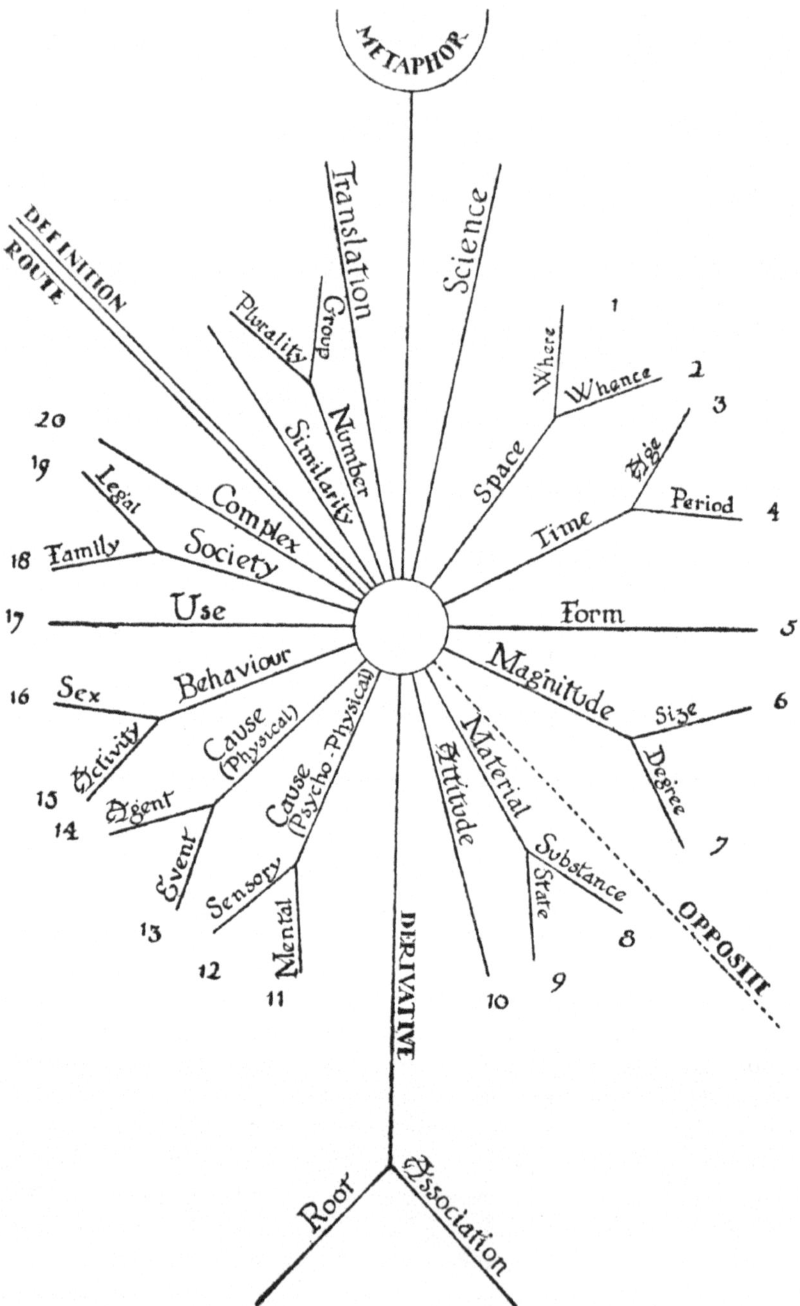

Figure 3.1 Panoptic conjugation
Ogden 1930: 12.

how a given field of reference may be covered with the greatest economy [. . .] What is
really required is a scientifically selected vocabulary minimum. (Ogden 1929b: 9; see
also Walpole 1937; Myers 1938: 55–70)

The possibilities of derivation and metaphor did receive detailed elaboration
from Ogden, but at the same time they reveal Basic's subservience to Standard
English and the problematic status of his claim of 850 words: we see that the core
vocabulary in fact consists of 850 word forms that are generally polysemous and
whose formal and semantic scope is bound by Standard English idiom. In terms
of derivation, only words that would be idiomatic in Standard English can be
created with the agentive suffix *-er/-or* (with the choice between *-er* and *-or* dic-
tated by the corresponding word in Standard English), the gerund and present
participle suffix *-ing*, and the past participle suffix *-ed* (see Ogden 1933 [1930]:
47–50). Compounding involves further difficulties: permissible compounds are
not only restricted by idiom, but their senses are often 'different from what
would be the normal suggestion of the parts', as in the cases of '*become* (= come
to be)' and '*outcome* (= what comes out)' (Ogden 1932a: 54–56).

In the processes of 'extension' and 'specialisation', the possibility of consistency between form and meaning is abandoned as Basic core words take on additional senses without any change in form (Ogden 1933 [1930]: 45–46). Extension
proceeds through metaphor, such as when 'letter', which in its simplest sense is
taken to be a letter of the alphabet, becomes 'letter', an epistle, or 'lift' the action
becomes 'lift', an elevator. In specialisation a word takes on a more specific
sense than it usually has, such as when 'judge' refers specifically to a judge at
law rather than a judge of any other sort. In addition, some words can be used
as different parts of speech without any formal marking: for example, the noun
back can become an adverb and the adjective *round* can become a preposition
(Ogden 1933 [1930]: 47). These various nuances and additional senses inherited
from the standard language are catalogued in *The Basic Words: a detailed account
of their uses* (Ogden 1932b) which, at 101 pages, is far from the panoptic ideal.

The claim to 850 words suffers further when it is revealed that Basic can, as
the need arises, take on 'special vocabularies' consisting of personal and place
names, trade terms, 'localized names', slang, 'measuring terms' (numbers and
units of measure), and scientific words (technical terms). It is thus legitimate
to say in Basic, 'He went to London in his Ford' (i.e. Ford-brand automobile;
Ogden 1929b: 12), where *London* and *Ford* qualify as supernumerary Basic words
because they are a place name and a trade name respectively. 'He went to "Town"
in his "bus"', is equally legitimate: *Town* is a 'localized name' and *bus* a slang term
(Ogden 1929b: 12). But there is an unacknowledged continuum of acceptability
in these *ad hoc* additions: localised names and slang receive quotation marks from
Ogden. In addition, onomatopoeic words are considered 'universally intelligible
without explanation' and can also be used freely in Basic. This includes such
unarguably onomatopoeic expressions as *pop* and *splash*, but also *cuckoo* (the bird
species), *hiccup* (the bodily action) and *tom-tom* (the drums; Ogden 1929b: 14–15).

The same provisos attached to the 'elimination formula' for selecting core words are operative in special vocabularies: we should prefer, for example, 'a word like *clay*, forming *fire-clay*, *china-clay*, *pipe-clay*, etc., [because it] has obvious uses in definition, as have also *filtration* and *distillation*, being key-operations in the definition or description of more complicated processes' (Ogden 1929c: 21–22).

In his pursuit of lexical minimalism Ogden may have fallen prey to his own 'word-magic'. He triumphantly cites the figure of '850 words', but behind many of these word forms lurks a tangled web of unpredictable and idiomatic additional senses. This problem did not go unnoticed by Basic's critics. Among them were Michael West (1888–1973) (1944 [1939]: 152) and Janet Aiken (1892–1944) (1944 [1936]: 147) – proponents of rival reduced Englishes, the 'Carnegie vocabulary' and 'Little English' respectively – as well as Morris Swadesh (1909–1967) (1944: 204), at the time a student of Sapir's engaged in cross-linguistic research for the IALA, who later went on to develop his own concept of a 'core vocabulary' in the form of the 'Swadesh list', a list of 100 words thought to be highly resistant to borrowing that could be used for lexicostatistical comparison of languages (see Swadesh 1955; final version in Swadesh 1972: 283–284). Aiken identified the source of Ogden's problem in an insufficient appreciation for the underlying structure of the language:

> The English language is like an iceberg – two-thirds below the surface. Words are what we see on a page. They are indeed necessary, but their importance is on the whole secondary to linguistic construction, pattern, or structure. Words are more easily learnt than inflections or grammatical rules. The vocabularies which have been devised thus far may be likened to a steeple without a church. What they need most of all is to have a solid underpinning of grammar and construction. If English can be simplified not only in words, but also in these more fundamental respects, then we shall have a result worthy of much praise. (Aiken 1944 [1936]: 147)

But it would seem that Ogden saw the situation precisely reversed: if first the 'words' were correct, the structural aspects of the language would follow. This is a departure from common practice in the international language movement at the time. In terms of their *a priori* theoretical commitments, the majority of language constructors in this period were concerned first and foremost with the formal aspects of language: the striving for analyticity in grammar and vocabulary was a question of the abstract structure of linguistic systems, not of the actual material from which they were to be constructed (see §III). But Ogden made lexical material his core concern and all formal properties contingent to it. As we demonstrate in the following section, Ogden saw the formal features of Basic issuing forth from his constrained, minimalist vocabulary. Although this attitude seems novel to Ogden, it was gaining ground: Morris, the founder of the IALA, emphasised the importance of words over grammar from at least 1924 (see Falk 1995: 244–245, 1999: 57–58, 65), and this view would become one of the main design principles of the later IALA Interlingua:

> It is, then, only a seeming reversal of the principle of grammar's precedence over vocabulary that after the vocabulary of a planned auxiliary language has been determined all that remains to be said by way of grammar must be completely subordinated to the structural characteristics of the vocabulary. The grammatical structure of a planned language determines its basic character precisely as does the structure of a natural language. But the determination of the vocabulary leaves few grammatical questions wholly indeterminate [. . .] The fundamental principle [. . .] must be that this grammar shall be the minimum or simplest possible system fit to govern the use of the chosen vocabulary in coherent speech. (Gode and Blair 1971 [1951]: ix)

Here grammar is made dependent on the vocabulary: grammar becomes nothing more than the 'minimum or simplest possible system' needed for putting words together to make sentences. This is a related but not identical line to the striving for analytic formal structures (cf. Falk 1995: 245–246, 1999: 57–58, 61–66). Rather than advocating the concerted construction of a transparent, analytic grammar, the view here seems to be, as it was with Ogden, that the desired grammar would simply emerge from a deftly assembled vocabulary, or at least that it would be a minimal veneer applied to such a vocabulary.

The shift from considering formal aspects of grammar in the abstract to concentrating on the material substance of words is perhaps unsurprising. On a pre-theoretical level, words are a more obvious, tangible component of language. They are the segmentally instantiated, corporeal forms of speech, unlike more abstract grammatical rules; at the same time they are the bearers of reference. These are among the features that Silverstein (2001 [1977]) recognises as particularly salient in languages cross-culturally and apt to impress themselves on speakers' awareness. That words should come to be seen as the core of language seems in this light understandable: the fascination with abstract formal structure characteristic of mainstream language constructors up to this point represents an intellectualised departure from our lay understanding of language. In a related vein, Joseph (1995; revisited and expanded in 2000: 93–140) argues for the existence of an enduring but not necessarily explicit tradition in western linguistic thought – beginning in the Cratylan naturalism versus conventionalism debate – which sees the natural at home in grammar and the conventional in the lexicon. Language constructors who, even tacitly, subscribe to this view need only concern themselves with the arbitrary and conventional lexicon; the grammar, in reverting to the natural, should take care of itself. This is indeed the programme Ogden pursued.

VI. Grammatical reform

In the preceding exposition a great difference in approach to grammar has emerged between Ogden and his contemporaries: while other language constructors sought simple and logical grammars through the regularisation of the best constructions modern Indo-European languages have to offer, Ogden felt that grammatical reform would proceed naturally from the scientifically selected Basic vocabulary. Whatever grammar exists in Basic is imported clinging to its words. The surprising consequence, in the context of grammars machined to precise rules and measures, is that Basic grammar is permeated by exceptions and irregularities, which go far beyond the quirks of derivation we have already seen above.

The attempt to control Basic grammar through word selection begins with the types of words adopted into the language. The parts of speech that manifest themselves in natural languages, Ogden claimed, are to a large extent simply artefacts of each language's historical development, and depart from the original scheme of 'universal grammar' based on human perception of the world, which recognises a division into 'objects', 'operations' and 'directions':

> [T]he level at which ordinary language is effective, is one where the distinctions between 'entity', 'state', 'change', 'process', 'event', 'behaviour' and 'relation' are reflected in a threefold symbolic differentiation. From the anthropomorphic standpoint, there are the *objects* which we wish to talk about, the *operations* which we perform on them, and the *directions* in which we operate. (Ogden 1929a: 3)

Later that same year, he proposed a different threefold scheme involving 'things', 'events' and 'qualities', recognising qualities as 'mentally differentiated though physically they are inseparable from the objects and happenings which they are said to qualify' (Ogden under the pseudonym More 1929: 31).[23] The Basic vocabulary should therefore not be populated by 'nouns', 'verbs' or 'pronouns', but by 'things' (corresponding to nouns), 'qualities' (adjectives), 'operators' (verbs) and 'directives' (prepositions) (Ogden 1932a: 2). These naturalised parts of speech are central to Basic: the first item in Ogden's (1933 [1930]: 12) list of the knowledge required to use Basic is 'the functions of the different parts of speech'. But unfortunately for Ogden's scheme, there remained several purely grammatical categories that he could not do without: pronouns, conjunctions, adverbs of manner derived from 'qualities', and sentence adverbs, such as 'tomorrow', 'together' and 'though'. These he subsumed in the Basic word list under the label 'etc.'.

Nouns, or 'things', are at the heart of the vocabulary since – even if our ontologies advance into the abstract – at base nouns are names of objects in the world. An immediate pedagogic advantage presents itself: a language based on nouns can be taught largely through 'the pictorial method, and particularly from the pictorial dictionary to which the various Larousse compilations are already pointing the way' (Ogden 1929c: 29). Only 200 of the 600 'things' in the Basic core vocabulary are explicitly marked as 'pictured', but Ogden's efforts to realise the 'pictorial method' for Basic would lead to his collaboration with one of the most visually minded of his contemporaries, the Vienna Circle philosopher Otto Neurath, and the further development of the latter's system of picture statistics to depict much more than simply the 200 pictured things: Neurath's system itself would become 'Isotype: international picture language' (see Chapter 4, §III). Richards went on to independently develop methods of teaching Basic using minimalist comics and animated cartoons, for which he spent the northern summer of 1942 at Walt Disney Studios in California to receive instruction in the relevant techniques (Russo 1988: 436).

Ogden's emphasis on the visible or otherwise observable carries over into the treatment of adjectives or 'qualities'. This is especially useful in the case of 'emotive adjectives', where it 'may not be possible to convey all the subtleties of mood and attitude, but the behaviour by which alone they are recognized is usually less elusive' (Ogden 1929b: 21). So, for example, in the place of 'coy' we describe the behaviour by which we recognise a coy woman: 'one who does not put forward her female attractions, or who does not give herself away readily to men' (Ogden 1929b: 21). Similarly, 'barbaric' is 'like the natives of Central Africa or the South Sea Islands', and 'envious' is 'feelings about some one in a much desired position' (Ogden 1929b: 21).

The most undesirable part of speech is the verb, since it is the antithesis of word-world isomorphy: it typically conflates many functions in a single inscrutable package. At its most extreme, argued Ogden, a verb can include all of an 'operation', an 'object' and a 'direction', as in the case of 'disembark', analytically paraphrased as 'get [operation] off [direction] a ship [object]'. In the various systems of tenses, moods and aspects attached to them, verbs also harbour the most formal complexity and irregularity among the parts of speech:

> When the most necessary *names*, the most fundamental *operators* and the essential *directives* have been determined, it can be shown that a verb is primarily a symbolic device for telescoping an operation and an object or a direction ('enter' for *go into*). Sometimes an operator, a directive *and* a name are thus telescoped, as in the odd word 'disembark' (*get, off,* a *ship*); Latin goes so far as to throw in a pronoun, and a tense auxiliary. (Ogden 1929a: 3; repeated in Ogden 1933 [1930]: 19–20)

Simultaneously reinforcing his naturalised grammatical scheme and his faith in English as its surest medium, especially in its American varieties, he adds:

> So long as the essentially contractive nature of the verb was concealed by the existing grammatical definitions, there could be no reduction in the vocabulary sufficiently radical to affect the problem of a Universal Language, *nor is this now possible in any language other than English*; and it is the continuous approximation of East and West (especially in its latest American developments), which makes this particular form of English *basic* for the whole world. (Ogden 1929a: 4; emphasis original; see also Ogden 1933 [1930]: 53–54)

The solution to the evils of verbs lies in dissecting them to reveal their semantic parts, their 'operators', 'objects' and 'directions'. This is the 'the chief grammatical provision for substitution in the grammar of Basic' (Ogden 1929b: 17).

The result is the 'operators' of Basic (*come, do, get, give, go, keep, let, make, put, take, send, say, seem, see*), which are supported by two auxiliaries (*be, have*), which can also act as operators (see Ogden 1932a: 20–24, 1933 [1930]: 53–60). These operators can be combined with 'directives' (prepositions) and 'things' (nouns) to paraphrase any verb in Standard English: for the Standard English word 'insert' Basic has the operator-directive equivalent *put in*. With a variety of different 'things' this can replace many more Standard English verbs, such as '*put* (a word) *in* = "interject", *put* (an account) *in* = "render", *put* (the tea) *in* = "infuse", *put* (the sheep) *in* = "fold", *put* (a request) *in* = "file", *put* (a seed) *in* (the earth) = "plant", *put* (the baby) *in* (the bath) = "immerse", *put* (things) *in* (a house) = "install", and so forth' (Ogden 1933 [1930]: 54–55). As we might expect in light of the role of Standard English idiom in word derivation (see §V), the range of objects that can enter into this relationship is similarly beholden to the standard language, drastically restricting the freedom and true compositionality of this technique.

Even though the parts of speech have been rechristened with their semantic labels, they continue to follow the morphological patterns of their Standard English equivalents, including all irregularities. 'Things' exhibit number inflection (including the distinction between mass and count nouns, irregular and semi-irregular forms such as 'feet' and 'knives', and forms that have zero inflection, such as 'sheep', or are always formally plural, such as 'trousers' and 'scissors'; Ogden 1932a: 10); the 'operators', like English verbs, agree with their subjects and have all the same tenses, including compound tenses with *be* and *have* auxiliaries; the 'qualities' have periphrastic comparative and superlative forms when they are more than one syllable long, or the endings *-er* and *-est* when only one syllable (with some exceptions: *bent, like, wrong, early*; Ogden 1933 [1930]: 51–52); and the pronouns inflect for case (Ogden 1932a: 73–77). 'These facts may be sad', Ogden (1932a: 10) tells us in Basic, 'but what are seven [irregular noun forms] among such a number?'

The continued observance of these irregularities, and indeed any form of morphology at all, was intended to be merely a concession to the standard language, designed not to offend the ears and eyes of Standard English speakers until Basic took hold, and designed to inculcate the right habits for those who would go on to learn 'Complete English'. But such concessions would have been only temporary. Ogden anticipated that it was only a matter of time before the 'analytic tendency' of the standard language went to completion and these 'sad facts' disappeared altogether:

> From this point of view it is an historical accident that the operator group still inflect [*sic*]. If *put* and *take* had developed as far as the model word *cut*, only the regular third person singular would differentiate them from the similar roots in an analytic language like Chinese.[24] 'I cut,' 'we cut,' 'they cut' – today and yesterday – 'I have cut,' 'the cake is cut,' 'a cut cake,' 'a cut off the cake,' and so on. But 'he cuts.' This lamentable and unmannerly hissing about a third person has been characterized by Sir Richard Paget

as un-English. It would probably have disappeared long ago in the normal course of events had not printers, lexicographers, and schoolmasters rallied so egregiously to its defence; and if any reform is overdue in our accidence, here is surely an appropriate casualty.

In due course, all irregular plurals and possibly all plurals – since we have already learnt to dispense with *sheeps* – might well follow it. (Ogden 1936: 57; see also Ogden 1931: 30–31)

Grammatical reform, Ogden insisted, could only proceed in a piecemeal fashion. The various failed attempts at English spelling reform show us how futile it is to overhaul a single aspect of the language at once. The only hope for Basic, and for Standard English, would be to isolate a reasonably well-behaved subset of the language and rely on the natural analytic tendency and the further simplifications of learners to effect grammatical reform: 'Basic, then, offers us for the first time a rational incentive to reform the essentials by degrees' (Ogden 1936: 58–59).

Complete change could propagate to the entire system quite rapidly – 'in a single generation' – in this modern age of 'printing, radio, and world-travel'. This could occur, says Ogden (1931: 30–31), wryly expressing his appreciation of American idiom, 'with much less of a shock than the average Englishman experiences when confronted by a youthful American – whose more elastic phraseology is nevertheless perfectly intelligible to him. He is slowly learning to "get busy" and "put over" his own "concepts". "Right now" his "co-ed" offspring are "talkie fans"; they get "psyched" and know all the "dope" – "and then some".' American English, according to Ogden, is the leading dialect in the analytic tendency. Later reflecting on work he had done in removing 'Americanisms' from a text for an English audience, he commented:

> I was unable to get away from the feeling that this foolish process was like putting wax lights back into a Club because certain old men had not got used to the electric system. But it was worse than a waste of time. From the point of view of an International Language it was clearly a step in the wrong direction. (Ogden 1993 [1932]: 42)

With the words and their behaviour in place, all that remained was putting them together to make sentences. To this end Ogden offered a simple schematic syntax based on that of Standard English. This would be imparted principally through 'model sentences', which are supposed to exhibit the full range of possible syntactic permutations. Several of these model sentences appear in the Basic pedagogic literature, and two of them, which are intended to illustrate maximally expanded sentences, where every possible sentence position is filled, appear in the fold-out list of the 850 words in all Basic books: 'The camera man who made an attempt to take a moving picture of the society women, before they got their hats off, did not get off the ship till he was questioned by the police', and 'We will give simple rules to you now.' In this connection Ogden revived

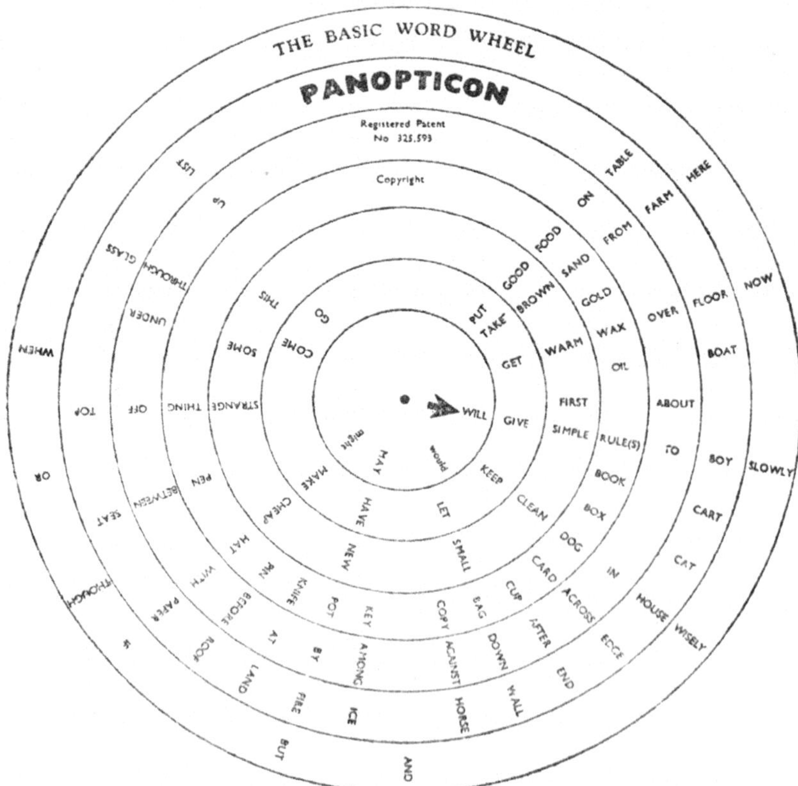

1 Price 2/6 (50 cents) from The Orthological Institute,
10, King's Parade, Cambridge, England.

Figure 3.2 Ogden's panopticon
Ogden 1932a: 183.

the 'panoptic' principle with his 'panopticon', or 'Basic Word Wheel' (shown in
Figure 3.2).

Each of the concentric discs of Ogden's panopticon contains all words of one
part of speech, and by rotating them it is possible to make grammatically correct
sentences. Grammar has become so natural that it is amenable to mechanical manipulation using the simplest of human inventions, the wheel. Ever the
technocrat, Ogden (1931: 32) saw 'modern mechanical aids' as crucial to Basic's
success: 'The teaching of grammar without the use of modern mechanical aids
cannot long survive, and Basic English has been designed to profit by the visual
and mechanical factor in a very high degree' (see also Ogden 1929a: 6–7, 1930a:
8).

VII. Bentham and beyond

In a fashion characteristic of him, Ogden made very little reference to the wider international language movement. Other projects were mentioned only in order to demonstrate their inferiority to Basic (see, e.g., his attack on the 'artificial' languages, Ogden 1935). He also expended very little effort on expounding and justifying the philosophical background to Basic; his energies seem to have been directed towards establishing and propagating a practical project. 'Basic', Ogden (1930: 1) says, 'must be presented like a radio set, with all the works concealed and only a few convenient knobs protruding for the public to twiddle'.

The only inspiration Ogden acknowledged for Basic was the English utilitarian philosopher Jeremy Bentham (1748–1832), to whom he attributed all the insights he saw embodied in the project. Indeed, his constant invocation of 'panopticism' was a deliberate attempt to claim Bentham's brand for Basic. Ogden (1928a: 2) tells us that he first encountered Bentham in 1914, but it was not until 1923, when translating Hans Vaihinger's (1852–1933) (1924 [1911]) *The Philosophy of As-If*, that he engaged with Bentham seriously (cf. Gordon 1990b: 45). By the time the first hints at Basic appeared in print (i.e. Ogden 1927b), Ogden was a confirmed Benthamite. But the unpublished traces of Basic predate Ogden's infatuation with Bentham, and Ogden himself described the emergence of Basic with the following words:

> The full application of these principles, some of which were being tested as long ago as 1908, others emerging with the completion of the *Meaning of Meaning* in 1923, while the final synthesis was not achieved until the spring of 1928, necessitated many months of unremitting labour on the part of several collaborators. (Ogden 1929a: 5)

Richards (1977: 108) tells us too that when writing *The Meaning of Meaning*, 'Ogden had long been deep in the history and theory of universal languages.' We may therefore legitimately ask what other ingredients, and in what quantities, are to be found in Basic. Because of Ogden's reticence on this issue, we must engage in some textual archaeology to find clues.

We might suspect Ogden's exclusive but generous acknowledgement of Bentham as being simply a bolster to his own originality and uniqueness. Bentham's name is known to all, but he is also suitably remote in time, not the current fashion and somewhat obscure: his devotee can claim to have rediscovered an illustrious predecessor, missed by ignorant contemporaries. Such a motive may have driven Ogden, but there would seem to be much more. By the 1930s Ogden emerged as a major Bentham scholar, on a mission to rehabilitate his work and image (see, for example, Ogden 1932d). Ogden clearly identified with Bentham, to the point that he sought out and acquired one of the Bentham silhouette rings, which he wore (see Gordon's introduction to Ogden 1993 [1932]: vii).[25] In Ogden's view, both he and Bentham were geniuses ahead of their time, misunderstood and unappreciated by their contemporaries:

[A] careful study of his [Bentham's] writings [. . .] make it clear that Orthology, [26] the science of correct symbolism based upon an elaborate analysis of the technique of communication, was the corner-stone of Bentham's system. That this has so seldom been realised by subsequent writers is due to the fact that Bentham was in this respect more than a century ahead of his times. (Ogden 1928b: 5; see also Ogden 1993 [1932]: 35–36).

In one of the few passages where he wrote about the theoretical background to Basic, and at that pseudonymously, Ogden tells us that there are 'five main principles' that underlie the system. These are:

[T]he elimination of verbs, the analysis of the thirteen operators and twenty-one directives which replace them in universal grammar, the use of panoptic conjugation in systematic definition, the projectional interpretation of emotive adjectives, and the development of Bentham's theory of Fictions in the treatment of metaphor. (Ogden, as More 1929: 3)

The fact that Bentham is named explicitly in only one of these principles belies his significance: Ogden credited him with inspiring every one of these points, and the one that bears his name, the theory of Fictions, is the centrepiece of the entire system of Basic. In fact, Ogden credited Bentham with the idea of developing English for universal communication, albeit without a specific citation to Bentham's work. 'It is to be noted that Bentham did not devote attention to the question of a synthetic language', Ogden (1993 [1932]: 21) says, 'not because he was not familiar with the controversy, but because he believed in the development of English for universal needs'. But in addition to the acknowledged debt to Bentham, we find for each of the principles underlying Basic earlier precedents in sources that Ogden would have known.

The theory of Fictions, at least under Ogden's interpretation, looks very much like the theory of word-magic. To say to what extent Bentham and Ogden's ideas really do resemble one another we would have to carefully separate Bentham from Ogden's interpretation, a task that goes beyond the immediate requirements of the intellectual genealogy we are tracing here. By Ogden's account, he had already written chapter 2 of *The Meaning of Meaning*, 'The power of words', before he read Bentham and was surprised and pleased at the similarities when he later learnt of Bentham's theory (Ogden 1928a: 2). At the foundation of Bentham's theory is the distinction between 'real' and 'fictitious' entities: the former are those that have an actual existence in the world and the latter are mere artefacts of our use of language. 'To language, then – to language alone – it is, that fictitious entities owe their existence; their impossible, yet indispensable existence', Bentham tells us (quoted in Ogden 1932d: 15). They are indispensable because we need them to conceptualise anything beyond what is immediately present before us. But, as in word-magic, trouble arises when we do not recognise fictitious entities as such and assume their real existence.

At least this much was a fairly common foundation of the language-critical philosophies current in the early twentieth century. We have already seen the various connections between Ogden and Richards, Welby, Moore, Russell and Wittgenstein (see Chapter 2). Vaihinger's (1924 [1911]) *The Philosophy of As-If* – the translation of which into English, it will be remembered, Ogden credited with giving him the opportunity to study Bentham more closely – was an expression of many similar sentiments popular in the German-speaking world and, if we follow Carus (2007), was probably among the indigenous German ideas that influenced the Vienna Circle, and in particular the young Rudolf Carnap (see Chapter 4, §I). Ogden repeatedly insisted on Bentham's priority and superiority in this area of thought: 'He [Bentham] anticipated, and went far beyond, Vaihinger's *Philosophie des Als-Ob* [Philosophy of As-If]; and, *a fortiori*, the relevant analyses of [French philosopher Henri] Bergson' (Ogden 1993 [1932]: 40; see also Ogden 1928b: 4).

As Ogden said himself, Bentham's theory of Fictions found direct application in creating metaphorical extensions in Basic, but this is not the only place Ogden could have found inspiration. Welby's intensive focus on metaphor as the engine of signification in language must of course have still exercised some influence as Ogden was working on Basic. Indeed, we have seen that Ogden's first hints at English as an international language are recorded in his 'significs' manuscript written just before the First World War, and later Ogden explicitly tied his Basic-era panoptic conjugation to the theory of definition in *The Meaning of Meaning*, which owed much to Welby (see Chapter 2, §V): 'The Panoptic Eliminator shows its place in the general scheme of the substitution, where the Theory of Definition discussed in *The Meaning of Meaning* is developed and applied to Lexicography in general and to Conjugation in particular' (Ogden 1930: 1; see also Ogden 1952: 12–13).

Looking further back in time, to Wilkins, Ogden's Enlightenment predecessor in language construction, we see that he also placed special importance on regular metaphorical processes as a means to enlarging the senses expressible in his language. Wilkins (1968 [1668]: 318) noted that in existing languages 'there are two ways used [. . .] for varying the sense of words; either by *Tropes:* or by such a kind of *Composition* as doth *alter the termination* of them'. In Latin and English, Wilkins' principal control languages, 'tropes' are generally unmarked but, in order to retain the unambiguous nature of his language, Wilkins included explicit markers for tropes in his series of 'transcendental particles', which perform functions generally achieved through derivation in natural languages (see Wilkins 1968 [1668]: 318–351; Maat 2004: 225–229).

First among the transcendental particles are those for 'metaphor', for 'enlarging the sense of that word [to which it is applied], from that strict restrained acception which it had in the Tables, to a more comprehensive signification', and 'like', which 'doth denote a varying of the sense of that word [to which it is affixed], upon the Account of some similitude' (Wilkins 1968 [1668]: 323–324). 'Prophesie' and 'suiter', for example, with the metaphor particle, mean 'prediction' and 'candidate' respectively. The 'like' particle, applied to 'Pitch', would mean 'deep black' and, applied to 'Arme', could mean 'Arme of Tree, Sea' (Wilkins 1968 [1668]: 323–325). The effects of these particles exhibit clear parallels to Ogden's, albeit unmarked, 'extension' (see §V).

The elimination of verbs, also among the 'five main principles' of Basic, is another suggestion found in Bentham's work, based on his theory of Fictions. 'A verb', says Bentham (quoted in Ogden 1932d: cvii), 'slips through your fingers like an eel'. Nouns are to be preferred to verbs, according to Bentham, because actions expressed as nouns are more clearly recognisable as fictions and as such are more manipulable:

> The verbal noun [i.e. the noun that denotes an action] – when thus obtained in a state of separation from these adjuncts, which form so many parts in the composition of the very complex part of speech called a verb; and which, in this its separate state, becomes the name of a sort of fictitious entity, of a sort of fictitious body or substance – is, in this state, rendered more prehensible. (Bentham, quoted in Ogden 1932d: lxxxvi)

The situation in language, Bentham continues, is comparable to the use of algebra: algebraic variables represent a problem at an abstract level, and when the variables are replaced with actual numerals, the problem becomes concrete. If the 'slippery' parts of speech – the verbs, adverbs, conjunctions, etc. – were to be decomposed into a complex made up of just a noun, a verb and an adjective, then what is said would become immediately apparent:

> In like manner, when of a sentence of which a preposition, an adverb, or a conjunction, makes a part, the equivalent is given in a sentence in which no part of speech other than a substantive, a verb, and an adjective, or some other substantive, is employed – then, and then only, is the import respectively attached to these mysterious parts of speech at once clear, correct, and complete. (Bentham, quoted in Ogden 1932d: lxxxvii; see also Ogden as More 1928)

Once again, these ideas do not seem to originate with Bentham: earlier precedents can be found in sources with which Ogden was undoubtedly familiar. Both Dalgarno and Wilkins sought to do away with verbs, and the alternative forms they proposed are strikingly similar to Bentham's. Dalgarno wanted to recognise only one part of speech, nouns, the names of things; all of the other traditional parts of speech simply represent modifications of and relations between nouns and so 'should be counted as inflexions and cases of the noun' (Dalgarno, quoted in Maat 2004: 103, see also 104–110). He modelled the structure of sentences on syllogistic propositions, thereby eliminating verbs, since under this scheme sentences become a combination of copula and predicate. Wilkins allowed for a more diverse ecosystem of word classes, but still targeted verbs for elimination, seeing them, like Dalgarno, as either derivatives of nouns or complex structures playing the role of a copula and adjective (see Maat 2004: 235). But just as Ogden would later have trouble maintaining his remoulded parts of speech, both Dalgarno and Wilkins took recourse to traditional grammatical categories and terminology in their projects, even after they had presented their new schemes (see Maat 2004: 110–117, 249).

Dalgarno and Wilkins were driven, within the limits of practicability, by a desire to reach 'universal grammar', a term that Ogden also used (see §VI), and a keenly sought after ideal of the Enlightenment. The goal, in short, was to attempt to find a deeper basis for linguistic categories (see Padley 1976: 154–209, in particular p. 157, and 1985). Ogden built his universal categories on psychology, appealing to human perception of the world. Dalgarno and Wilkins had similar ideas. Dalgarno says, 'The grammarian must assign names to things according to the ideas and logical rules derived from the nature of externally existing things themselves' (Dalgarno, quoted in Maat 2004: 65; see p. 153 for Wilkins' similar position). A corollary of this position is the belief in 'natural' syntax: both Dalgarno and Wilkins, like Ogden later, felt no need for the detailed description and explanation of syntax in their languages (see Maat 2004: 117–119, 248–249; cf. §III above).

One aspect of syntactic questions was the nature of the parts of speech. In Ogden's contemporary milieu, Malinowski proposed a natural evolution of the parts of speech based on his functional theory of language, and went on to speculate about how the various parts of speech might emerge from the view of the world shared by children and 'primitive' peoples:

> The grammatical categories with all their peculiarities, exceptions, and refractory insubordination to rule, are the reflection of the makeshift, unsystematic, practical outlook imposed by man's struggle for existence in the widest sense of this word. It would be futile to hope that we might be able to reconstruct exactly this pragmatic world vision of the primitive, the savage or the child, or to trace in detail its correlation to grammar. But a broad outline and a general correspondence can be found; and the realization of this frees us anyhow from logical shackles and grammatical barrenness. (Malinowski 1989 [1923]: 328)

The remaining two of the five main principles of Basic, panoptic conjugation and the 'projectional interpretation of emotive adjectives' (that is, the paraphrasing of adjectives in terms of visible features; see §V) may not have fully formed antecedents in Bentham's work, but the seeds of these ideas are definitely there. As we see in the following section, Ogden's use of 'panoptic' and his own 'panopticon' were not simply the repetition of a happy coinage from Bentham, but also involved the bringing on board of many of the design principles and social connotations associated with Bentham's project. In the projectional interpretation of emotive adjectives we are reminded of Bentham's warnings about the need to identify and isolate the emotive component of words, warnings which are common to Ogden's own word-magic and which his approach in describing the visible manifestations of emotive content heeds (see Bentham quoted in Ogden 1932d: lxxii).

In the visual aspect of 'projectional interpretation', which is both an ideal and a pedagogic principle throughout the Basic vocabulary (see §VI), we are also reminded of the Enlightenment's fascination with a real character, where the symbol would directly pick out its referent, without the intermediary of spoken language (see §I). Ogden's language retained speech, but in the attempt to tie words to visual representation – or at least to teach words using visual representation – it revived the duality of a real or universal character and a philosophical language.

Ogden himself said that the principles of Basic grew out of the theory of definition in *The Meaning of Meaning*, and we have seen that hints at what would become Basic are visible even when his stated allegiance was to Welby's significs. But appearances would suggest a caesura between *The Meaning of Meaning* and Basic: the former, in the spirit of Welby, focuses attention on the process of interpretation; the latter, by contrast, legislates a specific medium of communication to restrict the freedom of interpretation. Of course, dissimilarity in phenotype does not proscribe underlying genetic affinity: perhaps Basic, the theory of definition and significs are not so far apart after all. Ogden's scribbled assertion that '[s]ymbolic language would unite sense and meaning' suggests that he already saw a solution to the problem of misunderstanding in the creation of a certain form of language rather than in the case-by-case examination of interpretation that Welby advocated.

There are also indications that Welby would have at least in part endorsed a constructed language of the type Ogden had in mind. Welby, who insisted on the inherently context-dependent nature of language, rejected any possibility of there being 'Plain Meaning'. This position entails a rejection of any plan for an ideal language that would be unambiguous or aspire to a perfectly logical structure. She specifically cited Wilkins' project, Schleyer's Volapük and Jespersen's earliest work as examples of such misguided goals:

At present we have not even attained to an adequate conception of what an ideal language should be: we think of it, if at all, as the impossible thing that Bishop Wilkins proposed, a formalised dialect of culture with its phrases "rendered according to the genuine and natural importance of words," as if this were anything but what their speakers intended by them! Or we try to invent an artificial 'Volapük.' It is surely time that the fetish of a possible Plain Meaning, the same at all times and places and to all, were thoroughly exposed, and students more explicitly warned against anything approaching it, except on the narrowest basis of technical notation. Even Dr Jespersen tells us that an ideal language would "always express the same thing by the same, and similar things by similar means; any irregularity and ambiguity would be banished; sound and sense would be in perfect harmony; any number of delicate shades of meaning could be expressed with equal ease: poetry and prose, beauty and truth, thinking and feeling would be equally provided for: the human spirit would have

found a garment combining freedom and gracefulness, fitting it closely and yet allow-
ing full play to any movement" ([Jespersen 1894] p. 365). (Welby 1985 [1896]: 192)

But elsewhere Welby allowed for the possibility that a small selection of words
with precise and refined meanings could be a path to clarity in language:
'Perhaps, just as we have twenty-six letters and a vast store of combinations, so
a relatively small vocabulary might be made immensely more adequate' (Welby
1983 [1903]: 62). This could be seen as an anticipation of Ogden's word elimination. Although she believed we should try to maintain the existing, natural form
of expression, which contains our 'precious psychological heritage', we should
not allow 'it to divide us, or to silence that which, being everywhere the highest
thought of the highest man, is most of all worthy of expression' (Welby 1983
[1903]: 212; cf. Gordon 1990a).

Welby's supporters repeatedly drew her in the direction of constructed languages. The winner of the 'Welby Prize' for the best essay on '[t]he causes of
the present obscurity and confusion in psychological and philosophical terminology, and the directions in which we may hope for an efficient practical
remedy' (Anonymous 1896; see Schmitz 1985a: liii–lv), the German sociologist
Ferdinand Tönnies (1855–1936), proposed in his winning essay a continuum
of languages, at one end of which meaning is understood only tacitly and at the
other end of which it is established explicitly by convention; that is, laid down
(Tönnies 1899–1900: 326). Tönnies (1899–1900: 316–317) raised the possibility of 'a whole language in which all word-meanings would have a conventional
character' (see Schmitz 1985a: cxvii–cxli; and Schmitz 1985b for commentary). It was this possibility of establishing a strictly conventional language that
Tönnies pursued in his later work, and it is a sentiment that Ogden echoed in
his talk on the 'Progress of significs' in his suggestion that we should take active
steps to identify and eliminate ambiguous terminology in argument and discussion (Ogden 1994 [1911]: 25–34; see also Chapter 2, §V).

Gerrit Mannoury (1867–1956), a prominent member of the later Dutch significs movement (see Chapter 2, §V), wrote one of his later works in Esperanto,
'because only in this language are the meanings of words selected intentionally
and with consideration and so they offer more stability and objectivity than the
natural languages' (Mannoury 1937: 407).[27] The use of Esperanto in this work
was so important to Mannoury that he pursued it 'even though this was to delay
publication by several years' (Mannoury 1987 [1938]: 164), while he became sufficiently proficient in the language.

Other Welby supporters included the French philosopher André Lalande
(1867–1963) and Couturat, joint founders of the Société française de philosophie, which from 1902 produced the *Vocabulaire technique et critique de la
philosophie* (Lalande 1988 [1902–1923]), a dictionary of French philosophical
terminology with translation equivalents in other major European languages.
One of the primary goals of the *Vocabulaire* was to help standardise the terminology within French and across other European languages (see Schmitz

1985a: cxv). Welby also corresponded with Lalande in this connection and several entries in the *Vocabulaire* make reference to her (Schmitz 1985a: cxvi–cxvii).

Couturat was of course also a leader of the Délégation, and twice, in 1901 and 1902, he sought, through Tönnies, to secure Welby's signature on his declaration for an international auxiliary language. He made a third attempt in 1903, through the Scottish sociologist Patrick Geddes (1854–1932) (see Schmitz 1985a: cxv–cxvi). Even Bertrand Russell was persuaded to sign the declaration in 1903, although presumably with reservations, given his later comments: '[Couturat] lamented that the word Ido did not lend itself to the formation of a word similar to Esperantist. I suggested "idiot", but he was not quite pleased' (Russell 1967–1969, volume 1: 135–136).

Ogden's sole but repeated citation of Bentham and his habit of referring to his contemporaries only to say how they were wrong misrepresents the genealogy of his ideas. Bentham, it is true, was a great inspiration to Ogden, and many of his ideas, mostly stemming from his theory of 'Fictions', are implemented in Basic. But some of the most prominent features of Basic – the treatment of metaphor, the notion of 'universal grammar' with a campaign against verbs, the emphasis on the visible – have quite probable antecedents in the Enlightenment projects of Dalgarno and Wilkins, with which Ogden was almost certainly familiar. Even if Bentham gave Ogden an overarching philosophy in the theory of Fictions, individual ideas within Ogden's subsequent developments on it could have been informed by these other projects.

Before he declared himself a Benthamite, Ogden articulated his own detailed philosophy of language, recorded in *The Meaning of Meaning*, and he did not simply forget it in his conversion: he in fact explicitly tied its practical aspect, the theory of definition, to his new 'panoptic' method. Basic therefore has a further pedigree descending from Welby's significs, a semiotic, interpretation-based philosophy that may appear superficially incompatible with the legislated code of Basic. But this apparent incompatibility begins to dissolve under closer examination of Welby's comments on language engineering and the interpretation she was subject to in her time.

VIII. Totalitarianism and Newspeak

As we have seen, Ogden and his supporters cast Basic as a scientifically engineered tool for liberating thought, for making language the servant of reason, rather than forcing thought to follow the strictures of language. At the beginning of the 1930s – with modernist optimism at its height, despite, or perhaps because of, the financial, social and political troubles across Europe – such goals were respectable, but with the hardening of ideological fronts over the following decade and the descent into actual war – total war on a destructive scale never before seen in Europe – a sense of malaise and suspicion at grand social engineering projects set in. Technocrats and their schemes, whether from the left or right of the political spectrum, became the subject of criticism, and to the lips of many intellectuals came a mantra of 'freedom'.

Many intellectuals who had previously considered themselves socialists of one form or another, or were sympathetic to left-wing causes, abandoned the ideologies and movements they had previously supported, in the belief that any all-encompassing, centralised social planning inevitably led to totalitarianism. Basic English was neither 'socialist' nor 'fascist', but was most certainly a manifestation of the kind of technocratic social engineering that came to be seen as so problematic. A puzzling episode in this story is George Orwell's (1903–1950) ambiguous engagement with Basic. On the one hand, his fictional constructed language 'Newspeak' in the novel *Nineteen Eighty-Four* (Orwell 1989 [1949]) clearly parodies contemporary language projects in many respects, and bears in particular a number of similarities to Basic. On the other hand, in his personal and professional contact with Ogden, Orwell seems to have been quite supportive of Basic.

A monument marking the new intellectual trend against social planning is the 1944 book *Road to Serfdom*, written in England by the Austrian émigré economist Friedrich von Hayek (1899–1992). The book argued that the totalitarianism of the contemporary Soviet Union and Germany were two manifestations of a common impulse to comprehensive economic and social planning, an impulse that was winning increasing support in Britain, to the detriment of that country's tradition of liberalism. Britain, too, was being led down the totalitarian path:

> Few are ready to recognise that the rise of fascism and naziism [*sic*] was not a reaction against the socialist trends of the preceding period but a necessary outcome of those tendencies. This is a truth which most people were unwilling to see even when the similarities of many of the repellent features of the internal regimes in communist Russia and National Socialist Germany were widely recognized. As a result, many who think themselves infinitely superior to the aberrations of naziism and sincerely hate all its manifestations, work at the same time for ideals whose realisation would lead straight to the abhorred tyranny. (Hayek 2007 [1944]: 59)

Karl Popper (1902–1994) – likewise an exile from fascist Vienna, first in Christchurch, New Zealand, and then in London, who would become one of the most renowned philosophers of science in the twentieth century – staged at the same time a similar attack on social planners driven by high ideals and grand schemes in his two-volume *The Open Society and its Enemies*, written, Popper (1945: xi) tells us, from 1938 to 1943, and first published in 1945. The first volume took on Plato's idealism and the overt totalitarianism – to describe it anachronistically – of his *Republic*; the second volume treated Marx and his Hegelian notion of the inevitable march of history towards communism, without concern for what might be trodden on in the process.

Popper contrasted two poles of political intervention in society: 'Utopian engineering', the attempted implementation of grandiose social plans with the highest ideals; and 'piecemeal engineering', the identification of specific social problems with narrowly focused solutions, such as 'health and unemployment insurance', 'arbitration courts', 'anti-depression budgeting', and 'educational reform' (Popper 1945: 168). The first 'demands a strong centralized rule of a few' and 'therefore is to lead to a dictatorship' (Popper 1945: 169). The second, however, can engage the majority's 'reason' and allow them to rationally recognise the actual, concrete problems they face and look to a direct compromise solution:

> [I]f it is easier to reach a reasonable agreement about existing evils and the means of combating them than it is about an ideal good and the means of its realization, then there is also more hope that by using the piecemeal method we may get over the very greatest practical difficulty of all reasonable political reform, namely, the use of reason, instead of passion and violence, in executing the programme. There will be the possibility of reaching a reasonable compromise and therefore of achieving the improvement by democratic methods. (Popper 1945: 168–169)

In the same vein, but on a linguistic plane, Orwell's Newspeak is conceived of as an instrument of social engineering, intended to establish wide-scale social conformity through the control of thought. Here Newspeak seems to satirise Basic and like-minded projects. As we have seen, guiding thought through rectified language was a central theme of Ogden's philosophy of language, which was incorporated into the design of Basic. Such control was not viewed negatively, however, but as an enlightened and benevolent improvement on natural language. This is no more apparent than in Ogden's use of Bentham's term 'Panopticon' and his derivative 'panoptic'. These are no innocent neohellenisms, but rather terms with unavoidable connotations. Rather than shying away from these connotations, Ogden flirted with them.

As is well known, Bentham's panopticon was an architectural plan, an ideal design for public institutions centred on supervision: '*perpetual prisons* in the room of death; or *prisons for confinement* before trial, or *penitentiary-houses*, or *houses of correction*, or *work-houses*, or *manufactories*, or *mad-houses*, or *hospitals*, or *schools*' (Bentham 1843 [1791]: 40; emphasis original). The panopticon was an architectural contrivance for 'obtaining power of mind over mind, in a quantity hitherto without example: and that, to a degree equally without example, secured by whoever chooses to have it so, against abuse' (Bentham 1843 [1791]: 39). This would be achieved through '*seeing without being seen*' (Bentham 1843 [1791]: 44; emphasis original). The proposed panopticon would be a circular building with a watchtower in the middle: the 'inspector' would remain in his watchtower and look out at the inmates of the panopticon, each isolated in their own cell around the circumference.

At any moment the inspector could potentially be watching any inmate, but through the special arrangement of lighting and blinds installed in the tower, all the inmates should be able to see of the inspector is his silhouette; they could not tell if they were being observed or if the inspector was even present in the tower. Although the single inspector could not possibly have his eye on everyone simultaneously, Bentham advocated a range of technical devices and psychological games to heighten the impression of his omnipresence and omniscience. Through a series of 'tin tubes' that would connect his tower to each cell, the inspector could talk privately to any inmate at any time, without the others knowing that he was elsewhere occupied (Bentham 1843 [1791]: 41). 'Untoward' inmates should be allowed for a period to test the limits of their freedom. But during this time, particularly close watch would be kept on them, and their every misdeed would be observed and noted. One day, chosen at random to maximise surprise, the inmate would be presented with a catalogue of their transgressions, revealing that they were being observed and controlled all along:

> I will soon put an end to his [the inmate's] experiments: or rather, to be beforehand with him, I will take care he shall not think of making any. I will single out one of the most untoward of the prisoners. I will keep an unintermitted watch upon him. I will watch until I observe a transgression. I will minute it down. I will wait for another: I will note that down too. I will lie by for a whole day: he shall do as he pleases that day, so long as he does not venture at something too serious to be endured. The next day I produce the list to him. – *You thought yourself undiscovered: you abused my indulgence: see how you were mistaken. Another time, you may have rope for two days, ten days: the longer it is, the heavier it will fall upon you. Learn from this, all of you, that in this house transgressions never can be safe.* Will the policy be cruel? – No; it will be kind: it will prevent transgressing; it will save punishing. (Bentham 1843 [1791]: 81–82; emphasis original)

Although the psychology applied here may strike many modern readers as rather sinister, Bentham, it would seem, was oblivious to these implications. He saw only good in this atmosphere of pervasive surveillance, and the potential for his design to overcome the faults of existing prisons. In contrast to the existing state of affairs, there would be no direct contact between the inspector and the inmates, and any warders who must stray out into the cells would be subject to the same 'irresistable controul [*sic*]' from the inspector: these two features should reduce the opportunities for 'neglect or oppression' (Bentham 1843 [1791]: 45). But the sinister aspect of his project takes on a new dimension when Bentham argues for the suitability of his design to 'work-houses', 'manufactories', 'mad-houses', 'hospitals' and 'schools', with the suggestion that overbearing omnipotence, or at least the appearance of it, is a fitting model for such a variety of public institutions, a point that Foucault (1979 [1973]) emphasised in his classic study of the panopticon (see Semple 1993: 9–11 *et passim* for a counterbalance to Foucault's view).

In light of these potential sinister connotations, it might seem odd that

Ogden would embrace 'panopticism' as a guiding principle in Basic, central to its design; indeed, in the earliest publications the project goes by the name of 'Panoptic English' (e.g. Ogden 1928a). Ogden even played with the connotations: of his own 'panopticon', used for teaching and practising Basic syntax (shown in Figure 3.2, §VI), he commented that 'it enables the entire vocabulary imprisoned in this procrustean structure to be envisaged at a glance' (Ogden 1936: 59–61).

Control is a goal of Basic: at the very least, Basic is a technological instrument for taking control of the individual's own mind – of overcoming word-magic – and at most it is a contrivance for 'obtaining power of mind over mind', as Bentham claimed for his panopticon. We must not forget that Richards was actively propagating Basic in China as part of mental training for the Chinese to bring them into the modern world, and of course Churchill's fateful words in 1943 that opened the prospect of future 'empires of the mind' (see §IV). But again this was seen as humane and benevolent control, control for the subject's own good. This is nowhere clearer than in the work of Basic's greatest literary champion, H. G. Wells. In his mock history textbook from the future, *The Shape of Things to Come* (Wells 1933), where the problems of his day are turned into a narrative with a resolution, Wells fantasised about an enlightened technology-based 'Air Dictatorship' – so called because its authority is exercised by aeroplane, the modern technology that most impressed Wells – that brings peace and order to the whole world. On the linguistic front, worldwide communication and rational thought and discourse are secured by the Air Dictatorship's lingua franca, Basic English (see §7 in 'Book the Fifth' of Wells 1933 *et passim*).

This vision of Wells', a recurring theme in his work, made Orwell uncomfortable. Writing at the most hopeless point of the Second World War, in 1941, Orwell emphatically rejected it as naïve and misguided. The most technologically advanced society today, he wrote, is Nazi Germany, and the power of their totalitarian dictatorship is based not on reason, but on the emotional appeal of crude, folkish romanticism, against which Britain and the Allies have nothing to offer:

> Modern Germany is far more scientific than England, and far more barbarous. Much of what Wells has imagined and worked for is physically there in Nazi Germany. The order, the planning, the State encouragement of science, the steel, the concrete, the aeroplanes, are all there, but all in the service of ideas appropriate to the Stone Age. Science is fighting on the side of superstition. (Orwell 1968 [1941]: 170)

The critique became more pointed in *Nineteen Eighty-Four*, where the world is divided into three ideologically indistinguishable, continuously warring technocratic dictatorships, whose only reason for existence is the maintenance of power, and where scorning the welfare of their subjects is treated as proof of this power. Newspeak is a key tool of the state apparatus in *Nineteen Eighty-Four*. As in Basic, word elimination plays a central role in Newspeak, but as a means of limiting the thought of its speakers rather than freeing it. The elimination of words prevents mention of the associated thoughts, and leads ultimately to the elimination of the thoughts themselves:

> [R]eduction of vocabulary was regarded as an end in itself, and no word that could be dispensed with was allowed to survive. Newspeak was designed not to extend but to *diminish* the range of thought, and this purpose was indirectly assisted by cutting the choice of words down to a minimum. (Orwell 1989 [1949]: 313)

Orwell's Newspeak was the product of many influences, including other constructed languages like Esperanto: during his time in Paris as a young man Orwell lived with his aunt Nellie Limouzin and her partner Eugène Adam, better known as 'Lanti', the founder of the Esperanto SAT organisation (see Shelden 1991: 136–137; Bowker 2003: 105–107; see §I for SAT). Orwell's perception of political and bureaucratic discourse also clearly colours Newspeak (see e.g. Orwell 1968 [1946]). But in its main contours, Newspeak is particularly reminiscent of Basic (see Orwell 1989 [1949]: 312–326 for his 'grammar' of Newspeak; cf. Fink 1971).

Orwell was in fact at one point professionally involved with Basic. In 1942, Orwell, then Talks Producer in the Indian Section of the BBC, produced a programme in which Leonora Wilhelmina Lockhart (1906–1985), Ogden's assistant and collaborator on Basic (see Chapter 4), introduced the principles of the language to an Indian audience (see Fink 1971; Joseph 2001). At this time, Orwell would seem to have been supportive of Basic. In sporadic correspondence with Ogden, he mentions that he had wanted to do 'a series of talks giving lessons in Basic English' but that the project had unfortunately '[. . .] come up against a great deal of discouragement and opposition, some of which I understand and some not' (Orwell to Ogden, 16 December 1942).[28] Two years later, Orwell maintains his support and concurs with Ogden's identification and assessment of Basic's alleged enemies:

> I was aware, of course, that you have much to put up with from the Esperanto people [. . .] We have had them on to us since mentioning Basic, but I have choked them off. Also the Ido people.
>
> As I told you when I was in the B.B.C. (I have left there now) there was great resistance against doing anything over the air about Basic, at any rate for India. I rather gathered that its chief enemies were the writers of English textbooks, but that all Indians whose English is good are hostile to the idea, for obvious reasons. At any rate it was with great difficulty that I got Miss Lockhart on the air. (Orwell to Ogden, 1 March 1944)

As late as two years before he started drafting *Nineteen Eighty-Four*, in the year 1946 (see Bowker 2003: 368–370), Orwell therefore appears still to be sympathetic towards Ogden's project. In his classic essay 'Politics and the English language' (Orwell 1968 [1946]), in which he targeted thoughtless political sloganeering, we can see what Orwell would have found attractive in Basic:

> In prose, the worst thing one can do with words is surrender to them. When you think of a concrete object, you think wordlessly, and then, if you want to describe the thing you have been visualising you probably hunt about until you find the exact words that seem to fit it. When you think of something abstract you are more inclined to use words from the start, and unless you make a conscious effort to prevent it, the existing dialect will come rushing in and do the job for you, at the expense of blurring or even changing your meaning. Probably it is better to put off using words as long as possible and get one's meaning as clear as one can through pictures and sensations. (Orwell 1968 [1946]: 138–139)

Needless to say, this passage could have been written by Ogden: the power of empty words over thought, Ogden's 'word-magic', is there, as well as Ogden's preferred solution, the careful thinking out of what is to be said, starting from 'pictures and sensations', no less. But it is difficult to see how the solution offered by Basic, a legislated, restricted code, and the official language of the Wellsian world dictatorship, could possibly have appealed to Orwell.

The notion of the panopticon, so central to Ogden's thinking and rhetoric on Basic, was similarly anathema to Orwell. *Nineteen Eighty-Four* is in fact a critique of totalitarianism realised as an implementation of panopticism. The citizens of *Nineteen Eighty-Four* are under constant surveillance – 'Big Brother is watching you' – through 'telescreens', from which the inspectors of the 'Thought Police' can both observe and speak privately to any individual at any time:

> The telescreen received and transmitted simultaneously. Any sound that Winston made, above the level of a very low whisper, would be picked up by it; moreover, so long as he remained within the field of vision which the metal plaque commanded, he could be seen as well as heard. There was of course no way of knowing whether you were being watched at any given moment. How often, or on what system, the Thought Police plugged in on any individual wire was guesswork. It was even conceivable that they watched everybody all the time. (Orwell 1989 [1949]: 4–5)

Later in the novel (Orwell 1989 [1949]: 230–231), Winston Smith, the protagonist, and his girlfriend Julia are surprised when the telescreen speaks to them, to tell them to stay still, shortly before their arrest. Surveillance takes other non-technological forms in *Nineteen Eighty-Four*: the Thought Police regularly patrol the streets and can look in windows, and higher windows can be watched from helicopters; average citizens, and family members, including children, are encouraged to watch and inform on each other. Even the programme of cumulative surveillance to stifle the subject's will to test the boundaries is present: Winston and Julia are permitted for some time to carry on an affair and take part in what they believe is a seditionary movement, until they are apprehended. We never know Julia's fate, but we watch as Winston's crimes are paraded before him and exposed to him as delusional (for commentaries on Orwell's critique of panopticism, see Strub 1989; Lyon 1994: 57–67).

Basic, in its technocratic endeavour to control meaning and thought and its accompanying high-flown rhetoric, was a manifestation of precisely the kind of grand project for the betterment of the world that was denounced by disillusioned social thinkers in the wake of the Second World War. In this context, Orwell's engagement with Basic presents an ambiguous and puzzling case. In terms of their underlying philosophy of language, there are many points of contact between Ogden and Orwell, and this is no doubt the reason why Orwell was both publicly and privately supportive of Basic as late as two years before he began writing *Nineteen Eighty-Four*. However, the endorsement of Basic by Wells and its unashamed invocation of Bentham could have hardly appealed to Orwell, and key principles animating Basic – word elimination and Ogden's interpretation of 'panopticism' – are clearly parodied in *Nineteen Eighty-Four*. While Orwell's final position regarding Basic is far from clear, Ogden's affinity with other large-scale technocratic reform projects is quite evident through his interaction with the logical positivists of the Vienna Circle. As we see in the next chapter, Ogden, through his efforts to promote Basic during the 1930s, came into contact and collaboration with the Viennese philosophers. They held similar hopes and shared a similar fate.

Notes

1. The discussion of Basic English in this chapter is based largely on Ogden's publications from the period in which he was actively developing and promoting the project. The final statement on Basic, which was published a decade after Ogden's death, is Ogden (1968), a 'revised and expanded version of The System of Basic English [Ogden 1934a]'.

2. There are numerous histories of the international language movement and surveys of international language projects with varying degrees of discussion of their historical background. It must be noted that most of these histories were written by active participants in the movement and so tend to be partisan: the line between propaganda and scholarly research is frequently unclear. The best examples include Couturat and Leau (1903, 1907), Guérard (1922), the annotated bibliography of Stojan (1929), and Pei (1968 [1958]). Among more recent scholarly studies are the survey by Blanke (1985); the historical studies by Forster (1982) and Lins (1988), which look at various aspects of the Esperanto movement; and Haupenthal (2005b), which offers a contrastive examination of the beginnings of the Volapük and Esperanto movements. Two recent popular accounts of the history of constructed languages – including, to varying degrees, the modern international language movement – are Large (1985) and Eco (1995 [1993]). Unfortunately, the scholarship presented in both these books is rather derivative and in many respects limited (see the reviews Tonkin 1988; Maat 1999). See chapter 4 of Blanke (2006)

and the accompanying bibliography for an up-to-date guide to the interlinguistic literature.

3. Couturat's (1901: 55–56) original text from which these excerpts are taken: 'Le dessein de fonder une Langue universelle qui remplaçât toutes les langues nationales, soit dans le commerce entre les divers pays, soit surtout dans les relations entre les savants de toute l'Europe, procède évidemment du mouvement intellectuel de la Renaissance, qui, en renouvellant toutes les sciences et la philosophie, avait révélé l'unité fondamentale de l'esprit humain et avait fait naître l'idée de l'union internationale de tous les savants, si bien experimée par la locution de "République des Lettres". D'ailleurs, la Renaissance, en émancipant la pensée de l'autorité des anciens et surtout du joug d'Aristote, dont la Logique avait régné pendant tout le moyen âge et cognait encore dans les écoles, avait donné l'essor aux recherches scientifiques, et par suite fait naître le désir d'une Logique plus moderne, mieux appropriée aux besoins des sciences nouvelles. La raison prenait conscience de sa force et de son indépendance, et tendait à s'affranchir de toutes les entraves de la tradition et de la routine; on commençait à s'apercevoir qu'on pouvait dépasser l'antiquité dans la connaissance de l'univers, et à entrevoir la possibilité d'un progrès indéfini.'

4. It should be noted that Enlightenment projects did not have the single-minded focus on a spoken language that is a feature of most mainstream modern projects, but rather recognised a distinction between a written 'character' and a spoken language, and sought to offer both (see Maat 2004: 16–28). The great hope, popularised by such figures as Francis Bacon (1561–1626), was that a true character, unlike parasitic alphabetic writing, would circumvent the confusions of spoken language, as 'in China and the provinces of the furthest East', where, thought Bacon (unfortunately, naïvely), 'there are in use at this day certain real characters, not nominal; characters, I mean, which represent neither letters nor words, but things and notions' (Bacon, quoted in Maat 2004: 17, see also pp. 16–23). These ideas perhaps live on in obscured form in various 'picture theories' of language and meaning, such as those of Wittgenstein, Ogden and Neurath (see §IV; Chapter 4, §III).

5. While there were numerous other philosophical language projects in this period, we focus on these three – those of Wilkins, Dalgarno and Leibniz – because they have been the subject of the most secondary research and, as we demonstrate, were the most significant to language constructors in the modern period. See chapter 3 of Knowlson (1975), part II of Slaughter (1982) and Maat and Cram (2000) for information on other projects.

6. Schleyer's original text: 'Durch Eisenbahnen, Dampffschiffe, Telegrafi und Telefoni ist der Erdball zeitlich und räumlich gleichsam zusammengeschrumpft. Die Länder der Erde haben sich so zu sagen bedeutend genähert. Darum sind die Zeiten für kleinlichen, engherzigen Nazionalstolz wol für immer dahin. Die Menschheit wird täglich kosmopolitischer, und sent sich nach **Einigung**. Durch die grosartige **Weltpost** ist ein gewaltiger Schritt zu disem schönen Zile vorwärz gemacht worden. Auch inbezug auf Geld, Mas, Gewicht, Zeiteinteilung, Geseze und **Sprache** sollte sich das Brudergeschlecht der Menschen mer und mer einigen! Zu diser **Sprach-Einigung** im grosartigsten Mastabe will vorliegendes Werkchen

den ersten Anstos geben [. . .] Nachdem sich die Menschheit zur Weltpost geeignigt hat, muß sie sich auch zu einer **Weltschrift, -sprache** und -Grammatik einigen! Dises ist für sie unstreitig der grosartige, geistigmaterielle Gewinn und Fortschritt.' Schleyer's enthusiasm for language reform extended to reforming German orthography; this is why his spelling in German frequently seems unusual. The 'world post' that he refers to is most probably the Universal Postal Union, an agreement between European and Europeanised countries reached in 1878 – but based on the earlier General Postal Union of 1874 – that guaranteed carriage and provided for uniform tariffs for international post between the member countries (see Francis Lyons 1963: 43–48).

7. At the back of his earliest 1880 grammar of the language is a diploma of proficiency which lists the seventeen rules Schleyer laid down to govern the language movement. Here the *datuval volapüka*, the 'creator of the world language', is declared the sole authority on the language, with the exclusive right to determine its future development. As Forster (1982: 46) notes, in coining his title, Schleyer has reached for the superlative extremes his language allows. There are two suffixes in Volapük to indicate a 'person concerned with', *-el* and *-al*, the first being the normal form and the second the elevated form, so *sanel* is 'doctor', but *Sanal* 'The Saviour'. A normal inventor would then be *datuvel*, and *datuval* one much greater.

8. In 1892 the academy's name was changed and its affiliation became the language project Idiom Neutral (which is set out in Rosenberger 1902). In 1908, with another name change, it moved to Italy and adopted Latino sine Flexione, the project of Giuseppe Peano, the mathematician who inspired Russell in his logicism (see Chapter 2, §III), a state of affairs that continued until 1939, when the Academy was shut down by Mussolini. In the Netherlands a small Volapük movement, speaking a reformed version of the language proposed by Arie de Jong (1865–1957), grew up in the inter-war years, but it was wiped out during the Second World War, with the banning of the language in Germany and German-occupied territories (see Schmidt 1998 [1963] and Haupenthal 2005b for detailed histories of the Volapük movement).

9. A German supporter of Esperanto made an English translation of Zamenhof's brochure in 1887, the same year that the Russian, Polish, French and German originals appeared. This initial English translation is, however, generally considered to be of very poor quality; the authorised English translation is by the Irish supporter Richard H. Geoghegan from 1889.

10. Zamenhof's original letter is in Russian, but the English translation above is based on the commonly accepted Esperanto translation: 'Mi naskiĝis en Bjelostoko, gubernio de Grodno. Tiu ĉi loko de mia naskiĝo kaj de miaj infanaj jaroj donis la direkton al ĉiuj miaj estontaj celadoj. En Bjelostoko la loĝantaro konsistas el kvar diversaj elementoj: rusoj, poloj, germanoj kaj hebreoj; ĉiuj el tiuj ĉi elementoj parolas apartan lingvon kaj neamike rilatas la aliajn elementojn. En tia urbo pli ol ie la impresema naturo sentas la multepezan malfeliĉon de diverslingveco kaj konvinkiĝas ĉe ĉiu paŝo, ke la diverseco de lingvoj estas la sola, aŭ almenaŭ la ĉefa, kaŭzo kiu disigas la homan familion kaj dividas ĝin en malamikaj partoj. Oni edukadis min kiel idealiston; oni min instruis, ke ĉiuj homoj estas fratoj, kaj dume sur la strato kaj sur la

korto, ĉio ĉe ĉiu paŝo igis min senti, ke homoj ne ekzistas: ekzistas sole rusoj, poloj, germanoj, hebreoj k.t.p. Tio ĉi ĉiam forte turmentis mian infanan animon, kvankam multaj eble ridetos pro tiu ĉi "doloro pro la mondo" ĉe la infano. Ĉar al mi tiam ŝajnis, ke la "grandaĝaj" posedas ian ĉiopovan forton, mi ripetadis al mi, ke kiam mi estos grandaĝa, mi nepre forigos tiun ĉi malbonon.'

11. His dual dreams of superimposed linguistic and religious unity have been pursued by other modern religions. Bahá'u'lláh (1817–1892), the founder of the Bahá'í Faith, hoped for 'the origination of one language that may be spread universally among the people [. . .] in order that this universal language may eliminate misunderstandings from among mankind' (quoted in Stojan 1929: 149). Many Bahá'í consider Esperanto a viable universal language. There is also a familial connection in this regard: Zamenhof's daughter, Lydia Zamenhof, was an active member of the Bahá'í community and promoted Esperanto among them.

12. Original text: 'C'est un lieu commun que de constater les progrès inouïs des moyens de communication: on pourra bientôt faire le tour du monde en quarante jours; on télégraphie (même sans fil) d'un côté à l'autre d'Atlantique; on téléphone de Paris à Londres, à Berlin, à Turin. Ces facilités de communications ont entraîné une extension correspondantes des relations économiques: le marché européen s'étend sur toute la terre, et c'est sur tous les points du globe que les principaux pays producteurs entrent en concurrence. Les grands nations possèdent des colonies jusqu'aux antipodes et elles ont des intérêts dans les pays de les plus lointains. Leur politique n'est plus confinée sur l'échiquier européen; elle devient coloniale et "mondiale". Toujours pour la même raison, elles sont de plus en plus obligées de s'entendre et de s'unir, soit dans un intérêt commercial (Convention de Bruxelles relative au régime des sucres), soit dans un intérêt moral (Convention internationale relative à la traite des blanches).' See Francis Lyons (1963: 103–109, 274–285) for more information about the Brussels Sugar Conventions and the International Convention on the White Slave Trade.

13. Jespersen (1960 [1921]: 744) provides us with this colourful titbit revealing the linguistic situation at the committee's meetings: most business was conducted in French, although Baudouin de Courtenay occasionally preferred to speak German, and Peano spoke his Latino sine Flexione.

14. Of all of them, Ostwald had perhaps distinguished himself the most with his efforts at international standardisation and co-operation: he developed the *Weltformat*, the immediate ancestor of the modern ISO 216 paper sizes that are used almost universally today; he proposed the introduction of *Weltgeld*, which the Euro realises in limited form, and he was the financial backer of the *Brücke* organisation in Munich that sought to catalogue all scientific work as a way of removing boundaries between scientists working in different fields and countries (see Domschke and Hansel 2000; Domschke and Lewandrowski 1982; Krajewski 2006).

15. Schleicher's original words are: '[U]nsere Wörter nehmen sich gotischen gegenüber aus, wie etwa eine Statue, die durch langes Rollen in einem Flußbette um ihre Glieder gekommen und von der nicht viel mehr als eine abgeschliffene Steinwalze mit schwachen Andeutungen des einst vorhandenen geblieben ist [. . .]'. The

English translation given above is from Jespersen (1922: 326), a slightly corrected version of the translation in Jespersen (1894: 11).

16. Note that in the quotations Kant is talking in terms of traditional subject-predicate propositions. In modern first-order propositional logics, as developed by Frege, Peano and Russell (see Chapter 2, §III), the structure of a proposition is not limited to the relation between the predicate and its subject.

17. The exclamation marks are original. Original text: 'Alle Künstelei, Unklarheit und Verschrobenheit sei in ihr [der Sprache] auf's äusserste verpönt!! [. . .] In ihr soll man die Sprache nicht haben, um seine Gedanken zu verbergen, sondern sie mitzuteilen!'

18. Original text: 'Rein lateinische [. . .] Wörter einfach in eine Pfuschersprache nur so herübernehmen, wie *homo*, *sed*, u. dgl., das kann jeder Sprachen-Pfuscher, der sich die Sache l e i c h t machen und etwa nur Geld verdienen will, und das haben vor S. schon viele andere Vp. nachäffer unternommen, jedoch auch e r f o l g l o s.'

19. It is interesting to note that the mathematician René de Saussure (1868–1943), brother of the linguist and founder of structuralism Ferdinand de Saussure (1857–1913), defended Esperanto derivation against the Idists under the pseudonym 'Antido' (anti-Ido). His zeal for Esperanto ultimately went unrewarded, however: his later proposals for reforms to Esperanto were not only rejected by the Esperanto Academy, but also resulted in his expulsion (see Forster 1982: 150–151; Künzli 2001; see also Joseph 2012: 516–519).

20. Original text: 'Der Weltsprache ligt die englische Volkssprache zugrunde, weil dise von allen Sprachen gebildeter Völker die leichteste und verbreiteste ist', and he continued, '(abgesehen von ihrer heillos verwirrten Ortografi)'.

21. The contrast Ogden makes between 'Chinese', 'Cantonese' and 'Hakka' suggests that by 'Chinese' he means the standard northern variety usually referred to as 'Mandarin' in English.

22. The 'realtor from Zenith' to whom Guérard refers is George F. Babbit, the title character of Sinclair Lewis' (1885–1951) 1922 novel *Babbit*.

23. 'Adelyne More' was a playful pseudonym Ogden used frequently when writing in *The Cambridge Magazine* and *Psyche*. His main motivations for employing a pseudonym may have been to create the appearance of greater diversity in the editorial content of these magazines, and also to distance himself from more controversial or experimental ideas. Under this name he wrote *Uncontrolled Breeding, or fecundity versus civilization, a contribution to the study of over population as the cause of war and the chief obstacle to the emancipation of women* (More 1916), an inevitably controversial feminist and pacifist tract. An apparently female author would also no doubt lend extra credibility to such a book. Ogden had other pseudonyms that he used on occasion (see Gordon 1990b: 136, notes 5 and 6).

24. Ogden's example of 'cut' as a morphologically invariable verb is probably due to Jespersen (1922: 333).

25. Bentham had directed in his will that rings bearing his portrait should be made as commemorative gifts for his twenty-six closest friends (see Atkinson 1987).

26. 'Orthology' is a term that Ogden elevated to utmost importance in his work: he named the institute that he set up to promote Basic the 'Orthological Institute'.

Ogden (1952: 11–12) described the term so: 'It was with the object of focussing attention on these normative possibilities [in improving communication] that the term "Orthology" was selected in 1927. Except by [British mathematician Karl] Pearson, from its first appearance in 1622 in Fotherby's *Atheomastix*, it has been used only in a grammatical or pedagogical context – to cover that part of grammar which deals with "the right imposition of names." It was therefore associated with propriety in language as opposed either to the "incorrect" use of words or to neology. To extend this normative approach to the "logos" – to the control of words and symbols in general – involves also a change of orientation as regards correctness. Our language is said to be "correct" when it conforms to current usage or to the usage of the "best" writers of a given period; an improvement of our linguistic tools, on the other hand, may often be effected by deviation from current usage, whether by innovation (including neology) or systematization. Orthology is therefore concerned both with the changes desirable in our attitude towards words and symbols and with the changes in language itself which a scientific study of Thoughts, Words and Things may require' (see also volume 3 of Gordon 1994: xviii, note 20; Gordon 2006: 2582).

27. Original Esperanto text: '[. . .] ĉar nur in tiu lingvo la vortsignifoj estas intence kaj pripense elektikaj kaj pro tio ili havas pli da stabileco kaj objektiveco ol la interrilatigiloj de la naturaj lingvoj'.

28. The correspondence between Orwell and Ogden quoted here is held in the Orwell archive of University College London Special Collections. The letter from Orwell to Ogden, 1 March 1944, is also published in Davidson (2010: 226–227).

Chapter 4

Ogden and the Vienna Circle

By the beginning of the 1930s the centre of gravity of the new analytic approach to philosophy had moved from Cambridge to Vienna. Russell and Wittgenstein's various versions of logical atomism, mixed with indigenous strands of German philosophy, became the *wissenschaftliche Weltauffassung*, or 'scientific world conception', embodied in a set of doctrines known variously as 'logical positivism' or 'logical empiricism'. Although not wholly uncritical of their innovations, Russell himself recognised the pre-eminence of the direction taken by the Viennese philosophers, commenting later that he was, 'as regards method, more in sympathy with the logical positivists than with any other existing school' (Russell 1940: 7). The Viennese proponents of these new doctrines did not consider themselves '*pure* philosophers', but scientists striving to secure the epistemological foundations of science in order to do away with the accumulated confusions of philosophy. Their target was 'metaphysics' as practised by the German idealists, but in their mouths this word became a disparaging term for any philosophy that did not meet their standards of logical rigour. The aim was modern thought for the modern world, and an escape from the mysticism and mystification of the past.

Ogden came into personal contact with two of the most prominent members of the Vienna Circle, as the group is known, Otto Neurath (1882–1945) and Rudolf Carnap (1891–1970), in 1933, just after Basic English had appeared on the scene and was being vigorously promoted, and just after the members of the Circle had published some of their foundational papers and were gaining attention around the world.[1] Ogden's intentions were, in the case of Neurath, directed towards collaboration and, in the case of Carnap, towards business. Ogden wanted to adapt Neurath's 'Vienna method of picture statistics' for the teaching of Basic, fulfilling a long-held hope for a visual educational adjunct to his project (Ogden 1929b: 29; cf. Chapter 3, §VI). From Carnap he wanted to secure the English translation rights to his recent philosophical papers, which were already being keenly discussed in the English-speaking world.

By the time they became aware of each other, both Ogden on the one side and Carnap and Neurath on the other had already formulated the key ideas that constituted their doctrines and were busy promoting them. For this reason it is not possible to discern any major mutual influence. But both sides had a lot in common and, especially in the collaboration between Ogden and Neurath, many peripheral but significant aspects of their thought became aligned. Both sides took language as central to philosophical problems, which they saw as impinging on the everyday life of ordinary people. The ideal approach to combat traditional philosophical confusions, they felt, would be to develop an improved language, whose validity would depend on everyday language, variously conceived. The positions Carnap and Neurath shared with Ogden emerged from a background that had much in common with the tradition of Cambridge analysis and which interacted with it in a number of ways.

I. The Viennese scene

Vienna, in the decades leading up to and following the turn of the nineteenth century to the twentieth, was home to a vibrant intellectual culture, a world romanticised today as one of discussion groups meeting in cafés and private homes, as well as formally organised associations offering public lectures and courses to the average person. The Vienna Circle, which defies precise delineation from its environment, manifested itself as both a private discussion group organised from 1924 by Moritz Schlick (1882–1936), and a formal association, the Verein Ernst Mach, founded in 1928.[2] Its participants were also active in many other areas of intellectual life, in Vienna and other cities of Central and Eastern Europe (see further Haller 1993: chapter 6).

The default image we have of the Circle today derives principally from a document intended to be its manifesto, published in August 1929 (Verein Ernst Mach 2006 [1929]). As stated on its title page, the manifesto has 'no officially named author', but the preface is signed by Neurath, Carnap and Hans Hahn (1879–1934), a mathematician, friend and brother-in-law of Neurath (see Stadler 1997: 693–694). Documentary evidence as well as the themes and phrasing of the manifesto reveal the text to be very much a joint product, although Neurath and Carnap were among the most significant authors (see Uebel 2008; cf. Mulder 1968; Haller 1993: 70; Stadler 1997: 372). In the manifesto the 'scientific world conception' is pitted against the confusions and deceptions of 'metaphysics'. This was not simply an academic project, but an effort 'to fulfil a demand of the present day[, …] to fashion tools of thought for the everyday, not only for the everyday of scholars, but also for the everyday of all who in whatever way are involved in the conscious work on shaping our lives' (Verein Ernst Mach 2006 [1929]: 10–11).[3] The Circle's professed goal, in Neurath's words, was to make a better world and a better life through the enlightenment that science brings. This is of course the same sentiment driving Ogden's researches into meaning and language (see Chapter 2, §I–II), and his efforts at developing Basic (see Chapter 3, §IV).

The writing of the manifesto was prompted by Schlick's decision to decline a call to a professorship in Bonn in favour of staying in Vienna, which made it 'clear to him and to us that there is such a thing as the "Vienna Circle" of the scientific conception of the world, which goes on developing this mode of thought in a collaborative effort', as the manifesto declares (Verein Ernst Mach 2006 [1929]: 299). Although gratified by the honour shown to him through the dedication of the manifesto, Schlick complained that he could not agree with its advertisement-like style and seemingly dogmatic formulations (Mulder 1968: 390; cf. Uebel 2008: 93).

This difference in understanding of the political and social duties of the Circle, along with differences in philosophical doctrine, lay at the base of the main division in the Circle – that between the 'left wing', represented chiefly by Neurath, and the 'right wing', represented primarily by Schlick. Carnap stood in between these two poles: starting with views more closely aligned to the right wing, he later drifted towards Neurath (Haller 1993: 70; Carus 2007: 243). The key doctrinal divisions between the two wings took on their clearest lines during the so-called 'protocol sentence debate', to which we come in the next section. In the face of theoretical innovations driven by Neurath – and adopted to some extent by Carnap – Schlick and his student Friedrich Waismann maintained a conservative attitude to the problem of 'verification' of sentences that leant heavily on the evolving ideas of Wittgenstein (cf. Chapter 2, §III).[4]

The Circle was conscious of its place in the history of ideas: the manifesto contains a section on its historical background (Verein Ernst Mach 2006 [1929]: 301–304), which both highlights fellow 'anti-metaphysical' philosophers around the world – here Russell and Moore are named as exponents of a long English tradition – and provides a catalogue of empirically minded thinkers active in Vienna in previous decades, along with the foreign authors they translated and interpreted. Prominent among the Viennese philosophers, and representative of the direction of their thought, is Ernst Mach (1836–1916), after whom the Verein Ernst Mach was named, and for whom the chair that Schlick later occupied in Vienna was originally established.

Mach was known as much for his research in physics as his work in the philosophical foundations of science. In his epistemology, we see the same sort of realism and faith in immediate experience that characterises Russell's later doctrines (see Haller 1993: chapter 4; cf. Chapter 2, §III). The evolution of Schlick's thought independently followed a similar course to Russell's: although long interested in philosophical questions, he only officially turned to philosophy after completing his doctorate in physics, under the supervision of the German physicist Max Planck (see Stadler 1997: 775). He had arrived at many of the epistemological positions that united him with Russell and Wittgenstein before he became aware of their work (see Haller 1993: 104–107): perhaps he was drawn to Wittgenstein more for the confirmation he provided for his existing views, and the eloquence with which he provided it, than for any instruction he offered.

Similar backgrounds straddling multiple disciplines were common also to Carnap and Neurath. Carnap began with studies in physics, mathematics and philosophy, under Gottlob Frege in Jena (see Chapter 2, §III), among others.

This set him on the 'scientifically' oriented course, anchored in rigorous formalised argumentation, confirmed in his doctoral dissertation (published as Carnap 1922), a study of conceptions of space in physics supervised by Bruno Bauch (1877–1942), a neo-Kantian of the Southwest School (see Carnap 1963: 11–12; Carus 2007). In Vienna – where he was active, but not always present, from 1925 onwards – this developed into an ever more aggressive campaign for the scientific world conception and assault on 'metaphysics', a line that Neurath most strongly represented and which Schlick frequently found uncomfortable (see chapter 11 of Stadler 1997 for examination of the tensions between Neurath and Schlick).

But whereas Neurath was engaged in bringing the scientific world conception to the general population, Carnap stayed largely within the boundaries of academia. His organisational activities extended only to other academic groups, such as the lectures he arranged at the Bauhaus school of design (see Dahms 2004), and his attacks on metaphysics were highly technical and directed at an academic audience. His general approach was to use the logical techniques developed in his more constructive works to dissolve 'pseudo-problems' that have occupied philosophers, as in his essay *Scheinprobleme in der Philosophie* (Pseudo-Problems in Philosophy; Carnap 1967 [1928]), where he argues that the opposing arguments for realism and idealism are simply products of linguistic and logical confusion. The tone of these essays is generally superior and summary, much like that adopted by Ogden and Richards in *The Meaning of Meaning* (see Chapter 2). Carnap concludes *Scheinprobleme* with what he believes is a comprehensive list of all objections that could be raised against his arguments, and adds: 'For the sake of clarity, all critics are requested to admit explicitly to one of these viewpoints' (Carnap 1967 [1928]: 343).

Neurath, more socially and politically engaged than Carnap, began in Vienna with studies in areas as diverse as mathematics and natural science to history, and earned his doctorate in Berlin with a dissertation on ancient notions of commerce, trade and agriculture (published as Neurath 1906–1907 [1906]).[5] The social engagement that Neurath would show after his return to Vienna in 1919 had a period of incubation during the First World War: in 1916 he was appointed director of the *Kriegswirtschaftsmuseum* (Museum of War Economy) in Leipzig, founded in order to explain to the average citizen the workings of the war economy (see Schumann 1973 and Cartwright *et al.* 1996: 20), which Neurath idealised as a model of economic efficiency. It was at this time that he began to develop his system of picture statistics, as a means of communicating complex economic facts to a lay audience. The common beliefs and goals that underlie this work and Ogden's Basic were apparent to both Neurath and Ogden, and resulted in their later collaboration.

After the war Neurath had the opportunity to implement his ideas for a thoroughly planned, socialised economy as president of the Bavarian Central Economic Administration in the short-lived Bavarian *Räterrepublik* (Soviet Republic). When this experiment failed economically and politically, Neurath

was imprisoned for treason, but his release was soon secured by the socialist government of 'Red Vienna' (see Cartwright *et al.* 1996: 43–63). After
being deported to Vienna, Neurath continued his work in the *Gesellschafts-
und Wirtschaftsmuseum* (Museum of Society and Economy), founded in 1920,
which remained his main occupation during his period of contact with the
Vienna Circle. The principal goal of this museum was to make better citizens
by educating the people about the economic policies and achievements of the
Viennese government, and represented the union of Neurath's existing pedagogic, economic and political interests (see Neurath 1991 [1926], 1991 [1933]).
Neurath's public efforts on the intellectual front lacked the detail of Carnap's
anti-metaphysical evangelism, but he was still given to making programmatic
statements and to singling out the Circle's intellectual enemies (such as in
Neurath 1983 [1930–1931], 1983 [1931]).[6]

The most widespread image we have today of the Vienna Circle reflects, and
is the conscious propagandistic product of, the Circle's 'left wing', dominated
by Neurath and cautiously supported by Carnap. Neurath and Carnap took
up the fight for the Circle's radical anti-metaphysical philosophy in the wider
academic community, as well as in the general population. The views they held
share an unmistakable and freely acknowledged kinship with those developed
near-simultaneously in Cambridge, but are rooted also in indigenous German-
speaking traditions. Vienna and Cambridge were bound together by the same
epistemological questions and the same approach to answering them. For the
politically engaged Neurath, in particular, just as for Ogden, these were urgent
problems that impacted on everyday life. In both centres, everyday experience
was taken to be the foundation of knowledge, and the means to exploring this
experience was the language in which it is expressed. The problem remained,
however, of exactly how to pin down the everyday. The solutions arrived at by
Neurath and Carnap mirror those proposed by Ogden.

II. The everyday versus metaphysics

The target of Neurath's and Carnap's attacks was 'metaphysics': for them this
included not only doctrines explicitly labelled as such, but any philosophy that
failed to meet the standards of 'scientific' epistemological rigour they set. In fact,
they did not even consider their own work to be philosophy in the traditional
sense, but rather the elimination of philosophy and its replacement with a new
'unified science', a notion that originates with Neurath and that would become
an increasingly important platform associated with the Circle. 'Unified science'
would facilitate free co-operation and communication among scientists, breaking down the disciplinary boundaries that presently separate them. As Neurath
put it:

> It is one of the tasks of our time to aid scientific reasoning to attain its goal without
> hindrance. Whoever undertakes this is concerned not so much with "philosophy,"

properly speaking, as with "anti-philosophy." For him there is but one science with subdivisions – a unified science of sciences. We have a science that deals with rocks, another that deals with plants, a third that deals with animals, but we need a science that unites them all. (Neurath 1983 [1931]: 48)

In this wholesale denunciation of 'metaphysics' as the product of logical and linguistic confusions and the striving for a new 'scientific' solution, we are of course reminded of Ogden and Richards' crusade against 'word-magic' (see Chapter 2). The similarities do not end here, a fact of which all parties were aware. Early in his correspondence with Carnap, Ogden sent him a copy of *The Meaning of Meaning*, where he marked out the point at which Ogden and Richards give their own assessment of 'metaphysics'. Carnap replied, 'From the marked point (p. 222) I see, that our views about metaphysics will be in good agreement. With great interest I will see the details of your views' (postscript dated 30 December 1933 to a letter from Carnap to Ogden, 29 December 1933). The 'marked point' was most probably in the second paragraph on p. 222 of the third revised edition, published in 1930, where Ogden and Richards address 'metaphysics':

[T]he set of confusions known as metaphysics has arisen through lack of this true grammatical approach, *the critical scrutiny of symbolic procedure*. In the same manner our analyses of Beauty and Meaning are typical instances of what grammar might long ago have achieved had grammarians only possessed a better insight into the necessities of intelligent intercourse, and a livelier sense of the practical importance of their science. (Ogden and Richards 1989 [1923]: 222; same page as the edition of 1930; emphasis original)

In the details Carnap will have discovered that Ogden and Richards' method of definition involved a procedure highly similar to the technique he used himself in one of his most famous anti-metaphysical passages, his attack on Heidegger's proposition 'Das Nichts selbst nichtet' (The nothing itself nothings). This proposition, Carnap argued, is 'meaningless [. . .] in [the] strictest sense' (Carnap 1959 [1931]: 61), and contains merely an expression of a *Lebensgefühl* (attitude to life), perhaps partly assimilable to the 'emotive' connotation in Ogden and Richards' terminology (see Chapter 2, §I). He demonstrated, in the sort of diagrammatic form also eagerly employed by Ogden, how an originally meaningful expression could have strayed into the realm of the meaningless. In the left-hand column below we start with perfectly meaningful expressions of the everyday language. Meaningless sentences are then built from these in the middle column by using words in the same sentence structure that logically do not fit. Natural languages permit such logical misuses of words, but a logically correct language, as in the third column, would forbid such expressions (Carnap 1959 [1931]: 70).[7]

I. Meaningful sentences of ordinary language	*II. Transition from sense to nonsense in ordinary language*	*III. Logically correct language*
A. What is outside? Ou(?) Rain is outside. Ou(r)	A. What is outside? Ou(?) Nothing is outside. Ou(no)	A. There is nothing (does not exist anything) that is outside. ~(∃x) . Ou(x)
B. What about this rain? (i.e. what does the rain do? or: what else can be said about this rain?) ?(r) 1. We know the rain. K(r) 2. The rain rains R(r)	B. 'What about this Nothing?' ?(no) 1. 'We seek the Nothing' 'We find the Nothing' 'We know the Nothing' K(no) 2. 'The Nothing nothings' No(no) 3. 'The Nothing exists only because . . .' Ex(no)	B. None of these forms can even be constructed.

The key to exploding these metaphysical statements, in Carnap's view, lies in realising that, because they break the rules of logic, they cannot be made to say anything about the world. If a statement can be tested for correspondence to the world then it is valid; if not, it is meaningless metaphysics. Philosophy must pass the same epistemic tests as science, and science derives its validity from observation of the world. Observation, for its part, takes place at the level of phenomenal experience. Chemists cannot see the individual hydrogen and oxygen atoms that make up water, but they assume their existence because when they run an electric current through water, they produce two kinds of gas: one that ignites when exposed to a flame (hydrogen) and another that promotes the burning of an existing flame (oxygen). But scientific facts extend into the domain of the intangible: physicists, for example, cannot see or feel gravity as such, but they posit its existence because it provides the most economical explanation and reliable predictions of such observable facts as the falling of apples to the ground and the movement of the moon through the sky. This is to say, the epistemic basis of science is experience of the world as it comes to us through our eyes, ears, skin, and so on. Scientific facts are the stories we tell to connect and explain these experiences.

The elevation of scientific practice to epistemological principle led Carnap to measure his philosophy against the phenomena of the world as we experience them, rather than appealing to such abstract entities as sense-data, as Russell had done, or Wittgenstein's atomic *Tatsachen* (see Chapter 2, §III; Wittgenstein 1922: prop. 2). In this context the language of the everyday, as the language in which we express our experiences, gains a new significance. Carnap's elevation of phenomenal experience to the epistemic basis goes back to at least 1926, when he completed the manuscript of *Der logische Aufbau der Welt* (The logical construction of the world; Carnap 1967 [1928]).

By the time Carnap had come into contact with Ogden in 1933, however, he had retreated to the less strict position of 'physicalism'. This doctrine was originally proposed by Neurath, but finds its classical exposition in Carnap's (1934 [1931]) essay 'Die physikalische Sprache als Universalsprache der Wissenschaft' (The physical language as the universal language of science). The English translation of this essay was published under Ogden's editorship in 1934 with the title *The Unity of Science*, a title shared with a series of conferences from 1934 to 1941, organised primarily by Neurath (see Stadler 1997: 395–436). The doctrine of physicalism arose around 'late 1929' out of Neurath's objections to the Wittgensteinian atomistic epistemology prevailing in the Vienna Circle, and Carnap's phenomenalistic developments on it (Uebel 2007: 137; see also Carnap 1934 [1931]: 28; Carus 2007: 239–251). The dialogue in which physicalism was developed and refined within the Circle is known as the 'protocol sentence debate', named after the subject of discussion, the 'protocol sentences', the statements in which observations are recorded, as in a scientist's 'protocol' of their experiment.

At the centre of Carnap's (1934 [1931]) physicalism is the 'physical language'. This is indeed the language of the scientific discipline of physics, although not necessarily in the form it has today or in the form it has had in any historical period (Carnap 1934 [1931]: 54). The defining property of this language is that it talks objectively about physical entities in the world in quantitative terms (Carnap 1934 [1931]: 52–67). That is, it talks of goings-on in the world in a mathematically precise way independent of the perceptions of any individual. It is possible to verify any statement of this physical language by translating it into a 'protocol language' – a language used to record the experiences of an individual observer – and there are as many of these protocol languages as there are observers. The phenomenon comes first and the analysis later, argued Carnap (1934 [1931]: 46–47), turning to then recent research among the *Gestalt* psychologists.

Carnap took the physical language as his basis for two reasons. First, it is objective, or rather *inter-subjective*. That is, it talks about the world in absolute terms, divorced from the perspective of any single speaker. This is in contrast to the protocol languages, each of which refers to the private experience of the individual and so is not available for public discussion. Second, so claimed Carnap, every statement in every scientifically valid language can be translated into the physical language. Statements in any of the 'sub-languages' of chemistry, biology, psychology, sociology and so on – that is, in any of the genuine sciences – can all be translated into the physical language.

It is in fact the possibility of effecting a translation of a sub-language into the physical language that confirms the scientific validity of the related discipline (Carnap 1934 [1931]: 67–74). A 'metaphysical' statement, by contrast, cannot be translated into the physical language and this is how we can identify it as such (we saw an illustration of this technique above in the case of 'The nothing itself nothings'). But not every statement in the physical language can be translated into one of the sub-languages. The physical statement may deal with a subject matter that lies outside the scope of a given sub-language: a statement that could be translated into chemical terms may not be translatable into sociological terms, for example. It is this possibility of translating any statement from the sub-languages into the physical language that makes it the 'universal language' that guarantees the 'unity of science' as a single undertaking, and simultaneously excludes everything that is not scientific – these are the constructive and exclusionary sides of the scientific world conception (Carnap 1934 [1931]: 96).

The protocol languages are similarly sub-languages of the physical language. Any statement in a protocol language can be translated into physical terms, but the reverse is not always possible: the physical statement may go beyond the limits of the private experience of any particular individual, but for every true physical statement there is a possibly existing protocol language into which it could be translated. Again, it is this possibility of translation that lends validity to the physical and protocol languages: a true statement in either in fact says precisely the same thing as its translation into the other; they differ only in terms of their form. It should be remembered here that the physical language really does talk in physical terms. The description of perception in the protocol language becomes in the physical language an account in such terms as the position in four dimensional space of the individual electrons that make up the electrical impulses in nerves:

> Hence, every statement in the protocol language of S can be translated into a physical statement and indeed into one which describes the physical state of S's body. In other words there is a correlation between S's protocol language and a very special sub-language of the physical language. This correlation is such that if any statement from S's protocol language is true the corresponding physical statement holds intersubjectively and conversely. Two languages isomorphic in this fashion differ only by the sounds of their sentences. (Carnap 1934 [1931]: 87–88)

Carnap admitted that this conclusion may seem astonishing, but claimed that it is quite obviously true; he contended that we in fact intuitively make such translations between the physical and protocol languages every time we think about other people's accounts of their perceptions:

> The reader may still hesitate, feeling that such a deduction is utopian and would need full knowledge of the physiology of the central nervous system for its performance. This is not however the case; derivation of the required physical statements is already

possible and is achieved in everyday life whenever communication occurs. It is true that what we know in such cases of the physical situation of other persons' bodies cannot as yet be formulated as a numerical distribution of physical coefficients of state but it can be formulated in other expressions of the physical language which are just what we require. (Carnap 1934 [1931]: 85–86)

In Carnap's physicalist conception after 1929 the language of everyday experience therefore had a special and unrivalled role as the medium of immediate experience that correlates with the physical language. But this actually represented a step back from his position in *Der logische Aufbau der Welt* in 1926, where 'autopsychological objects', essentially the same entities of direct experience that are spoken about in the protocol language, form the basis of his system. He preferred this basis because of its epistemic primacy (Carnap 1967 [1928]: 101, §64), but he was forced to move away from it when it became apparent that it was incurably solipsistic.

The danger of solipsism was known to Carnap, and he wanted to characterise his approach as merely 'methodological solipsism'; that is, an approach that applies the 'form and method of solipsism' without acknowledging 'its central thesis' (Carnap 1967 [1928]: 102). He felt that he had escaped solipsism in practice, because he looked to the 'structure' of experience rather than its 'material'. The substance of individuals' experiences may not be the same, argued Carnap, but the relations of the elements that make up these experiences are comparable from individual to individual because they correspond to the relations between the entities in the world that are responsible for the experiences (see Carnap 1967 [1928]: §66, §16). This focus on formal relations as the basis of objective knowledge of course has an immediate precedent in Russell's 'logical constructions' (see Chapter 2, §III), and has roots extending back to Kant (cf. Richardson 1998: 35–51; Daston and Galison 2007: chapter 5).

Carnap (1967 [1928]: 101–106, §64, §65) tried further to side-step the problem of solipsism by making the additional point that 'the given does not have a subject'. A stream of experience simply exists; it only makes sense to identify a perceiving subject distinct from the world and other perceivers once the stream of experience has been analysed – or 'physically reconstructed', to use Carnap's term – and these elements have been separated out. There are no parts to a stream of experience, including no 'subject' or perceiver, until it has been processed in this way.

When Carnap came to actually sketch his analytical apparatus, however, he was not able to maintain the purely methodological character of his solipsism: his efforts at securing intersubjectivity depended on heteropsychological reconstruction of others' perceptions, which necessarily had to proceed over a physical step, anchored in the individual's own autopsychological basis. That is, to reach the intersubjective description, we must think about what other observers would perceive by imagining what the world would look like if we occupied the position they occupy and saw the world through their eyes. This approach appeals to agreement between perceivers on specific phenomena and weakens the assumption that intersubjectivity is guaranteed by the inherent structural correspondence of all streams of experience. As a result, argues Uebel (2007: 131–134), Carnap's system succumbed to anti-solipsistic arguments from Neurath and Heinrich Neider (1907–1990), another member of the Circle, at that time still a student.

But Neurath's objections to Carnap's philosophy went even deeper than his arguments against 'methodological solipsism'. Any form of epistemological certainty and an 'ideal language' in which this certain knowledge could be expressed, both notions which underlie Carnap's 'autopsychological objects' and his later 'protocol languages', were for Neurath metaphysical dreams. In his discussions with Carnap, Neurath continually returned to these topics (which he raised in the published record in Neurath 1981 [1928], 1983 [1930–1931], 1983 [1931]).

Among the clearest and best-known formulations of Neurath's position contra Carnap is Neurath's (1983 [1932]) 'Protokollsätze' (Protocol statements), his reply to Carnap's (1934 [1931]) 'Die physikalische Sprache als Universalsprache der Wissenschaft'. Even though with the advent of physicalism in 1929 Carnap had departed from 'methodological solipsism', in 1931 he still imagined a protocol language in which '[t]he simplest statements [. . .] refer to the given, and describe directly given experience or phenomena, i.e. the simplest states of which knowledge can be had' (Carnap 1934 [1931]: 45). But for Neurath, there could be no 'given'; every observation involves the application of some sort of theory, a notion frequently associated with the French physicist and philosopher of science Pierre Duhem (1861–1916), whom Neurath (1983 [1932]: 98) cited as an inspiration, among others (cf. Cartwright *et al.* 1996: 111–131).

Neurath's rejection of the 'given' in its semantic aspect – that is, the rejection of the possibility of observation statements that could only be interpreted as having one single, fixed reference without any ambiguity – may show some influence from Welby and her supporters (see Chapter 2, §III). Welby, it will be remembered, denied the possibility of what she called 'Plain Meaning', that is, literal, uninterpreted, unambiguous meaning. Neurath was certainly aware of her work: a strong influence on him in his early years was the sociologist Ferninand Tönnies, winner of the 'Welby Prize' (see Chapter 3, §VII; Cartwright *et al.* 1996: 10–11). He even saw in the work of the later Dutch significs movement a similar striving towards unified science (e.g. Neurath 1938: 19; Neurath 1987 [1938]: 136) and invited one of their members, Gerrit Mannoury, to the 1937 Unity of Science Congress (his talk is published as Mannoury 1987 [1938]; he also contributed to *Erkenntnis*, e.g. Mannoury 1934).

The impossibility of the 'given' means that there can be no clean separation between the protocol language and the physical language: the two are distinguished only in that the protocol language makes reference to observer, while the physical language does not (Neurath 1983 [1932]: 93). All we have, according to Neurath, is the 'trivial language' that is handed down to us from previous generations and is full of imprecise, unanalysed terms, which Neurath called *Ballungen* (a term Cohen, in his translation of Neurath 1983 [1932], renders as 'verbal clusters'). Instead of pursuing the inevitably fruitless goal of reaching an ideal language, we should simply seek to clean out the language we have of its metaphysical terms (Neurath 1983 [1932]: 91). This will give us a 'universal jargon', the best result that we can ever hope for (Neurath 1983 [1932]: 92). This is the view that Neurath summed up so elegantly in his well-known *Schiffer* [sailor] metaphor, a recurring motif in his writings (see Cartwright *et al.* 1996: 89–166 for the history of this metaphor):

> There is no way to establish fully secured, neat protocol statements as starting points of the sciences. There is no *tabula rasa*. We are like sailors who have to rebuild their ship on the open sea, without ever being able to dismantle it in dry-dock and reconstruct it from the best components. Only metaphysics can disappear without trace. Imprecise 'verbal clusters' ['*Ballungen*'] are somehow always part of the ship. If imprecision is diminished at one place, it may well re-appear at another place to a strong degree. (Neurath 1983 [1932]: 92)

Carnap (1934 [1931]) was clearly already struggling with objections of this kind. He was prepared to acknowledge Neurath's point as a practical difficulty, but not as an insurmountable theoretical barrier. There may be *Ballungen* in actual protocol languages, but that does not mean that there can be no 'primitive protocols' in which they have been entirely eliminated:

> Owing to the great clumsiness of primitive protocols it is necessary in practice to include terms of derivative application in the protocol itself. This is true of the physicist's protocol and true in far greater measure of the protocols made by biologists, psychologists and anthropologists. (Carnap 1934 [1931]: 44)

In the face of Neurath's critique, Carnap (1932–1933) accepted the possible existence of many different kinds of protocol languages. This was the beginning of Carnap's new programme of 'logical tolerance', which had little to say about the question of a single epistemological foundation and instead concentrated attention on the technical details of translation between languages (see Carnap 1937 [1934], a work also published in English by Ogden).

But Carnap always strove for precision and formal rigour in his theorising and no amount of tolerance would lead him to leave his finely specified logical systems floating coherently but without correspondence to the world. Inspired by the logical theory of truth developed by the Warsaw School of logicians, which has its classical formulation in the work of Alfred Tarski (1901–1983), first presented publicly in 1931 (but first published in Tarski 1956 [1933]), Carnap elaborated, in his 1942 *Introduction to Semantics*, a theory of 'pure semantics'. This is a theory of the possibilities of 'semantical systems', abstracted away from the 'pragmatics' of actual instances of language in use, and even from the 'descriptive semantics' of any particular language (Carnap 1942: 8–15). Carnap's semantical system consists of rules laid down in a metalanguage that specify the designation of signs in an object language and the conditions under which sentences in the object language are true, since 'to understand a sentence, to know what is asserted by it, is the same as to know under what conditions it would be true' (Carnap 1942: 22).[8]

Of course, this talk of 'truth' and the formal, rigid stipulation of the possibilities of interpretation in the abstract could never appeal to Neurath. In his correspondence with Carnap after the appearance of *Introduction to Semantics*, Neurath objected to Carnap's scheme, and the realist ontology that he believed it suggests through the implication that there is an object language at the very bottom of the hierarchy that refers to the 'given' (see Reisch 2005: chapter 10). Carnap, no doubt reflecting on many discussions that had taken place in previous years, anticipated Neurath's reaction in his preface to the book, and urged an open mind to experimentation to see what results might present themselves from admitting consideration of meaning and truth in the abstract:

> While many philosophers today urge the construction of a system of semantics, others, especially among my fellow empiricists, are rather sceptical. They seem to think that pragmatics – as a theory of the use of language – is unobjectionable, along with syntax as a purely formal analysis; but semantics arouses their suspicions. They are afraid that a discussion of propositions – as distinguished from sentences expressing them – and of truth – as distinguished from confirmation by observations – will open a back door to speculative metaphysics, which was put out at the front door. Some metaphysicians have indeed raised futile issues concerning truth, or rather the Truth, and I certainly should not like to help in reviving them. The same, however, holds for many other concepts, e.g. number, space, time, quality, structure, physical law, etc. Should we then refrain from talking about them in a non-metaphysical, scientific way? It seems to me that the only question that matters for our decision in accepting or rejecting a certain concept is whether or not we expect fruitful results from the use of that concept, irrespective of any earlier metaphysical or theological doctrines concerning it. (Carnap 1942: vii–viii)

Neurath pursued his preferred course of cleaning out the 'trivial language' to create a 'scientific jargon'. In this direction he produced his *Index Verborum Prohibitorum* – a pun on the Catholic Church's *Index Librorum Prohibitorum* and all that it implies – a list of words forbidden for their unavoidable slipperiness, which would inevitably drive their users to metaphysics. This he alluded to in Neurath (1983 [1932]: 91), but only explicitly mentioned first in print in Neurath (1987 [1933]: 8), although the idea would seem to go back to his days as a doctoral student (see Neurath and Cohen 1973: 7; Reisch 1997). He also constantly urged the use of concrete terms in place of more abstract expressions: instead of talking of 'magnetism' and the 'kingdom of animals', for instance, talk should be of magnets and individual species (Neurath 1996: 257–258, 304–305).

While Carnap followed the formal route in elaborating an ideal language for the sciences, Neurath pursued the practical course of providing a forum for specialists to present their sciences in the universal scientific jargon. Inspired by the *Encyclopédie* of the French Enlightenment figures D'Alembert (1717–1783) and Diderot (1713–1784) (see Neurath 1937: 134; Dahms 1996), Neurath began a project that eventually became *The International Encyclopedia of Unified Science*, which 'aim[ed] to show how various scientific activities such as observation, experimentation, and reasoning can be synthesized, and how all these together help to evolve unified science' (Neurath 1938: 2).[9] The single unique system of science does not exist, says Neurath, so the best that can be hoped for is a collaboratively compiled encyclopaedia of scientific wisdom. In places it may be inconsistent, but it is the best possible edifice we can construct for our scientific knowledge:

> [A]n encyclopedia (in contradistinction to an anticipated system or a system constructed a priori) can be regarded as the model of man's knowledge. For, since one cannot compare the historically given science with "the real science," the most one can achieve in integration of scientific work seems to be an encyclopedia, constructed by scientists in co-operation. (Neurath 1938: 20; see also Neurath 1983 [1935]a).

Many of the points Neurath raised in this period find expression around the same time – but still before they made contact – in the writings of Ogden and his assistant Leonora Wilhelmina Lockhart (1906–1985), who developed a theory of 'word economy' (Lockhart 1928, 1931a). Lockhart, much of whose wording resembles Ogden's own, saw the best approach to the 'scientific' study of meaning and symbolism in the 'science of Symbolism' that had grown out of *The Meaning of Meaning* and manifested itself in Basic (Lockhart 1931a: 12, 63). This gives us the means to make language 'a more precise instrument of thought', she argued, and in fashioning this instrument 'we are faced with the [. . .] problem of reduction' (Lockhart 1931a: 56). Reduction can be understood as grammatical reduction and as reduction of words: the elimination of complex rules of syntax and morphology and the elimination of excessively fine-grained and compositionally inscrutable words. English, with its 'analytic tendency' (see Chapter 3, §IV), provides the perfect basis for both: it is a language 'in which the elements entering into one construction may be reassembled and used in another' (Lockhart 1931a: 23).

Lockhart did not see 'analysis' of an expression as an end in itself: analysis is only useful insofar as it helps to establish a reference. But analytical expressions are generally better for establishing references, since they allow us to 'systematize our knowledge', and so are perhaps the best 'antidote to the habit of using words without adequate reference' (Lockhart 1931a: 56–57). In writings undertaken at Ogden's prompting (Wisdom 1930: 11, note 1), the British philosopher John Wisdom (1904–1993), a student of Moore and the transitionary Wittgenstein, argued that there is a fundamental difference between 'analysis' and 'interpretation', which Ogden's hero Bentham and like-minded philosophers failed to fully appreciate (cf. Chapter 3, §VII). Wisdom essentially took analysis to be the analysis of a concept, through which the fundamental elements and structure of facts in the world are revealed, while interpretation he treated as merely establishing what particular words mean; through interpretation we simply replace one set of words for picking out a referent with another, without necessarily offering a more philosophically motivated description (see Wisdom 1930, 1931). Lockhart (1931b) rejected the distinction and claimed that it presupposed the possibility of some sort of ultimate, 'metaphysical' knowledge beyond that which can be expressed verbally.

Ogden and Richards (1989 [1923]: 110) had already dealt with this issue in their discussion of definition when they denied that there was any contrast between 'real' and 'verbal' (i.e. 'nominal', or 'symbolic') definitions. This is the contrast between knowing what thought to attach to a word, which is provided by the verbal definition, and knowing the underlying properties of the object referred to by the word, expounded in the real definition. It is rooted in Aristotle's theory of essences, and received the formulation referred to by Ogden and Richards in the work of Locke (cf. Gupta 2015: §1.1). Ogden and Richards argued that words are only ever convenient symbols and a definition simply provides a more convenient set of symbols for picking out a referent, while a so-called real definition would be an enumeration of the properties of an object in the world. Although such an enumeration could also serve as a more convenient paraphrase, its target is the referent, not the symbols that refer to it, and so it goes beyond the domain of the science of symbolism.

By limiting analysis to whatever is most expedient for making reference, Lockhart was following a principle established already in *The Meaning of Meaning*. In the absence of absolute 'god-given concepts', as she put it, that ought to underlie analyses, she was left with the question of where any given analysis should stop, that is, what the correct bottom level of analysis should be. There is no single correct level, she concluded; any analysis can be reduced to a lower explanatory level (Lockhart 1931a: 58):

> [E]ven within the confines of a single language, the basis of definition is determined by the particular aspect of knowledge with which we are, for the moment, concerned. The 'species' on which the botanist's classification is based may be resolved in the chemist's test tube into a variety of substances; and the simple elements of the chemist's world will be turned by the physicist's electroscope into a complex system of energy. Each account of phenomena has its legitimate starting point. And as there seems to be no means of escape from the bias attaching to individual systems, linguistic or scientific, it is difficult to see how an absolute analysis of the constituents of the universe is possible. (Lockhart 1931a: 50–51)

In the place of ultimate analysis Lockhart adopted analysis at the level of our everyday phenomenal experience:

> If language is to consult human convenience – and being a tool fashioned by the human mind for its own purposes, this can scarcely be denied – it should symbolize objects, as far as possible, at the level of our perceptions. Facts that cannot be inferred directly from contact with the object should not be covered by the unit symbols. (Lockhart 1931a: 60; cf. Walpole 1937; Myers 1938)

We see in Lockhart's writings sentiments familiar from Carnap's conception of protocol languages and Neurath's universal jargon. Further strengthening the resemblance, we hear Susan Stebbing (1885–1943), a philosopher in the Cambridge tradition, echoing the critique Wisdom made of Bentham – and, by implication, Ogden and Lockhart – when she criticised the Vienna Circle philosophers for failing to distinguish between different kinds of analysis (Stebbing 1933; see also Beaney 2003; Milkov 2003). Comparing the logical constructions of logical atomism and related theories (see Chapter 2, §III) to the 'fictions' of Bentham (see Chapter 3, §VII), Ogden claimed that if logical analysts took their logical constructions seriously and admitted them as an essential part of language, as Bentham did his fictions, they would discover that many logical constructions cannot in fact be reduced to purported atomic facts. His comments at this time in support of analysis at the level of everyday language, as advocated by Lockhart, and in opposition to the search for the 'ideal language', could have been written by Neurath:

> Bentham believed that language must contain fictions in order to remain a language, *i.e.*, that a language which "mirrored" reality would be impossible. If the logico-analysts were to believe that "logical constructions" must *necessarily* occur in language they would profoundly modify their attitude to the problem; for it would follow that there could be no atomic proposition and all analyses would be relative. Whether some hierarchical analysis is possible must remain doubtful. What is at any rate clear is that we could not talk of *the* analysis of a given proposition. This is the real bone of contention between the logic-analytic temperament and the technological approach of Bentham. The latter realized that the problem is eminently a *practical* one – the classification of thought by simplifying and revealing the structure of language; and therefore a task for whose performance no eternally valid rules can be promulgated. The logico-analysts postulate an ideal language – perfect even in its well disposed irregularities – which requires methodical articulation in accordance with a preconceived metaphysical scheme. (Ogden 1932d: l–li; emphasis original)

Neurath and Carnap, in the name of the Vienna Circle, sought to proselytise the modern scientific world conception, to achieve the 'unity of science', which would bring all sciences together and exclude the unscientific. Carnap, like Ogden, targeted 'metaphysical' philosophers to expose their nonsensical doctrines. The weapon he used was also the same: *reductio ad absurdum* executed through an analysis of his opponents' language. In this battle, the language of the everyday became the anchor that prevented talk from drifting off into the metaphysical. But Neurath objected to Carnap's 'everyday'. Carnap wanted phenomenal experience to be his 'given', his solid foundation. For Neurath, even this reeked of metaphysics. All we have is our everyday language, our 'trivial language'; all we can hope for is to continually purge it of those expressions that lead to metaphysical misconceptions, in order to approach a universal jargon. The unity of science can then be achieved through the compilation of an encyclopaedia, where each scientist relates their discipline to the wider world in the jargon. But both Carnap and Neurath's notions of everyday language resonate with Ogden and Lockhart's postulates about performing analysis in language at the level of everyday experience. Neurath would draw further on these insights in his collaboration with Ogden, in which his 'Viennese method of picture statistics' became the 'Isotype: international picture language'.

III. International picture language

Neurath had already begun experimenting with the visual representation of statistical information during his time at the *Kriegswirtschaftsmuseum* in Leipzig, but it was at the Viennese *Gesellschafts- und Wirtschaftsmuseum* in the 1920s that the method reached new heights of sophistication and systematisation and became a top intellectual export product, with exhibits being lent to museums overseas and the establishment of branch museums in Berlin, the Hague, London and Moscow.

A typical example of the method from this period can be seen in Figure 4.1, which illustrates the different types of economies found in the world and their distribution over various population groups, with their sizes. The toothed wheel represents modern industrial economies, the hammer economies based around skilled trades and agriculture, and the bow and arrow hunter and gatherer economies with primitive agriculture. Each figure represents 100 million people; the outlined figures with hats represent Europeans; the brown figures with turbans represent 'orientals', Indians and Malays; the black figures Africans and 'mulattoes'; and the yellow figures with pointed hats represent 'Mongols'.

During the course of the 1930s, Neurath developed his picture statistics to deal with an ever broader range of material, going beyond the purely statistical to cover historical narrative and procedural instructions, addressed to an ever wider audience. The method eventually became the 'international picture language'. It is not entirely clear what lay behind this new designation; even as he introduced the 'international picture language', Neurath was careful to point out its continuing dependence on 'normal language':

> There are simple picture languages in which no other sorts of signs are used. What we have to do with here, however, is a picture language which is not able to give the story by itself, but only with the help of the words of a normal language. (Neurath 1936: 16; Marie Neurath 2009: 49 makes a similar point)

Wirtschaftsformen der Erde

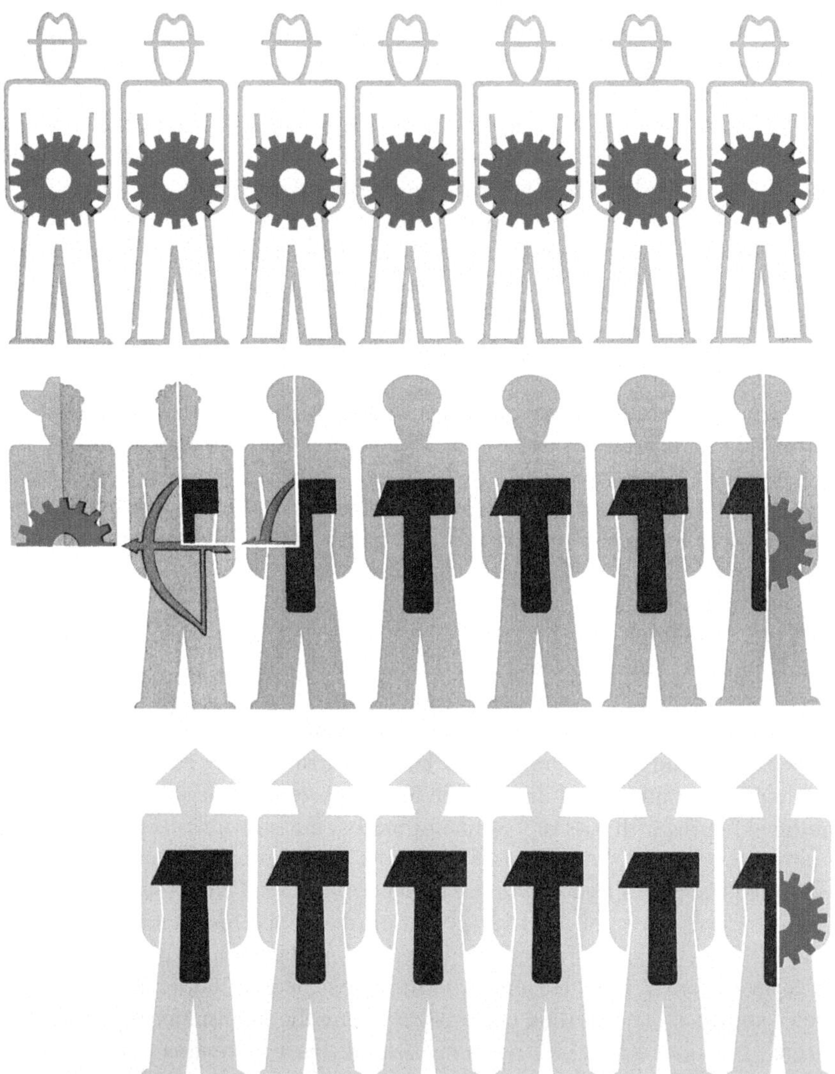

Figure 4.1 Economic systems of the earth
Gesellschafts- und Wirtschaftsmuseum 1930: 97.

Among later commentators, there are those, such as Müller (1991), who take the designation 'picture language' quite literally and examine it in light of the linguistic theories current in Neurath's milieu; others, such as Burke (2011), dispute that Neurath ever thought of Isotype as a linguistic system, despite the rhetoric that suggests as much. Whatever the precise status Neurath accorded to the method, it is clear that he saw it as some sort of system of communication and that his approach was deeply bound up with his philosophical convictions about the place of 'everyday' language (as discussed in §II above). These are convictions that he shared to a large extent with Ogden, and which came to manifest themselves through Neurath and Ogden's collaboration.[10]

Ogden's influence on Neurath's picture statistics extended to one of the most conspicuous features of the approach, its name. From 1935 onwards the method was called 'Isotype', which, like Ogden's 'Basic', is an acronym: 'International System Of TYpographic Picture Education'; a name, incidentally, that would seem to emphasise the system's pedagogic character rather than its claims to being an international auxiliary language. Marie Neurath (1898–1986; née Reidemeister) – a major proponent of Isotype, coiner of the name, and for many years the companion and later wife of Neurath – recalled the inspiration she drew from Ogden's Basic in the rebranding:

> The two Basic books [Neurath 1936 and Neurath 1937] forced us to find a new name for the method and the formation of the word 'Basic' ('British American Scientific International Commercial') helped in this. One afternoon I sat down and played around with it. I arrived at 'International System Of Teaching in Pictures' – Isotip; that did not sound quite right yet, except for the first syllable. It was then only a short step to 'Isotype'; but I did not succeed in finding a good sequence of words for it, and we stayed with the not entirely satisfactory solution of 'International System Of Typographic Picture Education'. When Neurath returned in the evening from a meeting in Amsterdam he was pleased with the name, and the next day, asked Arntz [chief graphic designer on the project; introduced below] to design a symbol for it. Both name and symbol were then published, for the first time, in *International picture language*. (Marie Neurath 2009: 47)

The first of two books published in collaboration with Ogden, *Isotype: international picture language* (Neurath 1936), sets out the system of Isotype and makes a case for its use in pedagogic and international contexts. With the obvious and acknowledged influence that Ogden had on the name 'Isotype', it can be imagined that he, an active participant in the international language movement, played a role in bringing Neurath into the fold and casting Isotype as an 'international picture language', despite whatever misgivings Neurath may have had about pressing the linguistic status of the method. Even if Neurath wanted to keep the linguistic claims of Isotype within limits, pictures and visual representation certainly occupied an important place in his philosophy of language. According to Neurath, pictures show – and can only show – concrete, tangible objects; they are incapable of expressing the abstract entities that populate the metaphysician's world. Pictures perhaps offer the best medium for Neurath's 'universal jargon'. There is freedom in the possible abstractness of the spoken language, but also metaphysical danger; a picture language protects us from this:

> What a triumph it was, when people freed themselves from the limits of pictographic writing, what a triumph, when language adapted itself flexibly and in multiple forms to the demands of scientific work, when people learnt to control this logical tool. Of course, liberation from the picture led also to diversions, led into the realm of the meaningless. Nominalisation created new problems. In particular the German language leads to such metaphysical diversions; it allows numerous statements about 'the nothing that nothings' (Heidegger), about the 'being' – as if the 'being' could be used in a sentence like the sword or the table. The pure pictographic writing recognises a sword and a table, but no being. (Neurath 1991 [1933]: 269)[11]

We see here Neurath's repetition of Carnap's earlier elevation of Heidegger to a paradigmatic example of metaphysical nonsense.[12]

The faith in pictures that Neurath demonstrates is not unique or even original to him. Ogden, we have already seen, preferred nouns to verbs because, among other reasons, nouns generally name things that can be 'pictured', while verbs do not. Additionally, in his Basic paraphrases for adjectives he preferred descriptions of the observable behaviour that the target of an adjectival qualification exhibits to the elusive qualities adjectives might otherwise be taken to convey (see Chapter 3, §VI). In Neurath's immediate philosophical milieu, Wittgenstein proposed his 'picture theory of language', where the 'pictures' we make of the world correspond to it exactly, and Russell also spoke of 'images' in our minds, although he was of course careful to emphasise that he did not necessarily mean visual images (see Chapter 2, §III).

Müller (1991: 239–230) specifically warns against looking for 'family resemblances' between Neurath's thought and the Wittgenstein of the *Tractatus*, pointing out Neurath's extreme negative reaction to the work (cf. §I). Despite their differences, however, we can still observe the quite clear common ground they had, along with others, in treating pictures as direct representations of the world. Müller does not deny this: his warning is probably directed at those who would posit an *influence* of the early Wittgenstein on Neurath that goes beyond observing their shared positions in their common milieu.

'Words divide, pictures unite', first attested in German as 'Worte trennen – Bilder verbinden' (Neurath 1991 [1933]: 273), and eventually gaining a Basic translation, 'Words make division, pictures make connection' (Neurath 1936: 18), was Neurath's repeated slogan for Isotype. It echoes his call for unified science, *Metaphysical terms divide – scientific terms unite* (Neurath 1987 [1933]: 23, emphasis original; see also Haller 1993: 175–176; Cartwright *et al.* 1996: 179), and in so doing classes 'word' with 'metaphysical terms' and 'pictures' with 'scientific terms'. But the 'division' and 'connection' that Neurath had in mind were not necessarily of an international character. The roots of the system were pedagogic: the original purpose was to explain economic details to the uneducated visitors to the Vienna *Gesellschafts- und Wirtschaftsmuseum*. Here the division is not between peoples, but between the social classes of a single people. Neurath (1983 [1946]: 236) later commented that '[w]hen I created "Isotype," together with my collaborators, as an international technique of visual information, I was thinking mainly of the masses, who could now grasp something more than before of the present knowledge of mankind'.

Neither is it just any pictures that unite. Isotype employs a distinctive style motivated by a similar spirit of minimalism to that found in Basic. The system of Isotype must make use of the minimum number of pictures possible, and the pictures themselves must be reduced to the barest outlines, containing only the details that are necessary for them to be recognisable. At the same time, the pictures have to be as clear and engaging as possible: they should be 'living signs' that talk directly to the viewer (see Neurath 1936: 32–33, 1991 [1933]: 269). The viewer should be drawn into a dialectical, 'meditative' process when they look at an Isotype picture; as they look and think about the picture, more details should become apparent, but only to a certain point:

> A picture that makes good use of the system gives all the important facts in the statement it is picturing. At the first look you see the most important points, at the second, the less important points, at the third, the details, at the fourth, nothing more – if you see more, the teaching picture is bad. (Neurath 1936: 27)

The style arrived at for this minimalistic depiction was a form of silhouette drawing stamped out from linocuts, visible in Figure 4.1 above, where each picture takes on the form of a 'type' (see Neurath 1991 [1935]: 342). This style was largely the product of the German artist Gerd Arntz (1900–1988), who came to work at the Vienna museum in its early days (see Annink and Bruinsma 2010).

Neurath spoke of the individual symbols as the 'vocabulary' of the system and the method of their combination as the 'grammar', although he always maintained a distance from the implications of linguistic status these terms carry (see Neurath 1936: 56). The basic principle of the grammar is that symbols should be overlaid to produce compounds representing concepts that belong together. In Figure 4.1 we can see this principle at work: the symbols for the different economic systems are placed on the symbols that represent the population groups. In this connection Neurath emphasised the need for independence of visual representation from the spoken language. Whereas in many spoken languages there is a metaphorical use of words that causes us to talk of 'a person's foot' and 'the foot of a mountain', no such metaphor should appear in a visual language, since there is no visual connection between these two concepts (Neurath 1936: 54–56). Most other grammatical principles in Isotype are of a practical rather than semantic nature and concern such issues as the layout of symbols, the use of colours, and, of course, given the system's original purpose of representing statistics, the representation of quantities (see Neurath 1936: 73–74 *et passim*; 1991 [1933]).

Isotype occupies a position in Neurath's thought and activities that has perhaps not yet been fully appreciated in subsequent scholarship on his work. From his return to Vienna after his imprisonment in Bavaria to the end of his life, Neurath's work on Isotype, through various institutions, was his main occupation and source of income. He used Isotype in his projects aimed at social reform, such as his museum work (represented in Gesellschafts- und Wirtschaftsmuseum 1930) and publications like *Modern Man in the Making* (Neurath 1939), a world history demonstrating the advance of civilisation, as well as in his more theoretically oriented projects, such as the *International Encyclopedia of Unified Science*, for which Neurath planned an unrealised '*Atlas* [. . .] worked out as an *Isotype Thesaurus* showing important facts by means of unified visual aids' (Neurath 1938: 25).

As Isotype entered its 'international picture language' phase, it was used increasingly for instructions and narratives where a series of iconic pictures was presented stepping through an action or a sequence of events. Figure 4.2, for example, instructs parents to take their children to the doctor to be cured when they exhibit the symptoms of rickets. This use of Isotype reached its peak after Neurath's death, when Marie Neurath was employed by the Nigerian government in the 1950s to produce a range of illustrated information booklets to explain government policy during the decolonisation period.

On a purely theoretical level, pictures appealed to Neurath as the basis of a system of communication, especially of scientific communication, because of what he saw as their inherent connectedness to the world. This ensured that they were accessible to everyone, he believed, regardless of their level of education or cultural background. He was not alone in seeing pictures in this light: Ogden, Wittgenstein and Russell all held similar views. Neurath, however, did not see the 'picture language' as having the same expressive range as spoken languages. But this could be an asset. Because so much cannot be expressed in the picture language, we are forced, as we are in Basic, to concentrate on the essentials and be clear about what we mean:

> But in the same way as Basic English is an education in clear thought – because the use of statements without sense is forced upon us less by Basic than by the normal languages, which are full of words without sense (for science) – so the picture language is an education in clear thought – by reason of its limits. (Neurath 1936: 20–22)

IV. Contact and collaboration

The course of Ogden's contact with Neurath and Carnap is revealed in their extensive correspondence.[13] In both cases the contact was initiated by Ogden and began with a proposal. Neurath he pursued because he wanted to develop

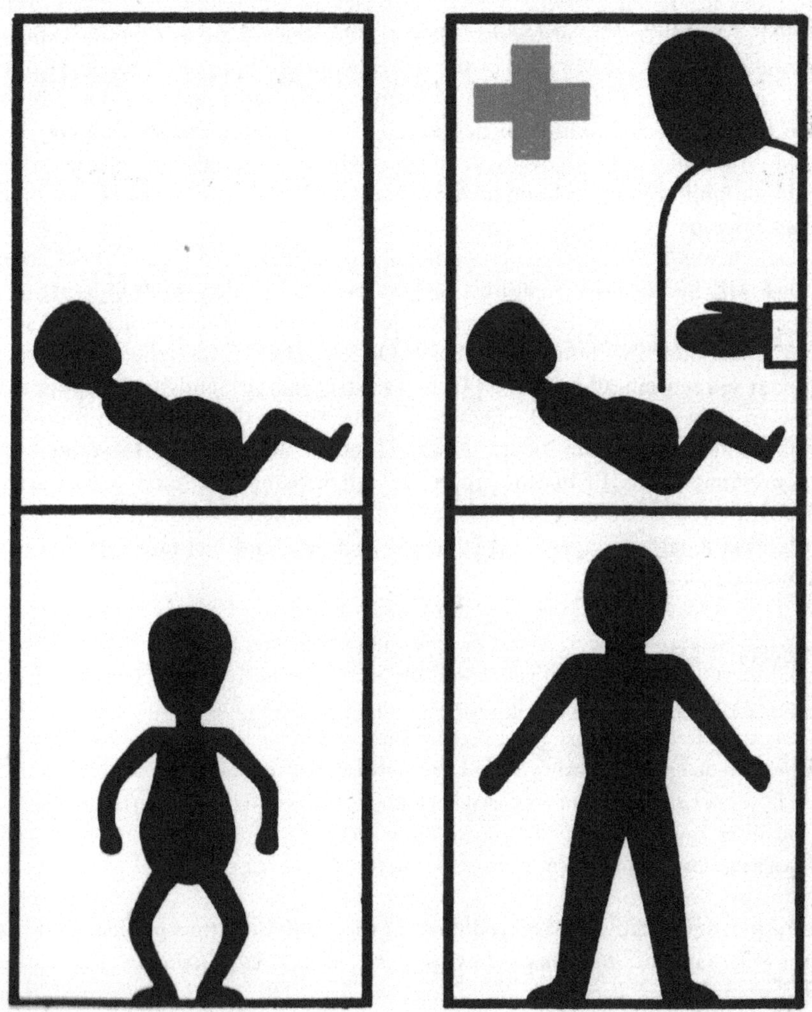

Figure 4.2 Rachitis
Neurath 1936: 55.

a visual education method for Basic; Carnap because he wanted to secure the English translation rights to his philosophical papers. In both instances he was successful. The collaboration with Neurath resulted in *Isotype: international picture language* (Neurath 1936) and *Basic by Isotype* (Neurath 1937). Carnap's 'Die physikalische Sprache als Universalsprache der Wissenschaft' (1931) appeared in Ogden's *Psyche Miniatures* series as *The Unity of Science* (1934), and his *Logische Syntax der Sprache* (1934) with Kegan Paul as *Logical Syntax of Language* (1937). A great deal of the correspondence between Ogden, Neurath and Carnap is made up of back-and-forth negotiations regarding the publication of these books, and often degenerates into brusque exchanges over such distasteful topics as fees, royalties and copyright. But amid these exchanges their common philosophical and linguistic interests still managed to emerge as topics of discussion.

Ogden was keen to win such eminent intellectuals as Neurath and Carnap over to the Basic cause. Neurath's earliest letters to Ogden, beginning in 1933, appear to be lost,[14] but from Ogden's side of the correspondence it can be seen that he responded with interest to Basic. Ogden writes, 'The Basic books named in your letter went all to you on October 7 (<u>registered</u>), and I am hoping that they are now in your hand' (Ogden to Neurath, 17 October 1933; underlining original), suggesting Neurath had expressed an interest in these books in his previous letter. In his first reply to Ogden, later that same year, Carnap also displayed some curiosity about Basic, prompted by his existing interest in international languages, in particular Esperanto, and Neurath's enthusiastic comments on Basic:

> When Neurath was here recently he spoke enthusiastically about your "Basic English". I'd be very grateful if you could send me something in the way of orientation. For many years I've had a lively interest in the problem of an international auxiliary language. In terms of theory I'm especially interested in the logical side of this problem, the question of logical syntax. But I've also been involved with the practical aspects (I can speak Esperanto, but am not dogmatically attached to this system). I consider an auxiliary language especially worthwhile and necessary for international relations in science. (Carnap to Ogden, 7 December 1933)[15]

In response Carnap also received most of the Basic literature published at that time. Ogden sent: *Bentham's Theory of Fictions*; *Jeremy Bentham 1832–2032*; *Opposition*; *Word Economy*; *Basic English*; *The ABC of Basic English*; *Basic English Applied: Science*; *Basic for Economics*; *Carl and Anna*; *Debabelization*; and the 1933 issue of *Psyche* (Ogden to Carnap, 11 December 1933). He commented that '[t]hese will give you a general picture of the theory on which the system is Based [*sic*].' Carnap further ordered (Carnap to Kegan Paul, 29 December 1933): *The Basic Words*; *The Basic Dictionary*; *The Basic Vocabulary*; and *Basic by Example*. Ogden later sent *The Meaning of Meaning* and Richards' *Basic Rules of Reason*, of which Carnap acknowledged receipt in a letter on 30 December 1933. Unwilling to allow any opportunity for propaganda to slip by, Ogden points out in his letter of 11 December 1933 that '[t]his letter is itself all in Basic English, and within the rules of the <u>ABC [of Basic English]</u>' (underlining original). He also frequently signs himself 'Yours (in Basic) very truly, C. K. Ogden'.

Neurath's initial interest in Basic appears to have continued through the

1930s. Apart from their collaboration, in 1935 Ogden was made a member of the international organising committee for the Unity of Science congresses (recorded in Neurath 1938: 26; Stadler 1997: 406), and Neurath invited him to speak at the 1937 Congrès Descartes in Paris (the Ninth International Congress of Philosophy), as well as inviting both Ogden and Lockhart to talk at the 1941 Unity of Science congress on 'the analysis of language making' and word economy respectively (the invitations are dated Neurath to Ogden, 10 June 1937, 26 September 1941; Neurath to Lockhart, 26 September 1941; Neurath also sent invitations to participate in the 1939 congress: Neurath to Ogden, 7 February 1939, 11 April 1939). Neither Ogden nor Lockhart presented at these conferences, however. The reason why remains an open question, but the invitations from Neurath imply that he wanted to encourage their programme or at least that he thought it was worthy of wider discussion and debate in such a high-level forum. A later letter from Neurath to Lockhart suggests that he found Basic English a useful source for his own work and had a desire to learn more about its historical and philosophical background:

> I had more than once [in recent lectures at Oxford, Nottingham, London and Exeter] an opportunity to discuss Basic English problems. Let me repeat how much I appreciate the General Basic Dictionary. It helps me really in preparing my Scientific Universal Jargon and to understand better some problems of Language Making. Where could I find a report, [*sic*] how Basic has been made? The history, so to speak, of this language? (Neurath to Lockhart, 19 July 1941)

Neurath's reaction to one of the most controversial aspects of Basic, its strident promotion of all that is 'British American' as a model for the world, is informative in respect to his political and philosophical orientation. In 1942 he writes to Ogden: 'Since I believe, more or less, in the Anglicization of the world, I anticipate success for BASIC, of course' (Neurath to Ogden, 23 January 1942). By the time he wrote these words, with the Second World War well underway, Neurath had been living in Great Britain for two years. He had arrived there after fleeing the German invasion of the Netherlands, where he had been based since 1934. In February of that year, the Verein Ernst Mach, the registered society that formed the public face of the Vienna Circle (see §I), was shut down by the Austro-Fascist regime of Austrian Chancellor Engelbert Dolfuß (who was himself assassinated in July of that same year in the political turmoil that gripped Austria). Neurath, who was at the time in Moscow disseminating his picture statistics in the USSR at the invitation of the Soviet government, decided not to return to Vienna.

The rise of fascism in central Europe was felt by other members of the Vienna Circle. Carnap, who took up a professorship in Prague in 1931, was already away from Vienna when events took their dramatic turn, but he continued to visit frequently until 1933. After setting out on a lecture tour in the United States in 1935, he did not return to Europe. Many of those who stayed in Vienna faced an even more unfortunate fate. Schlick, probably the Circle's least politically active member, was murdered by one of his students in 1936, an individual act, but one spurred on by the social and political climate (see Stadler 1997: 920–961).

Great Britain was Neurath's refuge and Ogden was among the friends who helped him to become established there. It would seem that Ogden assisted in Neurath's and Marie Reidemeister's (from 1941 Marie Neurath) release from internment as enemy aliens. Their main British supporter at this time was Susan Stebbing (introduced in §III above; see Reisch 2005: 15–16), but Ogden also assisted. Neurath writes to Ogden in 1940:

> I am like Reidemeister interned; we are reading, writing, designing and continuing our scientific and educational work. But we are handicapped by the lack of libraries and of contacts with scholars. The society for the pr. of sc. [promotion of science] and learning made an application for release. I ask you for help too. It will be too great to have a reference letter from you and Reidemeister's additional letter of Miss Lockhart could be useful too telling about our Institute in Holland. A doubt hardly can arise about our political reliability. (Neurath to Ogden, 11 September 1940)

The Neurath of the 1940s was a man satisfied with his new English homeland and the Anglo-American future he anticipated. Ogden's and Neurath's correspondence in this period consists mostly of queries from Neurath about the history of various English thinkers, in particular Ogden's hero, Jeremy Bentham. Ogden indulged him in each letter with pages of information and opinion. In a somewhat cryptic passage of a very long letter buried in this exchange, Neurath ruminated on the 'British Atmosphere' and its role in shaping the 'Modern Atmosphere':

> I do not know, how you think of the history of the science – I think that the empiricist parts of them become more and more elements of a common realm, the 'orchestration' seems to be increasing. The 'tools' are more and more unified – there is no particular physics in the USA, India, not even in Germany, in spite of stupid books on German or Aryan physics. This progress in 'unification' is related to some progress in unification also in the field of language reform, terminology in a wider sense etc. Condillac, Hobbes, Bentham, Mill, etc and then others too, play their role, creating the MODERN ATMOSPHERE. I think that Logical Empiricism is an element of this atmosphere of scientific encyclopedism. The fact that an archbishop of Dublin wrote Elements of Logic, MANY STATEMENTS IN IT WHICH YOU ACCEPT, TOO (objecting, very much, to other of course) impresses a continental scientist, who is accustomed to different types of archbishops, professors of universities in the middle of the 19th century. The point is, that I 'believe' very much in the British Atmosphere, compared with others, in spite of many things. (Neurath to Ogden, 26 February 1942; capitalisation original)

The worldwide 'progress in "unification"' that characterises the 'Modern Atmosphere', the scientific world conception, of which the logical empiricism of the Vienna Circle is a part, believed Neurath, is well-rooted in the 'British Atmosphere', to the point where it is perceptible even among the British clergy of the nineteenth century, as exemplified by Richard Whately, author of *Elements of Logic* (Whately 1845), where on the continent, by contrast, only reactionaries could be expected in such positions. Ogden, who maintained the image of the classical eccentric English gentleman scholar, would have been the perfect friend for a newcomer trying to assimilate to the 'British Atmosphere'.

Neurath even suggested that Ogden may have inspired some aspects of George Bernard Shaw's prototypical eccentric English academic, Henry Higgins, as he was portrayed in the 1938 film version of *Pygmalion*. Neurath commented (19 December 1944):

> I have just seen again the film PYGMALION and again, I felt that some details remind me of your studios, with a Chinaman's shaking head, a big Grammophon [*sic*] funnel and other paraphernalia, which let me feel at home in some intellectualized cosy climate. Did you realize that, too?

Ogden replied (24 December 1944):

> I haven't seen the Pygmalion film, but Bernard Shaw was a frequent visitor to the Institute in happier times to hear himself recorded on the big gramophones. If Peace be only lurking around the corner, it may not be too long before we can once more take up the threads left by V1, V2 ... V4.[16]

Neurath's praise for 'our British muddle' came out in his correspondence with Carnap at the same time (see Cartwright *et al.* 1996: 87). In one of his last writings, Neurath compared 'Anglo-Saxons' to 'Germans':

> [Germans] are, as individuals, on an average not less friendly than other people, but the German atmosphere is full of enthusiasm and exaltation, more than, for example, the Anglo-Saxon one; that is, full of preparedness to admire self-sacrifice, and to desire death in war for the highest good; and, from self-sacrifice it is but a short step to realizing that sacrifice of others is unavoidable for *the* cause. In the Anglo-Saxon atmosphere, people think more in terms of the little happiness of all little men in a human environment, and even the people on top regard themselves more often as people who like to have their weekends and who therefore could become potential victims of a future totalitarianism, rather than as people who are permanent commanders of guard formations. This would agree with the prevalence of empiricist utilitarianism in the western countries and of metaphysical idealism in Germany. (Neurath 1983 [1946]: 238)

Despite the early exploratory enthusiasm he expressed in his first exchanges with Ogden, Carnap's 'lively interest' in international auxiliary languages did not develop into the sort of support for Basic that Neurath showed. Much of Carnap's Christmas holiday of 1933, which followed shortly after his first contact with Ogden, was spent reading and digesting the books Ogden had sent him, and in his first letter after Christmas, whose opening could have served as a testimonial for Basic, he demonstrated an interest in the language that would have certainly pleased Ogden:

> [T]he best and most pleasing things of all I got this Christ-birthday are the books you sent me so kindly.[17] It was very interesting for me to get knowledge of your system of Basic English. And here you see the fruit of my reading. At school I was learning much Latin and Greek but very little English. Later I was sometimes reading English books and papers of my science range, but had no chance for talking and writing. My knowledge of English is so bad, that I not ever had the heart for writing an English letter. And now I am very happy to be able to do so by help of Basic English. (Carnap to Ogden, 29 December 1933)

Carnap goes on to endorse Lockhart's theory of 'word economy'. He writes:

> I am in full agreement with your (and Miss Lockharts [*sic*]) statement about word economy. I have the belief: if there would be a competition among the philosophical books and papers in German for the use of the least number of words, I possibly would be at the top. (Carnap to Ogden, 29 December 1933)

However, the winner of the winter holiday remained for Carnap Esperanto. In his next letter, he gave Ogden's permission to use his name on a petition in support of Basic – 'I give you with pleasure my approval to put my name on the list of those who give their support to Basic' (Carnap to Ogden, 7 February 1934) – but maintained a preference for Esperanto, which, he writes, 'is still more simple than Basic. (Much more, in my opinion, than you seem to see; what you say at some places f.e. about Esperanto is not quite right; but this question is not very important.)' (Carnap to Ogden, 7 February 1934).[18] In practice, however, perhaps only a language like Basic which is derived from a natural language has a chance, opined Carnap. But Carnap backed away from putting too much weight on such practical concerns; he only countenanced such issues because of the arguments of his pragmatic friend Neurath:

> [W]e see from the facts – or at least it seems very probable – that the much greater number of men are not ready to make use of a not-natural language system; they have even a disgust at such a one. For this reason a part language of a natural language has much more chance to be taken in use by a great number of men in the near future, on the condition that this language is simple enough (though not so simple as a con-structed one). Now, in my opinion, your Basic system is in this condition. It is possible to make use of it even at present in the relations to a very great number of men. You are right that this gives to Basic the greatest chance of beeing [*sic*] the help-language of the future.[19] I will say you openly, that I have a feeling of regret about the fact that a

constructed language – though much better, if seen from the angle of <u>theory</u> – has no chance in <u>fact</u>. But facts have more force than feelings; and so we have to take Basic. (I myself am a man more of theory and system than of fact and doing. That I am looking now at the question of Basic from the angle of fact is chiefly the effect of the words of my friend Neurath.) (Carnap to Ogden, 7 February 1934; underlining original)

In his reply, Ogden implied that he and Carnap were actually in agreement on the question of Basic versus Esperanto (12 March 1934): 'Delighted to have your signature. [What you say is what we mean by "not satisfactory for the purpose"; i.e. "men are not ready to make use of a made-up language."]' Note that Carnap did not consider Esperanto perfectly logical, however:

In consequence of the unsystematic and logically imperfect structure of the natural world-languages (such as German or Latin), the statement of their formal rules of formation and transformation [within Carnap's logical syntax project; see §II] would be so complicated that it would hardly be feasible in practice. And the same difficulty would arise in the case of the artificial world-languages (such as Esperanto); for, even though they avoid certain logical imperfections which characterize the natural world-languages, they must, of necessity, be still very complicated from the logical point of view owing to the fact that they are conversational languages, and hence still dependent upon the natural languages. (Carnap 1937 [1934]: 2)

In connection with the view expressed here, it is interesting to observe that Carnap later commented that the debate over natural versus constructed languages was one of the central points of disagreement that later drove the different schools of analytic philosophers in their respective directions. On one side were Moore, Wittgenstein and their followers, who concentrated on expression in natural language and, on the other side were the Vienna Circle philosophers, who focused on expression of scientific facts in the artificial languages of mathematics and logic:

Only slowly did I recognize how large the divergence is between the views of the two wings of analytic philosophy in the question of the natural versus constructed languages [. . .] It seems to me that one explanation of this divergence is the fact that in the Vienna Circle mathematics and empirical science were taken as models representing knowledge in its best, most systematized form, toward which all philosophical work on problems of knowledge should be oriented. By contrast, Wittgenstein's indifferent and sometimes even negative attitude toward mathematics and science was accepted by many of his followers, impairing the fruitfulness of their philosophical work. (Carnap 1963: 68–69)

The Wittgenstein that Carnap describes is surely one already on the way to his later views, one that could in no way be mistaken as striving to develop a 'logically perfect language' (see Chapter 2, §VI). Carnap also recollected

Wittgenstein's strong negative reaction to constructed languages at their first meeting, probably on 4 July 1927 (see Stadler 1997: 485):

> At our very first meeting with Wittgenstein, Schlick unfortunately mentioned that I was interested in the problem of an international language like Esperanto. As I had expected, Wittgenstein was definitely opposed to this idea. But I was surprised by the vehemence of his emotions. A language which had not 'grown organically' seemed to him not only useless but despicable. (Carnap 1963: 26, cf. 28–29, 34)

It is not possible to say from the correspondence with Ogden where Carnap stood in relation to the critique of Basic as Anglo-centric. He later cited two motivations for his interest in international languages: the simplicity of their structure, and 'the humanitarian ideal of improving the understanding between nations' (Carnap 1963: 69). In Carnap's mind, as we have seen, Basic did not meet the first of these ideals as well as the more artificial constructed languages, and it is easy to imagine that its Anglo-centrism, with its inevitable elevation of one national culture above all others, would have also detracted in his view from its ability to fulfil the second ideal. Basic is not even mentioned in Carnap's (1963: 67–71) retrospective survey of constructed language projects. Unlike Neurath in England, Carnap was not quite so infatuated with his new American home. Among many features that pleased him, he also found much to criticise in the new host culture, such as the 'strong conformism' he detected in American society:

> Once I referred in a talk with Einstein to the strong conformism in the United States, the insistence that the individual adjust his behavior to the generally accepted standards. He agreed emphatically and mentioned as an example that a complete stranger had written him that he ought to have his hair cut: 'Don't forget that you now live in America.' (Carnap 1963: 39)

Carnap's perception of American society was no doubt influenced by living through the chilliest parts of the Cold War, when the anti-communist paranoia of McCarthyism led to FBI investigations into the backgrounds and political persuasions of many American academics, Carnap included – a situation examined in detail by Reisch (2005). If Carnap found conformism objectionable, it is easy to imagine that he may have been disturbed by a project like Basic, with its 'panoptic' basis, and all that implies (see Chapter 3, §VIII).

By the spring of 1934 Carnap seems to have more or less given up on Basic. He began his first letter in April with: 'please allow me to write in normal English. My former letters were exercises in Basic, but it takes me a little more time to write in Basic, because of the right selection of words' (Carnap to Ogden, 13 April 1934). 'Nevertheless', he added, 'I would prefer to get your letters in Basic as before, if it does not cause you trouble or loss of time' (Carnap to Ogden, 13 April 1934). He announced also to Ogden that he had been invited to deliver a series of lectures in London in October of that year, and so now he

had reason to improve his knowledge of 'normal English'. This is in fact the trip
when Carnap first made the personal acquaintance of Ogden, later recalling that
'I talked often with C. K. Ogden, mainly about language and logic, his Basic
English and international languages' (Carnap 1963: 33–34).

Unperturbed, Ogden pursued Carnap further as a potential Basic English
speaker. In response to an apparent enquiry from Neurath on the possibility of
translating the proceedings of the 1934 meeting of the Unity of Science movement in Prague, he wrote: 'Carnap himself writes excellent Basic! Why not ask
him to be present, for Basic, at the Conference?' (Ogden to Neurath, 22 April
1934). As the date of Carnap's London lectures drew closer, Ogden urged him
to consider using some Basic: 'Why not do <u>one</u> of your "London Lectures" in
Basic? I would be happy to go through a rough copy in the simplest English
you are able to send. There would be no need to say that it was Basic till after
the event' (Ogden to Carnap, 21 July 1934; underlining original). Here Ogden
was urging Carnap to employ one of his favourite ruses for demonstrating the
efficacy of Basic: a text is delivered in the language and then at the end, with
a flourish, it is revealed that Basic was being used all along (Ogden 1943: 25,
among other texts, employs this technique).

Carnap politely but firmly rejected Ogden's advances, with some attempt at
consolation. He felt he would be 'too much restricted' if he had to speak Basic, a
suggestion that would have surely irritated Ogden:

> Your suggestion of giving one of the lectures in Basic has something attractive about it,
> and I had thought myself already before about this idea. But I think that this occasion
> would not be quite convenient, because these lectures contain a lot of technical terms;
> I should feel to [*sic*] much restricted, if I were to say these things in Basic. But I am
> considering the possibility of writing later on a paper and in this case I should be very
> obliged for your kind help to put it into Basic. (Carnap to Ogden, 30 August 1934)

The later published version of these lectures appeared under Ogden's editorship
(Carnap 1934, 1935), but in 'normal English', not Basic English. There do not
seem to be any extant papers by Carnap in Basic.

Amid these negotiations emerged one Basic enthusiast that Ogden never seems
to have really appreciated: Ina Carnap, the wife of Rudolf Carnap. She was keen
to contribute to the Basic project. Her first letter to Ogden is not dated but, from
the friendly insinuations it contains, it would seem that the two had recently met
each other in person: 'You see the result from my being friend with you. What
about C. K.??' she wrote, asking for permission to address Ogden as 'C. K.', as
was common among his friends (Ina Carnap to Ogden, undated). This is presumably shortly after Carnap's trip to London in October 1934 to deliver his lectures.
She told Ogden that 'at the time I give every free minute to Basic and I am very
pleased by doing it'. She offered her notes on Lockhart's translation of *Carl and
Anna* (Frank 1930 [1926]) into Basic, which seems to be 'a bright work' but 'there
are some points where [she] does not give [her] full agreement'.

Ogden replied with encouragement (Ogden to Ina Carnap, 14 November 1934). In her next letter Ina Carnap suggested translating the satirical book *Der Papalagi* (Scheurmann 1920) into Basic and offered her assistance to Paul Hempel (dates unknown), head of the German English teachers association and chief Basic-German lexicographer.[20] This letter she closed with some jesting uncertainty, which may have been a sign of healthy self-deprecation or of a sense that her advances were unwelcome: 'Dear Mr. Ogden, if you are unhappy with my violent Basic interests and about all the trouble you get by it, you may give me a stop and put me in my place. This would not be the cause of troubles with me' (Ina Carnap to Ogden, 21 November 1934).

Her fears would seem to have been founded. Within a week of this second letter Ogden replied with encouragement for her work – 'It is clear that you are quite an authority on Basic from the start' – and said that he was looking forward to her notes on *Carl and Anna* and the translation of *Der Papalagi*, and that Dr Hempel may indeed be pleased to have help with his dictionary work (Ogden to Ina Carnap, 26 November 1934). But this tone was probably more a sign of politeness than sincerity. Ogden passed on the materials to Lockhart and after a long delay and a follow-up enquiry from Rudolf Carnap – 'Mrs. Carnaps [*sic*] sends you her best thanks for "St.Marc" and Richards' "Basic in Teaching". Have you had time to give a look to the "Papalagi"?' (Carnap to Ogden, 26 March 1935) – Ogden finally replied five months later to say that Lockhart was still looking into it: '"Papalagi" is still with Miss Lockhart, and will not be waiting longer than the Stebbing story. Till then, I am hoping the Basic is going forward' (Ogden to Ina Carnap, 1 April 1935).

Lockhart eventually replied almost a year later with a response that was not particularly encouraging. Her closing claim that she knows 'practically no German' and for this reason requires the help of another colleague is difficult to reconcile with the fact that she is credited as translator of the Basic edition of *Carl and Anna*, as discussed above.

> I had a preliminary look through your sample when it first came in, and saw that it is amusing stuff and well worth taking trouble with, but also that it would need a good deal of time to get the Basic right.
>
> I put the manuscript on one side, as I gathered from Mr. Ogden that there was no great urgency about it, and I happened to be very busy just then. I should like to revise it now and send it back to you with full comments to guide you in the translation of the rest of the book, if you decide to persevere with it, but as I know practically no German, I must wait till Miss Graham is free to collaborate on the job.
>
> [. . .] With deep apologies for having let the matter for so long. (Lockhart to Ina Carnap, 12 March 1936)

Perhaps Ina Carnap did not have quite the cachet Ogden was looking for in a supporter of Basic.

V. Totalitarianism revisited

In an era darkened by the shadow of totalitarianism, within days of Nazi Germany's invasion of Poland in 1939, the final act of aggression that triggered the Second World War, the first expression of the kind of anti-technocratic sentiments that came into full bloom after the war were levelled at the logical positivists of the Vienna Circle, from within. Horace Kallen (1882–1974), at the Fifth International Congress for the Unity of Science, criticised the movement for what he saw as its totalitarian tendencies. The division between 'science' and 'metaphysics', the meaningful and the meaningless, current in the unity of science movement was, he argued, but another manifestation of the same absolutism and intolerance that characterised the political climate of Central Europe and had plunged the continent once again into war. What was needed, according to Kallen, was not a 'unity' of science, but an 'orchestration' of scientific activities, not a melding of 'scientific' and exclusion of everything else, but free co-operation between all scholars.

Kallen's critique taps into the revolt against interference in political and social life that Friedrich von Hayek and Karl Popper – both Viennese intellectuals sent into exile, like the members of the Vienna Circle, as a result of Central Europe's decline into fascism – would later stage against self-appointed planners and reformers who follow high-flown philosophical ideals. Orwell's *Nineteen Eighty-Four*, with its apparent parody of Ogden's Basic and like-minded constructed languages, also belongs to this current of thought (see Chapter 3, §VIII). The debate that Kallen's critique triggered resumed again after the war, and was carried out mostly between Kallen and Neurath: Neurath, the left-wing radical, in political as well as intellectual matters, was clearly disturbed by Kallen's attack, which he painstakingly tried to deflect, claiming it was the result of misunderstanding.[21]

'Like a union of lovers', Kallen (1940 [1939]: 87) maintained, the unity of science movement, 'far from being a fusion of plurality into unity, [should] multiply plurality and liberate diversification'. The goal should not be the one conquering system that subsumes and supersedes all others, but tolerance and a dialogue between all approaches to knowledge. This sentiment, of course, is found also in Neurath's writings, but Neurath's tolerance had limits: he was still one of the first to shout 'metaphysics' and condemn all doctrines not compatible with physicalism, in its various forms (see §I). '[I]n any process of enquiry', commented Kallen (1940 [1939]: 85), 'it is always the other fellow's meanings that we declare meaningless, not our own'. In Kallen's view, the logical positivists' efforts to establish a universal linguistic medium for science – which Carnap approached formally and Neurath informally with his 'universal jargon' – entail the exclusion of all other approaches. 'Logpu', as he dubbed their proposed universal language, has as its goal the imposition of a single, unified logic on others, which the logical positivists would control as members of an elite scientific caste:

[They] would need to conquer or to buy the status of a privileged hieratic class to whose exclusive custody the peculiar treasure would accrue; not only would they act as its consecrated keepers; it would become their sole and peculiar task to indoctrinate the chosen of the next generation in the sacred mystery, which would have to be made unintelligible as it was holy to the rest of mankind. The vernaculars of the latter would have to be depreciated as ignoble and vulgar, unworthy to be the vehicles of the superior deliverances of science. (Kallen 1940 [1939]: 91)

This inevitable course that 'unification' of this sort would take is visible all around, argued Kallen: in the totalitarian countries it had already gone to completion and, in the 'free countries', the same pressures could be felt from such forces as 'Big Business' and a reinvigorated 'ancient ecclesiastical authority'; the unity of science movement was just one more of these (Kallen 1940 [1939]: 82, 87).

Revisiting the topic in the resumed discussion immediately after the war in 1945, Kallen saw the power of institutionalised, 'unified' science as having only grown. This had led to scientific breakthroughs, he did not deny, but only because the insights of individual, unconstrained thinkers pointed the way for further research. A prominent example in the preceding six years was the project, involving 'some few men of science in England, some hundreds in the United States, [who] had an idea of the premises and procedures of the enterprise', 'some army men and politicians [who] had a notion of its goal', and 'some 65,000 human beings, in three different plants, their foremen, production managers, expert physicists, chemists, biologists, engineers', who were responsible for building of the 'uranium-bomb' (Kallen 1946a: 516). But the original work that made this project conceivable came from undirected enquiry into radioactivity and the 'structures and energies of the atom' by such individual physicists as James Clerk Maxwell, Ernest Rutherford, Frederick Soddy, Max Planck, Niels Bohr and Albert Einstein (Kallen 1946a: 519). There would have been no object for investigation through a systematic research programme if it were not for the discoveries they were led to by their unfettered creativity and genius.

In the place of 'unity', which he understood as an inevitably assimilating process, Kallen proposed 'orchestration', the free co-operation of individuals, a term Neurath readily adopted in the following discussion. Neurath acknowledged the dangers Kallen perceived, but denied that they are present in the unity of science movement:

It is the problem of any democracy, which any actual scientific research organization has also to solve: on the one hand the non-conformists must have sufficient support; on the other hand, scientific research needs some co-operation. This implies on the one hand that we have to leave something to chance, and that on the other hand we have to find some loyal compromise for actual collaboration, without suppressing personal convictions. What can we call this democracy of co-operation within the 'encyclopedism of logical empiricism'? I have no better word for that than Kallen's 'orchestra-tion'. (Neurath 1983 [1946]: 236)

The 'universal jargon' that Neurath proposed as the refined language of unified science – and here he also readily accepted Kallen's facetious term 'Logpu' – was not a means for segregating the scientist caste, it was not 'something highbrow and complicated' (Neurath 1983 [1946]: 237), but just the everyday language refined. If Kallen, Neurath and a 'Melanesian friend' were to have lunch in a New York restaurant, Neurath contended, they should have no difficulties understanding one another as long as they used terms like 'turkey', 'crackers', 'cold', 'hot', 'happy', and so on. The Melanesian may have no word for 'turkey', but would surely be able to substitute it with the term 'some fowl'. Difficulties would only arise if the language were to depart from the everyday with terms like 'causality' and 'inner experience' (Neurath 1983 [1946]: 237).

In his earlier arguments for scientific encyclopaedism, Neurath claimed that the 'unified-science-attitude' based on such empiricism had naturally become more prevalent in life all over the world. But in a concession to the kind of objection that Orwell would later make to Wells' scientific and technological optimism, he acknowledged that technological advance and the general scien-tific attitude do not always march in lock step, as the case of modern Germany showed: 'How much modern engineering and technical activity, together with all the helpful special sciences, were evolved, for instance, in Germany during the nineteenth century and how little comprehensive scientific empiri-cism!' (Neurath 1938: 22). The unparalleled technological advance of modern Germany, he argued, proceeded without any challenge to the reign of obscuran-tist traditional philosophy.

Kallen could not countenance Neurath's faith in the underlying unity of everyday experience and the language we use to describe it as the source of a growing empirical tendency: 'even such "sensory data" as "turkey," "cold," "hot," "happy," may have to start as incommensurable diversities and work their ways toward a consensus' (Kallen 1946a: 521). No language can carry uni-versal meanings:

> Even Neurath's clever and welcome isotypes [*sic*] are far from having the self-evidence he claims for them; they cannot say identical things to different people, nor can they say much to the same people without the explanatory texts which gives [*sic*] them their meanings. Vary texts and you vary the meanings. The parallel for *Logpu* need not be pressed. (Kallen 1946a: 521)

To Neurath's luncheon Kallen invited also 'a brahmin Hindu, an orthodox Jew, a Buddhist Chinese, and one of Stefansson's Eskimos'.[22] What the guests would wish to eat and how they would eat it depends on a range of 'attitudes, feelings and judgments' that they bring to the table, all of which may be inexpressible in Logpu. What unity they could achieve would be a 'free exchange' of some points of diet, some expressions and table manners, which would come about not through any underlying unity, but through the fact that they are all eating at the same table, with each participant respecting the right of others to carry on in their own way (Kallen 1946a: 521–522).

Kallen's critique of unity and planning can be seen as an expression of the sentiment against ideals and wide-scale schemes that grew during the polarisation of the European social and political scene in the 1930s and has its classical formulation in such post-war critiques as those of Hayek, Popper and Orwell. Popper's social critique has particular relevance to the debate between Kallen and Neurath when compared with his well-known position contra logical positivism, on which his reputation as a philosopher of science is built. Popper's signature doctrine of 'falsification' (first published Popper 1959 [1934]) exhibits the same pragmatic and 'piecemeal' attitude that motivates his social and political philosophy. Falsification, in contrast to the 'verification' associated in particular with the right wing of the Vienna Circle (see §I–II), lays weight only on the disconfirmation, or falsification, of propositions and the theories they express, rather than seeking to confirm, or verify, propositions by matching them to the world. Scientific progress, argued Popper, results from successively refining theories to overcome the points on which they have been falsified. There is no 'absolute' foundation to science; it is always provisional and open to gradual improvement:

> The empirical basis of objective science has thus nothing 'absolute' about it. Science does not rest upon rock-bottom. The bold structure of its theories rises, as it were, above a swamp. It is like a building erected on piles. The piles are driven down from above into the swamp, but not down to any natural or 'given' base; and when we cease our attempts to drive our piles into a deeper layer, it is not because we have reached firm ground. We simply stop when we are satisfied that they are firm enough to carry the structure, at least for the time being. (Popper 1959 [1934]: 111)

In the same way, social progress, under Popper's conception (see Chapter 3, §VIII), gradually results from identifying and solving specific social problems. Neurath (1983 [1935]b) attacked Popper for 'pseudorationalism', interpreting him as supposing that there are complete and definite theories that can be comprehended at once and that each one can be tested against an *experimentum crucis*. He also pointed out that Popper's claim that the goal in science should be to falsify existing theories hardly accords with the behaviour of actual scientists. Despite this, Popper's vision of approximation of theory to a complex world is not wholly incompatible with the views on epistemology that Neurath advanced within the Vienna Circle (cf. his *Schiffer* metaphor in §II; Glock 2008: 164–168). The difference lies in Neurath's unrelenting pluralism, while Popper imagines incremental improvement in one single system approximating to the world of experience.

Amid these discussions Neurath was becoming, in his social philosophy, sensitive to the totalitarian dangers of technocratic planning, as we have already seen in his admiration for the 'British Atmosphere' in his correspondence with Ogden. In his essay 'International planning for freedom' (Neurath 1973 [1942]), Neurath still envisaged a 'world commonwealth' organised by 'social engineers' to restore world order after the war, but he placed on the social engineers the obligation to factor 'happiness conditions' into their planning programmes, rather than reaching for particular targets measured on a single scale, such as production or profit, without regard for the hardship this may cause elsewhere (Neurath 1973 [1942]: 423–431). In fact, argued Neurath, a certain amount of 'muddle' may be necessary and even desirable in a free, democratic society, where everyone has the opportunity to follow, or at least voice, their own conscience. In the long run, a free organisation may even be more efficient than one that is strictly technocratic and directed to a single goal:

> Some muddle thus seems unavoidable in a society of free men and within a democratic
> world commonwealth. People who like freedom and see these relations, will not give
> bad names to a muddle without analyzing whether this muddle is perhaps related to
> civil liberty or not [. . .]. (Neurath 1973 [1942]: 430)

But it may not have been possible for those around him to take Neurath at his word. Neurath's strong, frequently uncompromising personality and his history of personal engagement in various 'undemocratic' governmental planning efforts undoubtedly played a role in forming his reputation for autocracy: he was after all in charge of socialising the Bavarian economy during their Soviet Republic, his disputes within the Vienna Circle often led to hurt feelings, and as editor of the *Encyclopedia* he changed the titles and content of many contributions from other authors without consultation (see Reisch 2005: 204–205). For those who were unsympathetic, Neurath could be seen as a reviled dictator, not of a state, but of an intellectual programme.

Kallen never pressed his position so far. Before their final exchange over the character of the unity of science movement could be published in 1945, Neurath passed away. In his obituary of Neurath, appended to their published discussion, Kallen insisted on Neurath's ultimate commitment to freedom:

> Of course he had his intolerances and rejections – who has not? – but the doctrines
> and disciplines which he excommunicated were those which experience had led him
> to hold as enemies of free men in a free society, as superstitions employed by malicious
> power to degrade and to starve the soul of mankind. (Kallen 1946b: 529–530)

Quoting from their final correspondence, Kallen allowed Neurath to once again state his position that the goal of unified science as realised through the universal jargon had been misunderstood:

> I do not assume that the Melanesian, the Jew and the Hundu [*sic*], You and I will agree
> about attitudes, tastes, and taboos. I do assume that we shall be in a position to tell each

other in an understandable way about our differences. To tell that Otto likes beef, to tell that the Hindu dislikes beef implies that Otto and the Hindu both use expressions which mean 'beef,' 'liking,' 'disliking.' Without a common vehicle to both they cannot tell one another of their differences.

But I go farther. I add that we cannot have a common language for the discussion of the 'Ding an sich' [thing in itself] or of 'vitalism.' (Neurath, quoted in Kallen 1946b: 531–532)

Notes

1. Some of the first publications about the work of the Vienna Circle to appear in English include Feigl and Blumberg (1931), Neurath (1983 [1931]) and Stebbing (1933).

2. Schlick, professor of 'philosophy of the inductive sciences' at the University of Vienna, initially organised the discussion group on the urging of his students Herbert Feigl (1902–1988) and Friedrich Waismann (1896–1959). The Verein Ernst Mach has traditionally been considered the public face of this discussion group because of the joint membership of many participants, including Schlick, who was chairman of the Verein from its inception to its dissolution. However, the Verein was more the creation of the *Freidenkerbund Österreichs* (Free-thinker Association of Austria), of which Neurath was a prominent member (Stadler 1997: 364–370, 1982; see also Neurath's 1930–1931 description of the Verein Ernst Mach). There was a great deal of tension between Schlick and Neurath: Schlick was uncomfortable about the intellectually aggressive and politically engaged attitude of Neurath and the Verein. The Vienna Circle is also identified by its journal, *Erkenntnis*, published from 1931 in co-operation with the like-minded *Gesellschaft für Empirische Philosophie* (Society for empirical philosophy) in Berlin (see Stadler 1997: 248–251).

3. The complete sentence reads in the original: 'Der Wiener Kreis glaubt durch seine Arbeit im Verein Ernst Mach eine Forderung des Tages zu erfüllen: Es gilt, Denkwerkzeuge für den Alltag zu formen, für den Alltag der Gelehrten, aber auch für den Alltag aller, die an der bewußten Lebensgestaltung irgendwie mitarbeiten.' An idiomatic English translation that does not quite capture the central place of the word *Alltag* in this quotation can be found in Neurath and Cohen (1973: 305).

4. Held up as a model by Schlick and present in Vienna in the final years of the 1920s, Wittgenstein granted small audiences to selected Circle members – eventually restricted to just Schlick and Waismann – where he expounded his ideas in transition (see McGuinness 1979, which contains records of Waismann's abortive efforts at writing an exposition of Wittgenstein's ideas). Neurath, for his part, could never tolerate this subservience to Wittgenstein: it is reported that in the Circle's discussions of the *Tractatus* Neurath continually interrupted the discussion by exclaiming 'metaphysics!' It was eventually suggested to him that he should just hum 'mmm' when he felt the discussion was becoming metaphysical rather than disturbing it with his interjections. In response, he said it would be more efficient to say 'not-m' when the discussion turned away from metaphysics (Neurath recounts this story in

his correspondence with Carnap and Charles Morris, 18 November 1944, quoted in Reisch 2005: 8; Cartwright *et al.* 1996: 5–6 also tell the anecdote, but without attribution).

5. Neurath's doctoral supervisors were the historian of the ancient world Eduard Meyer (1855–1930) and the economist and sociologist Gustav Schmoller (1838–1917). He in fact submitted two doctoral dissertations, only the second of which was actually examined. The reason for this is unknown (see Cartwright *et al.* 1996: 11–12).

6. For further biographical details on Neurath, see Neurath and Cohen (1973: 1–80).

7. In his detailed study of the intellectual interaction between Carnap, Heidegger and Ernst Cassirer (1874–1945), Friedman (2000) shows that the three were very well-informed about one another's work and that Carnap's critique of Heidegger was considerably subtler than it has traditionally been taken to be. Heidegger in fact responded to Carnap's critique in unpublished lectures from this period (see Friedman 2000: chapter 2).

8. The device of metalanguage and object language is employed as a way of liberating Carnap's account from Wittgenstein's (1922) distinction between *saying* and *showing*. Wittgenstein thought that it was impossible to *say* anything about the workings of language, logic, and the world as a whole using language and logic themselves. All that could be done was to *show* through the use of language and logic how they worked. The *Tractatus* itself only *showed* these principles; it was unable to *say* anything about them. Many theorists saw a potential escape from this limitation in metalanguages, languages of higher orders, which would be able to *say* something about their object languages. This possible solution occurred even to Russell in his introduction to the *Tractatus* (see Chapter 2, §VI; cf. Uebel 2007: chapter 5).

9. In this passage, his introduction to the first volume of the *Encyclopedia*, Neurath cites the 'famous French *Encyclopédie*' as an inspiration. Neurath's idea for the *Encyclopedia* was first publicly expressed at the Pre-Congress of the First International Congress for the Unity of Science in 1933. Concrete plans for the encyclopaedia were laid, under the direction of Neurath's Mundaeum Institute in the Hague (which Neurath founded after going into exile from Vienna), at the First International Congress for the Unity of Science in the following year, and a contract for publication was settled with the University of Chicago Press, where Charles Morris, a prominent native American supporter of logical empiricism was based (cf. Chapter 2, note 25), in 1937. Seven volumes appeared altogether; the first in 1938 and the last in 1969. The second volume contained the first publication of Kuhn's (1962) influential *The Structure of Scientific Revolutions*. See Cartwright *et al.* (1996) and Stadler (1997: 399–400) for discussion of Neurath's encyclopaedism.

10. The principles of Neurath's system and the philosophical ideas that lie behind them are recorded in numerous publications by Neurath. Most of these are collected, and translated into German for texts originally in other languages, in Haller and Kinross (1991). Neurath's earliest essay in which the basics of the method can be recognised is Neurath (1991 [1925]), written shortly after the founding of the Vienna *Gesellschafts- und Wirtschaftsmuseum*. Neurath (1991 [1933]) and Neurath

(1936) describe the system in detail. Neurath (1996) gives a thorough philosophical and pedagogic justification for the system, and Neurath (2010), his 'visual autobiography', tells the story of the development of the system from the perspective of his personal history. Examples of the system in action can be found in *Gesellschaft und Wirtschaft* (Gesellschafts- und Wirtschaftsmuseum 1930), which contains reproductions from the original exhibits in the Vienna museum. The bibliography compiled by Marie Neurath and Kinross (2009) contains references to many further primary and secondary sources.

11. Original: 'Welcher Triumph war es, als man sich von den Schranken der Bilderschrift befreit hatte, welcher Triumph, als die Sprache biegsam und vielgestaltig sich allen Anforderungen wissenschaftlicher Arbeit anpaßte, als man dieses logische Werkzeug beherrschen lernte. Freilich, die Befreiung vom Bild führte auch auf Abwege, führte ins Gebiet des Sinnleeren. Substantivierung gab Anlaß zu immer neuen Problemen. Insbesondere die deutsche Sprache verleitet zu solchen metaphysischen Abwegen, sie gestattet umfangreiche Erörterungen über "das Nichts, welches nichtet" (Heidegger), über das "Sein"; als ob das "Sein" ebenso in einem Satz verwendet werden könnte wie das Schwert oder der Tisch. Die reine Bildschrift kennt zwar ein Schwert und einen Tisch, aber kein Sein.'

12. Neurath's singling out of the German language as particularly inclined to lead to 'metaphysical diversions' is perhaps also a response to Heidegger's claim that German, along with Greek, 'is (in regard to its possibilities for thought) at once the most powerful and most spiritual of all languages' (Heidegger 1959 [1935]: 57). The lectures from which this quotation is taken were given only in 1935, but Heidegger may have made similar comments at an earlier date.

13. The correspondence quoted in this chapter between Ogden, Neurath, Carnap, Lockhart and Ina Carnap is kept in the Ogden collection of the William Ready Division of Archives and Research Collections, McMaster University Library. Copies of a subset of the Ogden-Neurath correspondence can also be found in the Noord-Hollands Archief (see Fabian 1996).

14. The first letters from Ogden to Neurath and Carnap in the McMaster Archives date from 1933 (29 September 1933 and 4 December 1933 respectively). In both cases, from the wording of the letters it appears that it is the first contact between the parties.

15. Original: 'Als Neurath kürzlich hier war, sprach er auch mit Begeisterung von Ihrem "Basic English". Ich wäre Ihnen sehr dankbar, wenn Sie mir etwas zur Orientierung schicken könnten. Ich bin seit vielen Jahren lebhaft interessiert an dem Problem einer internationalen Hilfssprache. Theoretisch interessiert mich besonders die logische Seite dieses Problems, die Fragen der logischen Syntax. Aber auch praktisch habe ich mich damit befasst (ich kann Esperanto, bin aber nicht dogmatisch festgelegt auf dieses System). Ich halte besonders für die internationalen Beziehungen auf dem Gebiet der Wissenschaft die Verwendung einer Hilfssprache für erstrebenswert und notwendig.'

16. Shaw's script for *Pygmalion* was first published in 1912, when Ogden was still a university student. It is therefore impossible for Ogden to have served as a model

for the original character of Henry Higgins, although it is still possible that some of his traits were incorporated into the Higgins character as portrayed in the later film version. Commonly cited inspirations for Higgins include the English phoneticians Henry Sweet (1845–1912) and Daniel Jones (1881–1967) (see Wainger 1930: 558; Collins and Mees 1998: 97–103).

17. Note that Carnap begins the first paragraph after the greeting formula in this letter with a lower-case letter; this is standard German practice, but of course not English practice. In the corrections to his Basic that Ogden sent back to Carnap (as Carnap requested him to do), Ogden silently corrected this point. Ogden may not have been aware of this difference himself: he also corrected without explicit mention a genitive apostrophe, although he explicitly corrected several commas.

18. There are some rather unidiomatic features of the passage quoted from Carnap's letter, such as the periphrastic comparative 'more simple' and the abbreviation 'f.e.' for 'for example', presumably formed on analogy with German 'z.B.'.

19. Carnap's term 'help-language' is perhaps a calque on the German word *Hilfssprache* or the Esperanto word *helplingvo*, which in Standard English usually has the more Romance form 'auxiliary language' and in Basic is 'helping language'.

20. Paul Hempel is not to be confused with Carl Hempel (1905–1997), a member of the Vienna Circle.

21. The debate between Kallen and Neurath is dealt with in great detail in chapter 9 of Reisch (2005). Neurath had long been involved in the planning and organisational debate in its purely economic aspect: Ludwig von Mises (1881–1973) – founder of the Austrian School of economics and mentor to Hayek – formulated many of his key liberal doctrines in response to Neurath's views on adapting the institutions of the war economy for use in peace time (see Caldwell in Hayek 1997: 5–10).

22. 'One of Stefansson's Eskimos' is presumably a reference to the ethnographic work of Arctic explorer and anthropologist Vilhjalmur Stefansson (1879–1962).

Chapter 5

Epilogue

The case studies of three episodes in the intellectual life of C. K. Ogden presented in the preceding pages have offered us a new perspective on attitudes and approaches to problems of language and meaning in the modernist age of the early twentieth century. Reflected in the ideas, rhetoric and plans we have examined are the characteristic modernist themes of a sense of crisis and the search for new solutions in science and technology. Ogden's efforts, and those of his contemporaries, follow the familiar pattern of the age: optimism and faith in science led to the 'scientific' treatment of language and meaning, the practical temperament of the age turned this into engineering projects, and finally the climate of disillusionment at the end of the Second World War precipitated their abandonment.

Our first case study looked at the philosophy of language expounded in *The Meaning of Meaning* and its place in the intellectual environment in which it was written. This book was Ogden and Richards' first major contribution to the ongoing discussion on the problem of meaning, a consuming concern of the period that shaded into broader issues in religion, metaphysics, epistemology and logic. *The Meaning of Meaning* was both a theoretical treatise on the place of meaning in language and life, as well as a practical manual for its artful manipulation and use (as we saw in Chapter 2, §I–II).

As a synthesis of, first and foremost, the logical doctrines of Russell and the semiotic theorising of Welby, with both of whom Ogden was in personal contact, *The Meaning of Meaning* reflects many of the key ideas relating to meaning that had currency in the modernist period. Of utmost importance here is the perception that there is a crisis in meaning, and an urgent need to tame language, the premier bearer of meaning in the human world. The method suggested by Ogden and Richards – consisting in periphrastic definitions supported by rules of best practice in using language – is essentially a hybrid of Russell's descriptions and Welby's focus on the process of interpretation (Chapter 2, §III–IV). But the two traditions represented by Russell and Welby were in many respects deeply antagonistic, and the kind of synthesis Ogden and Richards made could not be taken for granted: it would be decades before similar approaches entered the mainstream of English-speaking philosophy (Chapter 2, §V).

'Science', the saviour of the modernist age, was invoked by Ogden and Richards to support their project. Not only did they appeal, like Russell and many other linguistic theorists (Chapter 2, §VII), to the latest research by self-consciously 'scientific' modern psychologists to ground their work, but they also claimed the same scientific rigour and validity for their theory in dubbing it the 'science of Symbolism'.

Basic English – Ogden's next major endeavour and our second case study – turned the 'science of Symbolism' into an engineering project. Basic was Ogden's contribution to the thriving international language movement, where the contemporary sense of crisis was answered by the immensely practical temperament of the modernist age. The crisis was the difficulty of international communication in a rapidly shrinking multilingual world, the inefficiencies this imposed on international science and business, and the problem of nationalistic chauvinism that was seen to be fed by it. The best solution would be a language specially constructed for international use, which would realise the ideals of contemporary philosophy of language (Chapter 3, §II).

Ogden's Basic, as an implementation of the science of symbolism, conformed to the guiding philosophical and aesthetic norms of the wider movement. As it was elaborated and applied, Ogden's philosophy of language moved more in the direction of Russell – and the majority of language constructors – and away from Welby. Rather than inviting its speakers to contemplate the process of interpretation, Basic legislates forms to constrain the possibilities of interpretation (Chapter 3, §V–VI). Ogden also took on board the latest typological fashions in logic, linguistics and the international language movement, praising 'analytic' structures in language as forms that directly embody the meanings they represent (Chapter 3, §II).

But in other respects Basic was extremely unusual. While other language constructors agonised over the most inclusive 'international' forms for their languages, Ogden saw all that was needed in English. To create the best international language, argued Ogden, all that needed to be done was to constrain English and make it accessible to the foreigner, a view that found little sympathy among his fellow language constructors, but which seems to be a manifestation of a particularly British attitude to the world (Chapter 3, §IV).

In our final case study, in which we examined Ogden's contact with Neurath and Carnap, we saw the coming together of the major themes running through the other two case studies. When Ogden made contact with Neurath and Carnap, they had already arrived at their own all-encompassing, linguistically-oriented philosophical doctrines, which – despite their differences on certain key points – they subsumed under the common label 'physicalism' (Chapter 4, §II). Their views were highly compatible with Ogden's, a fact that was clear to them, as we saw through their correspondence, where all three engaged with one another and discussed the similarities and differences in their philosophy (Chapter 4, §IV). From this contact resulted a collaboration between Ogden and Neurath in which Neurath's system of picture statistics – which was deeply rooted in his philosophy of language – was brought into alignment with Basic, and with the wider international language movement (Chapter 4, §III).

The commonalities between Ogden and his Viennese counterparts came into even clearer relief in light of the shared political implications of their work. Distancing himself from his contemporaries, Ogden claimed that the chief insights informing Basic stemmed from Jeremy Bentham (Chapter 3, §VII). Ogden's enthusiasm for Bentham extended to aligning Basic with the thinking behind Bentham's panopticon: Basic was presented as an instrument of benevolent authoritarian mental control. These signals were received and amplified by such cultural promoters of Basic as H. G. Wells. Newspeak, George Orwell's parody of constructed languages in *Nineteen Eighty-Four*, seems to draw out the social and political implications of Basic and related projects, although his precise position on these matters is ambiguous. On the one hand, Newspeak appears to specifically parody characteristic features of Basic, in particular vocabulary reduction. Panopticism, variously conceived, is also a central theme of both Basic and Orwell's book. On the other hand, Orwell in fact endorsed many of the principles of expressive clarity underlying Basic and would seem to have been supportive of the project in the period before he started writing *Nineteen Eighty-Four* (Chapter 3, §VIII).

In the debate between Kallen and Neurath (Chapter 4, §V), logical positivism, and in particular the physicalist notion of common language, was similarly subject to criticism for its political implications. Floating in the air was the accusation that such projects were the unwitting servants of totalitarianism, those uncompromising and intolerant ideologies that trampled common sense and common decency in early twentieth-century Europe. This ideological malaise marks the decline of the modernist period: the technocrats' grand projects, built on wisdom derived from science, were seen as but another manifestation of the same inhumane impulses that brought catastrophe on the world. Whatever their intentions, the technocrats' aim of rapid, comprehensive reform was now subject to suspicion.

I. Linguistics

Linguistics, the discipline that occupies itself with the scientific study of language, has a rather peripheral place in the story told in this book. While not a major force in the events recounted here, the mainstream of linguistics in this period was in fact deeply involved with the schools and doctrines we have met. The perhaps paradoxical result of mainstream linguists' engagement with these currents was to drive them away from the questions that animated Ogden and his closest colleagues.

The approach that came to dominate linguistics by the middle of the twentieth century was that fostered in the school of American structuralism that grew up around Leonard Bloomfield (1887–1949). Bloomfield was familiar with *The Meaning of Meaning*, although he was not particularly impressed by it. An

adherent of a strict form of behaviourism that committed him to 'mechanis-
tic' psychology, he could not come to terms with the book's 'mentalism', its
appeal to unobservable mental processes (see Bloomfield 1927: 215–216, 1933:
515; cf. Gordon 2006: 2582–2583). He was also familiar with the doctrines of
logical positivism, and personally acquainted with Carnap and his American
supporter Charles Morris (1901–1979) (see Chapter 2, note 25; Chapter 4, note
9), with both of whom he worked for a period at the University of Chicago
(see Hiz and Swiggers 1990; Tomalin 2004). Bloomfield found logical positivism much more impressive: he even produced an invited contribution to
the *International Encyclopedia of Unified Science* on the 'Linguistic Aspects of
Science' (Bloomfield 1938).

Although he had much to say on topics in linguistic semantics, especially in
his earlier work (cf. Bloomfield 1914, 1933), Bloomfield had an ambivalent relationship to the issue of meaning in language. He recognised the central importance of meaning to language, but at the same time he saw semantics as 'the
weak point in language-study' (Bloomfield 1933: 140; cf. Koerner 1970; Hymes
and Fought 1981 [1975]). The proper domain of contemporary linguistics,
according to Bloomfield, should be the study of formal patterns in languages.
Logical positivism provided Bloomfield with the framework to conceptualise
the disciplinary role of linguistics: restricted to the formal aspects of language,
linguistics could rely on allied fields within unified science to gradually solve
the problems of meaning (see, e.g., Bloomfield 1933: 139–140, 1938: 24, 1970
[1943]: 401).

Through the 'revolution' instigated by Noam Chomsky (b. 1928) in the late
1950s, the reference point for mainstream linguistics became the generative
grammar he and his followers developed (on the Chomskyan 'revolution', see
Matthews 2001). Despite the revolutionary rhetoric surrounding Chomskyan
generative grammar, one very clear line of continuity between the generativ-
ists and their predecessors has been their concentration on the formal aspects
of language (see Chomsky 1957: chapter 9; see also Matthews 2001; Tomalin
2006). But early in his career Chomsky briefly flirted with the possibility that
the underlying forms he posited in what was at one time dubbed 'deep structure'
might directly represent meanings (e.g. Chomsky 1957: 92, 1964 [1962]: 936,
1965: 75–79, 135–136, 148–160, 1966: 33). Searching for putative underlying
forms that directly represent meanings became, in the 1960s and 1970s, the
guiding thesis of the 'generative semantics' movement. Chomsky and his loyal
followers kept their distance from such representational efforts and maintained
the independence of their formal investigations. After the so-called 'linguistics wars' between Chomsky's camp and the generative semanticists, generative
semantics as a school eventually faded from the academic scene in the 1980s (see
Newmeyer 1986 [1980]; Harris 1993; Huck and Goldsmith 1995; Seuren 1998:
chapter 7).

The latter-day efforts of the generative semanticists to establish scientifically motivated isomorphic notations for meaning may represent a reflex of

the modernist approaches we have examined in this book. Capturing meaning in precise, unambiguous forms was the overarching goal of all efforts from Russell's 'logically perfect language' to the technocratic projects of the international language movement, including Ogden's Basic (but these projects of course differed considerably in the use they hoped to make of these captured meanings; see Chapter 2, §III and §VI; Chapter 3, §I–III).

The views of Bloomfield and Chomsky were demonstrably formed by the same social and political forces we have witnessed acting in this book. The current of technocratic benevolent control that was at its strongest in the inter-war years – and which swept up Ogden and the logical positivists alike (see Chapter 3, §VIII; Chapter 4, §V) – also carried Bloomfield away. In his 1929 presidential address to the Linguistic Society of America, he prophesied a future in which linguistics and the other human sciences would contribute to the enlightened control of humanity for its own good:

> I believe that in the near future – in the next few generations, let us say – linguistics will be one of the main sectors of scientific advance, and that in this sector science will win through to the understanding and control of human conduct.
>
> In the domains of physics and biology science has for some time been working with success and has given us great power. In the domain of anthropology – that is, in the study of man's super-biological activities – science has been unsuccessful [. . .]
>
> The truth of this contrast and its tragic import appear plainly in the fact that our achievements in non-human science do us little good, because we cannot understand or control their human consequences. We make powerful engines, but we have no way of deciding who is to use them, and we have seen them used for our destruction. We can prevent suffering and widen the scope of life, but the fruition of these our powers is disturbed by such means as the hazards of gambling. (Bloomfield 1970 [1929]: 149; quoted partially in Harris 1993: 56)

Chomsky, whose career began in the period of disillusionment after the Second World War, reacted to professional scholarly encroachment on social and political life in much the same way that Orwell reacted to constructed languages, and Kallen to logical positivism. Chomsky has always emphasised the separation of his scientific and technical work from his equally prominent political activism and sees any claim of special academic expertise in this latter domain as suspect:

> [The intelligensia] pretend[s] to be engaged in an esoteric enterprise, inaccessible to simple people. But that's nonsense [. . .] The alleged complexity, depth, and obscurity of these questions [of the social sciences] is part of the illusion propagated by the system of ideological control, which aims to make the issues seem remote from the general population and to persuade them of their incapacity to organize their own affairs or to understand the social world in which they live without the tutelage of intermediaries. For that reason alone one should be careful not to link the analysis of social issues with scientific topics which, for their part, do require special training and

techniques, and thus a special intellectual frame of reference, before they can be seriously investigated. (Chomsky 1979: 4–5)

This attitude of Chomsky's played a decisive role in motivating his attacks on behaviourism (e.g. Chomsky 1959), the signature psychological theory associated with post-Bloomfieldian linguistics. According to Chomsky, behaviourism is not only scientifically inadequate, its political implications render it unconscionable (see Harris 1993: 55–56; Barsky 1997: 80, 99–100). Behaviourism, as Chomsky (2004 [1974]: 164–165) would later say, represents a methodology 'known to every good prison guard, or police interrogator' elevated to the status of scientific theory, 'giv[ing] a cloak of neutrality to the techniques of oppression and control'.

II. Natural Semantic Metalanguage

In present-day linguistic semantics, the clearest historical connection to the ideas explored in this book is to be found in the various 'formal' semantic theories. These grew directly out of the logical tradition established by Frege, Russell, Carnap, Tarski and others, and only came to be integrated into mainstream linguistics after the end of the generative semantics period discussed in the previous section (for standard historical accounts from practising formal semanticists, see Abbott 1999; Partee 2011).

Present-day linguistic semantics is, however, a hugely diverse field, of which formal approaches represent only a small part (see Riemer 2016 for a recent survey). One outlier in this field which exhibits suggestive similarities to Ogden's Basic, and related modernist approaches to meaning, is the Natural Semantic Metalanguage (NSM), whose founder and driving force is Anna Wierzbicka (b. 1938). The core activity of NSM is the definition, or 'explication', of word meanings using the method of 'reductive paraphrase', which seeks to restate these meanings in a form that breaks them down into their putative components while retaining the original sense (see Wierzbicka 1987: 12–13). The explication of the word 'mother' below is a typical example of a current NSM definition:

X is Y's mother. =
(a) at one time, before now, X was very small
(b) at that time, Y was inside X
(c) at that time, Y was like a part of X
(d) because of this, people can think something like this about X:
      "X wants to do good things for Y
      X doesn't want bad things to happen to Y"
(Wierzbicka 1996: 155)

The first line of this explication gives the canonical sentence context for the word being defined, in line with NSM practitioners' recognition of the fact that the sense a word carries is governed by the context in which it is used (see Wierzbicka 1987: 8; Goddard 1994: 23, 2002: 14; Goddard and Wierzbicka 2002: 42). Parts (a) to (c) of the explication, Wierzbicka (1996: 154–155) tells us in her commentary, deal with the biological side of motherhood, while part (d) addresses the 'social and psychological component'. In her commentary she also devotes some space to justifying her definition, contrasting it to several other lexicographers' definitions, all of which she finds inadequate.

The key assumption driving the NSM programme is that there are 'semantic primitives', a set of meanings or concepts (the two terms are used interchangeably in the NSM literature) that all humans possess, and out of which all other, more complex meanings are composed (Wierzbicka 1980: 12–13, 1996: 9–13). The ultimate goal of NSM practitioners is to discover these primitive meanings which, according to their 'strong lexicalisation hypothesis', are held to have lexical 'exponents' of one form or another in each of the world's languages (Goddard 1994: 13; Wierzbicka 1996: 14). Although Wierzbicka (2011: 381) recently stated that the inventory of semantic primitives may have reached its final form, it continues to fluctuate: it currently contains sixty-five items, with one further candidate under consideration (personal communication from Anna Wierzbicka via e-mail, 1 January 2013).

The treatment of definition as a fundamental device for securing understanding is a feature common to both NSM and Ogden's philosophy of language, as expressed in *The Meaning of Meaning* and as applied in Basic (see Chapter 2, §II; Chapter 3, §V). Both NSM and Basic also see the optimal basis for definitions in a vocabulary of limited size that contains only the 'simplest' words: in the case of NSM these are the semantic primitives, and in Basic they are those listed in the core vocabulary (see Chapter 3, §V). But there is a difference in the status accorded to these key words. In NSM the primitives are taken to be somehow innate (see, for example, Wierzbicka 2011: 379), while in Basic they are merely the words 'scientifically selected' for their practical utility in formulating definitions (see Chapter 3, §V). This difference in status most probably results from their different attitudes to analysis: Wierzbicka is strongly committed to decompositional, or 'reductive', analysis, whereas Ogden preferred transformative analysis in cases where it was more expedient (see Chapter 4, §II for discussion of this contrast). Wierzbicka's claims for innateness stem also from the rationalist turn in post-1960s linguistics, about which we say more below.

Between Ogden and Wierzbicka there is also a deep divide in the way the universal vocabulary is realised. For Ogden the actual Basic word forms were the units that constituted the universal vocabulary, but for Wierzbicka the word forms are merely the 'exponents' of the semantic primitives. Each language of the world is taken to have its own list of exponents, but each item in these lists corresponds to exactly one primitive, and the items are isomorphic with their equivalents across the lists (see, for example, Wierzbicka 1996: 22–23). Unlike Ogden, who recommended English for the world, Wierzbicka and her followers engage in considerable cross-cultural research in an effort to discover the putative universal meanings and their exponents in a geographically, culturally and typologically diverse range of languages (Goddard and Wierzbicka 2002 is representative of this work).

But the emphasis in NSM on finding lexical exponents betrays another similarity with Basic, the notion that words are the heart of language (see Chapter 3, §VI). In recent years, there has been work with the NSM programme on elaborating the 'universal syntax' of the semantic primitives, but this consists mainly in dividing them into classes based on their possibilities of combination with other primitives (see Wierzbicka 1996: chapter 3), coupled with several 'powerful iconic and indexical mechanisms' for representing these connections (Wierzbicka 1996: 146). Underlying this approach would seem to be the same assumption that was held by the technocratic language constructors, who sought completely 'analytic' grammars that transparently showed the interrelation of the ideas behind words (see Chapter 3, §III).

However, in actual NSM explications, which are rendered using the exponents of primitives in a given natural language, the structure of clauses and inflection of words follows the dictates of the natural language used (Goddard 2002: 31–32; cf. Wierzbicka 1996: 26–27). Again we are reminded of Basic, where Ogden strove to meet the demands of 'universal grammar', but still deferred in practice to the strictures of English. This comparison is not straightforward, however. NSM has at least two levels, the abstract level of the primitives and the surface level of their realisation in natural languages. The 'universal syntax' is a feature of the abstract level, while the idiomatic forms of explications exist at the surface level. Basic, on the other hand, has only the surface forms, which Ogden was coaxing towards 'universal grammar'.

The similarities between NSM and Basic and its allies extend to some aspects of the discourse in which they are couched. In all these projects there is an insistence on the need for an intuitive, common-sense approach to the representation of meaning. We have seen this quite clearly in Basic, as well as in Neurath's Isotype project (see Chapter 4, §II–III). In similar fashion, Wierzbicka is highly critical of the technical and remote-sounding metalanguages employed in many other semantic theories. Despite their commitment to the rationalist notion of innate semantic primitives, Wierzbicka and her followers constantly emphasise the empirical character of their undertaking. Their explications, they claim, can be 'verified' by being tested against native speaker intuitions (cf. the critiques of Riemer 2006; Willems 2012: 670–673).

The further development of NSM is a matter of refining inadequate explications and the list of primitives used in them (these ideas permeate NSM, but see, for example, Wierzbicka 1980: 17–18, 23, 1987: 2, 1988: 11–12, 1996: 217; Goddard 1994: 10–12). This conception of scientific progress through gradual refinement might remind us of Neurath's notion of the 'universal jargon' (see Chapter 4, §II), although the similarity is at such a generic level that no definite links can be postulated. Gradualism in present-day lay philosophy of science is in any case a commonplace, and has most probably achieved this status not through Neurath's efforts but those of his rival Popper (cf. Chapter 4, §V). It would therefore probably be unreasonable to seek a direct connection from Neurath to NSM in this area.

A somewhat surprising turn in the most recent NSM scholarship is that towards 'Minimal English', an international auxiliary language constructed on the basis of NSM. Minimal English, Wierzbicka (2014: 194) tells us, 'is not another simplified version of English analogous to Ogden's 1930 [*sic*] "Basic English" or Jean-Paul Nerrière's "Globish"' (see Chapter 3, §IV for Globish). Rather, Minimal English 'is, essentially, the English version of "Basic Human"' (Wierzbicka 2014: 195), the rendering in English exponents of the set of primitive concepts uncovered by NSM research. What sets Minimal English apart from all other reduced Englishes is its alleged culturally neutral standpoint. Its use should preserve the existing investment of the millions of second-language learners of English in acquiring the formal shell of that language – its phonology, word forms, grammar, and so on – while leaving the baggage of 'Anglo' culture behind. Any other language could be reduced in this way to serve as the medium for 'Basic Human', argues Wierzbicka, but in the context of present-day globalisation English is indisputably the best host:

> [G]iven the realities of today's globalizing world, at this point it is obviously a mini-English that is the most practical way out (or down) from the conceptual tower of Babel that the cultural evolution of humankind has erected, for better or worse. (Wierzbicka 2014: 194)

Minimal English has only just begun its iteration of the eternal return; we will have to await further developments before we can properly identify its place in history.

NSM itself has as yet attracted no serious historiographic commentary. By Wierzbicka's own anecdotal account, the idea of searching for semantic primitives was first suggested to her in a 1964 lecture on Leibniz's *characteristica universalis* and related seventeenth-century projects, which was given in Warsaw by her teacher Andrzej Bogusławski (b. 1931) (Wierzbicka 1992: 216–218, 1996: 11–13).[1] Wierzbicka and her supporters see their project as a continuation of Leibniz's work (as portrayed in Couturat 1901, 1903, among other places; cf. Chapter 3, §I), but now made achievable because of their empirical, scientific methodology as opposed to Leibniz's reliance on philosophical speculation.

More recent antecedents to her project, such as those explored in this book, are not unknown to Wierzbicka: she cites, in her various writings, such figures as Carnap, Ogden, Peirce, Russell, and both the early and late Wittgenstein. But her citations tend to deal only with particular, isolated points; she never tries to engage with their systems of thought as wholes. In linguistics, such leaps back into the Enlightenment and disregard of the immediately preceding generation represent a common strategy, embodied most saliently in Chomsky's (1966) *Cartesian Linguistics*. However, just like generative grammar, NSM is undoubtedly a product of the same mid-twentieth century milieu that emerged seamlessly from the preceding period examined in this book.

Despite all the refinements, reforms and revolutions that separate us from the treatment of language and meaning in the age of modernism, the era has left us with at least one lasting legacy. Up to the present day, all major theories of linguistic semantics affirm the generally unstated and unexamined consensus that the task of semantic theory is to find and account for some objective 'meaning' encoded in linguistic expressions. It might be modulated by contextual or other pragmatic factors, but there is always a single correct 'Plain Meaning', to use Welby's term. The turn taken by Ogden from *The Meaning of Meaning* to Basic therefore continues to characterise semantic reflection today: the legislated univocal code of logicians has devoured natural language, leaving hermeneutic reflection behind in the pre-scientific past. NSM, with its ultimate paraphrases that reveal the true meaning of any expression, is one of the most overt and unashamed representatives of this trend, but it is by no means alone in its commitment to reduction and absolutism (cf. Riemer 2016: 3–7).

Note

1. Wierzbicka (1992) gives the year 1964 for Bogusławski's lectures, while Wierzbicka (1996) has 1965. She has indicated that the correct year is 1964 (personal communication via e-mail, 1 January 2013).

Bibliography

Abbott, Barbara (1999), 'The formal approach to meaning: formal semantics and its recent developments', *Journal of Foreign Languages* 119:1, 2–20.

Aiken, Janet Rankin (1944 [1936]), 'Little English', in Johnsen (1944), pp. 142–147.

Alter, Stephen G. (2005), *William Dwight Whitney and the Science of Language*, Baltimore: Johns Hopkins University Press.

Anderson, John Richard Lane (1977), 'C.K. Ogden: a plea for reassessment', in Florence and Anderson (1977), pp. 231–244.

Annink, Ed and Max Bruinsma, eds. (2010), *Gerd Arntz: graphic designer*, Rotterdam: 010 Publishers.

Anonymous (1896), 'Advertisement of Welby Prize', *Mind* 5:20, 583.

Atkinson, Catherine (1987), 'The Jeremy Bentham silhouette rings', *The Bentham Newsletter* 11, 48–50.

Auroux, Sylvain and Simone Delasalle (1990), 'French semantics of the late nineteenth century and Lady Welby's significs', in *Essays on Significs*, ed. H. Walter Schmitz, Amsterdam: John Benjamins, pp. 105–131.

Ayer, Alfred Jules (1946 [1936]), *Language, Truth and Logic*, London: Victor Gollancz.

Baldwin, Thomas (2001), *Philosophy in English since 1945*, Oxford: Oxford University Press.

Bally, Charles (1965 [1913]), *Le Langage et la Vie*, Zurich: M. Niehans.

Barandovská-Frank, Veřa K. (2003), *De Latino sine Flexione Centenario, ein Jahrhundert Latino sine Flexione*, Berlin: Institut für Kybernetik.

Barsky, Robert (1997), *Noam Chomsky: a life of dissent*, Cambridge, MA: MIT Press.

Baumann, Adalbert (1915), *Wede, die Verständigungssprache der Zentralmächte und ihrer Freunde, die neue Welt-Hilfs-Sprache*, Diessen von München: Huber.

Beaney, Michael (2003), 'Susan Stebbing on Cambridge and Vienna analysis', in Stadler (2003), pp. 339–350.

Beaufront, Louis de (2004 [1925]), *Kompleta Gramatiko Detaloza di la Linguo Internaciona Ido*, Ponferrada: Ido-Societo Hispana.

Bentham, Jeremy (1843 [1791]), 'Panopticon; or, the Inspection-House', in *The Works of Jeremy Bentham*, vol. 4, ed. John Bowring, Edinburgh: William Tate, pp. 39–66.

Blanke, Detlev (1985), *Internationale Plansprachen: eine Einführung*, Berlin: Akademie-Verlag.

Blanke, Detlev (2006), *Interlinguistische Beiträge: zum Wesen und zur Funktion internationaler Plansprachen*, Frankfurt: Peter Lang.

Bloomfield, Leonard (1914), *Introduction to the Study of Language*, New York: Henry Holt and Company.

Bloomfield, Leonard (1927), 'On recent work in general linguistics', *Modern Philology* 25:2, 211–230.

Bloomfield, Leonard (1933), *Language*, New York: Henry Holt and Company.

Bloomfield, Leonard (1936), 'Language or ideas?' *Language* 12, 89–95.

Bloomfield, Leonard (1938), *Linguistic Aspects of Science* (= *International Encyclopedia of Unified Science*, vol. 1, no. 4), Chicago: University of Chicago Press.

Bloomfield, Leonard (1970 [1929]), 'Linguistics as a science', in Hockett (1970), pp. 149–152 (original in *Studies in Philology* 27, 553–557. [Vol. 27 of *Studies in Philology* was published in 1930; 1929 is the year Bloomfield's speech was originally delivered before the Modern Language Association of America].).

Bloomfield, Leonard (1970 [1943]), 'Meaning', in Hockett (1970), pp. 271–276 (original in *Monatshefte für deutschen Unterricht* 35, 101–106).

Bowker, Gordon (2003), *Inside George Orwell*, London: Little Brown.

Bradley, Francis H. (1893), *Appearance and Reality: a metaphysical essay*, London: Swan, Sonnenschein & Co.

Bréal, Michel (1900 [1897]), *Semantics: studies in the science of meaning*, trans. Nina Cust, London: Henry Holt (original *Essai de sémantique. Science des significations*, Paris: Hachette).

Brinton, Daniel Garrison, Henry Phillips, Jr. and Monroe B. Snyder (1888), 'Report of the committee appointed October 21, 1887, to examine into the scientific value of Volapük', *Proceedings of the American Philosophical Society* 25:127, 3–17.

Brower, Reuben, Helen Vendler and John Hollander, eds. (1973), *I. A. Richards: essays in his honor*, New York: Oxford University Press.

Brugmann, Karl and August Leskien (1907), *Zur Kritik der künstlichen Weltsprachen*, Straßburg: Trübner.

Bühler, Karl (1990 [1934]), *Theory of Language: the representational function of language*, trans. Donald Fraser Goodwin, Amsterdam: John Benjamins (trans. of *Sprachtheorie: die Darstellungsfunktion der Sprache*, Jena: Fischer).

Burke, Christopher (2011), 'The linguistic status of Isotype', in *Image and Imaging in Philosophy, Science and the Arts*, vol. 2, ed. Richard Heinrich, Elisabeth Nemeth, Wolfram Pichler, David Wagner, Frankfurt: Ontos, pp. 31–57.

Bynum, Terrell Ward, ed. (1972), *Conceptual Notation, and Related Articles*, Oxford: Oxford University Press.

Carington, Whately (1994 [1949]), 'Meaning', in Gordon (1994), vol. 5, pp. 155–211.

Carnap, Rudolf (1922), *Der Raum: ein Beitrag zur Wissenschaftslehre* (= Kant-Studien Ergänzungshefte, Nr. 56), Berlin: Reuther und Reichard.

Carnap, Rudolf (1932–1933), 'Über Protokollsätze', *Erkenntnis* 3, 215–228.

Carnap, Rudolf (1934 [1931]), *The Unity of Science*, trans. Max Black, London: Kegan Paul (trans. of 'Die physikalische Sprache als Universalsprache der Wissenschaft', *Erkenntnis* 2, 432–465).

Carnap, Rudolf (1934), 'The rejecton of metaphysics', *Psyche* 14, 100–111.

Carnap, Rudolf (1935), *Philosophy and Logical Syntax*, London: Kegan Paul.

Carnap, Rudolf (1937 [1934]), *Logical Syntax of Language*, trans. Amethe Smeaton, London: Kegan Paul (trans. of *Logische Syntax der Sprache*, Vienna: Springer).

Carnap, Rudolf (1942), *Introduction to Semantics*, Cambridge, MA: Harvard University Press.

Carnap, Rudolf (1947), *Meaning and Necessity: a study in semantics and modal logic*, Chicago: Chicago University Press.

Carnap, Rudolf (1959 [1931]), 'The elimination of metaphysics through logical analysis of language', trans. Arthur Pap, in *Logical Positivism*, ed. Alfred Jules Ayer, Glencoe, Illinois: The Free Press, pp. 60–81 (trans. of 'Überwindung der Metaphysik durch logische Analyse der Sprache', *Erkenntnis* 2, 219–241).

Carnap, Rudolf (1963), *Intellectual Autobiography*, in Schilpp (1963), pp. 3–84.

Carnap, Rudolf (1967 [1928]), *The Logical Construction of the World and Pseudo-Problems in Philosophy*, trans. Rolf A. George, Berkeley: University of California Press (trans. of *Der logische Aufbau der Welt*, Berlin: Weltkreis, and *Scheinprobleme in der Philosophie*, Berlin: Weltkreis).

Cartwright, Nancy, Jordi Cat, Lola Fleck and Thomas E. Uebel (1996), *Otto Neurath: philosophy between science and politics*, Cambridge: Cambridge University Press.

Carus, André W. (2007.), *Carnap and Twentieth-century Thought*, Cambridge: Cambridge University Press.

Chipchase, Paul (1990), 'Some account of the literary production of Lady Welby and her family', in Schmitz (1990), pp. 17–59.

Chomsky, Noam (1957), *Syntactic Structures*, The Hague: Mouton.

Chomsky, Noam (1959), Review of *Verbal Behavior*, Skinner (1957), *Language* 35, 26–58.

Chomsky, Noam (1964 [1962]), 'The logical basis of linguistic theory', in *Proceedings of the Ninth International Congress of Linguistics*, ed. Horace G. Lunt, The Hague: Mouton, pp. 914–978.

Chomsky, Noam (1965), *Aspects of the Theory of Syntax*, Cambridge, MA: MIT Press.

Chomsky, Noam (1966), *Cartesian Linguistics: a chapter in the history of rationalist thought*, New York: Harper and Row.

Chomsky, Noam (1979), *Language and Responsibility*, ed. and trans. Mitsou Ronat, New York: Pantheon Books.

Chomsky, Noam (2004 [1974]), 'Class consciousness and the ideology of power', in *Noam Chomsky: language and politics*, ed. Carlos-Peregrín Otero, Oakland: A.K. Press, pp. 143–170.

Churchill, Winston (1944 [1943]), 'Common tongue a basis for common citizenship', address at Harvard University, 6 September 1943, in Johnsen (1944), pp. 97–99 (original text in *New York Times*, 7 September 1943, p. 14).

Cohen, Robert S. and Marie Neurath, eds. (1983), *Otto Neurath – Philosophical Papers 1913–1946*, Dordrecht: Kluwer.

Collins, Beverley S. and Inger M. Mees (1998), *The Real Professor Higgins: the life and career of Daniel Jones*, Berlin: Walter de Gruyter.

Couturat, Louis (1901), *La Logique de Leibniz*, Paris: Ancien Libraire Germer Baillière et Cie.

Couturat, Louis (1903), *Opuscules et Fragments Inédits*, Paris: Ancien Libraire Germer Baillière et Cie.

Couturat, Louis (1907), *Étude sur la Dérivation en Espéranto*, Paris: Brodard.

Couturat, Louis (1910 [1909]), 'On the application of logic to the problem of an international language', in Couturat *et al.* (1910), pp. 42–52.

Couturat, Louis (1910), *Étude sur la Dérivation dans la Langue Internationale*, Paris: Delagrave.

Couturat, Louis and Léopold Leau (1903), *Histoire de la Langue Universelle*, Paris: Hachette.

Couturat, Louis and Léopold Leau (1907), *Les Nouvelles Langues Internationales*, Paris: Hachette.

Couturat, Louis, Otto Jespersen, Richard Lorenz, Wilhelm Ostwald and Leopold Pfaundler, eds. (1910), *International Language and Science*, London: Constable and Company.

Cram, David (1980), 'George Dalgarno on "Ars Signorum" and Wilkins' "essay"', in *Progress in Linguistic Historiography*, ed. E. F. K. Koerner, Amsterdam: John Benjamins, pp. 113–121.

Cram, David (1985), 'Universal language schemes in seventeenth-century Britain', *Histoire Epistémologie Langage* 7, 35–44.

Dahms, Hans-Joachim (1996), 'Vienna Circle and French Enlightenment – a comparison of Diderots *Encyclopédie* with Neurath's *International Encyclopedia of Unified Science*', in Nemeth and Stadler (1996), pp. 53–62.

Dahms, Hans-Joachim (2004), '*Neue Sachlichkeit* in the architecture and philosophy of the 1920s', in *Carnap Brought Home: the view from Jena*, ed. Steve Awodey and Carsten Klein, La Salle: Open Court, pp. 357–376.

Daston, Lorraine and Peter Galison. (2007), *Objectivity*, New York: Zone Books.

Davidson, Peter (2010), *George Orwell: a life in letters*, London: Harvill Secker.

Dittrich, Ottmar (1913), *Die Probleme der Sprachpsychologie und ihre gegenwärtigen Lösungsmöglichkeiten*, Leipzig: Quelle und Meyer.

Domschke, Jan-Peter and Karl Hansel (2000), *Wilhelm Ostwald: eine Kurzbiografie*, Großbothen: Vorstand der Wilhelm-Ostwald-Gesellschaft.

Domschke, Jan-Peter and Peter Lewandrowski (1982), *Wilhelm Ostwald: Chemiker, Wissenschaftstheoretiker, Organisator*, Cologne: Pahl-Rugenstein.

Drezen, Ernest (1931), *Historio de la Mondolingvo*, Leipzig: Ekrelo.

Dummett, Michael A. E. (1991), *Frege: philosophy of mathematics*, Cambridge, MA: Harvard University Press.

Eaton, Helen S. (1927), 'The educational value of an artificial language', *Modern Language Journal* 12, 87–94.

Eaton, Helen S. (1934a), *Comparative Frequency List*, New York: IALA.

Eaton, Helen S. (1934b), *General Language Course*, Dallas: Banks Upshaw and Company.

Eaton, Helen S. (1940), *Semantic Frequency List*, Chicago: University of Chicago Press.

Eco, Umberto (1995 [1993]), *The Search for the Perfect Language*, trans. James Fentress,

Oxford: Blackwell (trans. of *Ricerca della Lingua Perfetta nella Cultura Europea*, Rome: Edizione Laterza).

Ellis, Alexander John (1891), 'On the conditions of a universal language, in reference to the invitation of the American Philosophical Society of Philadelphia, U.S., to send delegates to a congress for perfecting a universal language on an Aryan basis, and its report on Volapük', *Transactions of the Philological Society 1888–1890*, 21:1, 59–98.

Erdmann, Karl Otto (1900), *Die Bedeutung des Wortes*, Leipzig: Eduard Avenarius.

Eschbach, Achim (1988), *Karl Bühler's Theory of Language*, Amsterdam: John Benjamins.

Esterhill, Frank (2000), *Interlingua Institute: a history*, New York: Interlingua Institute.

Fabian, Reinhard (1996), 'The Otto Neurath Nachlass in Haarlem', in Nemeth and Stadler (1996), pp. 337–356.

Falk, Julia S. (1995), 'Words without grammar: linguists and the international auxiliary language movement in the United States', *Language and Communication* 15, 241–259.

Falk, Julia S. (1999), *Women, Language and Linguistics: three American stories from the first half of the twentieth century*, London: Routledge.

Feigl, Herbert and Albert E. Blumberg (1931), 'Logical positivism', *Journal of Philosophy* 28:11, 281–296.

Fink, Howard (1971), 'Newspeak: the epitome of parody techniques in *Nineteen Eighty-Four*', *The Critical Survey* 5:2, 155–163.

Firth, John Rupert (1935), 'The technique of semantics', *Transactions of the Philological Society for 1935*, 36–72.

Firth, John Rupert (1957 [1950]), 'Personality and language in society', in *Papers in Linguistics 1934–1951*, ed. J. R. Firth, London: Oxford University Press, pp. 177–189 (original in *The Sociological Review* 42:2).

Florence, Philip Sargant and John Richard Lane Anderson, eds. (1977), *C. K. Ogden: a collective memoir*, London: Pemberton.

Forster, Peter G. (1982), *The Esperanto Movement*, The Hague: Mouton.

Foucault, Michel (1979 [1973]), *Discipline and Punish: the birth of the prison*, trans. Alan Sheridon, Harmondsworth: Penguin (trans. of *Surveiller et Punir: naissance de la prison*, Paris: Gallimard).

Frank, Leonhard (1930 [1926]), *Carl and Anna*, trans. Leonora Wilhelmina Lockhart, London: Kegan Paul (trans. of *Karl und Anna*, Leipzig: Reclam).

Frege, Gottlob (1959 [1884]), *The Foundations of Arithmetic*, trans. John L. Austin, Oxford: Blackwell (trans. of *Die Grundlagen der Arithmetik*, Breslau: Wilhelm Koebner).

Frege, Gottlob (1972 [1879]), 'Conceptual notation', in Bynum (1972), pp. 101–203 (trans. of *Begriffsschrift, eine der arithmetischen nachgebildete Formelsprache des reinen Denkens*, Halle an der Saale: L. Nebert).

Frege, Gottlob (1972 [1882]), 'On the aim of the conceptual notation', in Bynum (1972), pp. 90–100 (trans. of 'Über die Begriffsschrift des Herrn Peano und meine eigene', *Jenaische Zeitschrift für Naturwissenschaft* 16, 1–10).

Frege, Gottlob (1984 [1892]), 'On sense and meaning', in Frege (1984), pp. 157–177 (trans. of 'Über Sinn und Bedeutung', trans. Max Black, *Zeitschrift für Philosophie und philosophische Kritik* 100, 25–50).

Frege, Gottlob (1984 [1918–1919]), 'Thoughts', trans. Peter Geach and R. H. Stoothoff, in Frege (1984), pp. 351–372. (trans. of 'Der Gedanke', *Beiträge zur Philosophie des deutschen Idealismus* 2, 58–77).

Frege, Gottlob (1984), *Collected Papers on Mathematics, Logic, and Philosophy*, ed. Brian McGuinness, Oxford: Blackwell.

Friedman, Michael (2000), *A Parting of the Ways: Carnap, Cassirer and Heidegger*, Chicago: Open Court.

Gardiner, Alan Henderson. (1919), 'Some thoughts on the subject of language', *Man* 19:2, 2–6.

Gardiner, Alan Henderson (1922), 'Definition of word and sentence', *The British Journal of Psychology* 12:4, 352–361.

Gardiner, Alan Henderson (1951 [1932]), *The Theory of Speech and Language*, Oxford: Oxford University Press.

Gerhardt, Carl Immanuel, ed. (1890), *Die philosophischen Schriften von Gottfried Wilhelm Leibniz*, vol. 7, Berlin: Weidmannsche Buchhandlung.

Gesellschafts- und Wirtschaftsmuseum Wien (1930), *Gesellschaft und Wirtschaft: bild-statistische Elementarwerk*, Leipzig: Bibliographisches Institut.

Glock, Hans-Johann (2008), *What is Analytic Philosophy?* Cambridge: Cambridge University Press.

Goddard, Cliff (1994), 'Semantic theory and semantic universals', in *Semantic and Lexical Universals*, eds. Cliff Goddard and Anna Wierzbicka, Amsterdam: John Benjamins, pp. 7–29.

Goddard, Cliff (2002), 'The search for the shared semantic core of all languages', in Goddard and Wierzbicka (2002), vol. 1, pp. 5–40.

Goddard, Cliff and Anna Wierzbicka, eds. (2002), *Meaning and Universal Grammar: theory and empirical findings*, 2 vols, Amsterdam: John Benjamins.

Gode, Alexander (1959), "Manifesto de Interlingua", *Novas de Interlingua* 4, 21–35.

Gode, Alexander (1971 [1951]), *Interlingua-English: a dictionary of the international language prepared by the research staff of the International Auxiliary Language Association*, New York: Storm Publishers.

Gode, Alexander and Hugh E. Blair (1971 [1951]), *Interlingua: a grammar of the international language*, New York: Storm Publishers.

Gomperz, Heinrich (1908), *Weltanshauungslehre, zweiter Band: Noologie*, Jena: Eugen Diederichs.

Gomperz, Heinrich (1941), 'The meanings of "meaning"', *Philosophy of Science* 8, 157–183.

Gordon, W. Terrence (1982), *A History of Semantics*, Amsterdam: John Benjamins (reissued 2016 with new material as *A History of Lexical Semantics*, Saarbrücken: Scholars' Press).

Gordon, W. Terrence (1990a), 'Significs and C. K. Ogden: the influence of Lady Welby', in Schmitz (1990), pp. 179–196.

Gordon, W. Terrence (1990b), *C. K. Ogden: a bio-bibliographic study*, Metuchen, NJ: The Scarecrow Press.

Gordon, W. Terrence (1990c), 'C. K. Ogden, Edward Sapir, Leonard Bloomfield, and the geometry of semantics', *Papers from the Fourth International Conference on the History of Linguistics*, ed. H. J. Niederehe and E. F. K. Koerner, Amsterdam: John Benjamins, pp. 821–832.

Gordon, W. Terrence, ed. (1994), *C. K. Ogden and Linguistics*, 5 vols, London: Routledge/Thoemmes Press.

Gordon, W. Terrence (2006), 'Linguistics and semiotics I: the impact of Ogden and Richards' *The Meaning of Meaning*', in *History of the Language Sciences*, ed. Sylvain Auroux, E. F. K. Koerner, Hans-Josef Niederehe and K. Versteegh, vol. 3, Berlin: Walter de Gruyter, pp. 2579–2588.

Graham, Elsie (1977), 'Basic English as an international language', in Florence and Anderson (1977), pp. 153–160.

Grattan-Guinness, Ivor (1977), *Dear Russell, Dear Jourdain: a commentary on Russell's logic, based on his correspondence with Philip Jourdain*, London: Duckworth.

Grattan-Guinness, Ivor (2000), *The Search for Mathematical Roots, 1870–1940*, Princeton: Princeton University Press.

Grice, Herbert Paul (1961), 'The causal theory of perception', *Proceedings of the Aristotelian Society* 35, 121–52 (reproduced in chapter 15 of Grice 1989, pp. 224–247).

Grice, Herbert Paul (1989), *Studies in the Way of Words*, Cambridge, MA: Harvard University Press.

Griffin, Nicholas (1991), *Russell's Idealist Apprenticeship*, Oxford: Oxford University Press.

Griffin, Nicholas, ed. (1992), *The Selected Letters of Bertrand Russell*, vol. 1, London: Allen Lane.

Guérard, Albert Léon (1922), *A Short History of the International Language Movement*, London: T. Fisher Unwin.

Guérard, Albert Léon (1944 [1941]), 'International language and national cultures', in Johnsen (1944), pp. 129–142 (original in *American Scholar* 10, 170–183).

Gupta, Anil (2015), 'Definitions', in *The Stanford Encyclopedia of Philosophy*, ed. Edward N. Zalta <https://plato.stanford.edu/archives/sum2015/entries/definitions/> (accessed on 21 December 2016).

Haller, Rudolf (1993), *Neopositivismus. Eine historische Einführung in die Philosophie des Wiener Kreises*, Darmstadt: Wissenschaftliche Buchgesellschaft.

Haller, Rudolf and Robin Kinross, eds. (1991), *Otto Neurath: gesammelte bildpädagogische Schriften*, Wien: Hölder-Pichler-Tempsky.

Hardwick, Charles S. (1977), *Semiotic and Significs: the correspondence between Charles S. Peirce and Victoria Lady Welby*, Bloomington: Indiana University Press.

Harris, Randy Allen (1993), *The Linguistics Wars*, New York: Oxford University Press.

Haupenthal, Reinhard (1976), *Plansprachen*, Darmstadt: Wissenschaftliche Buchgesellschaft.

Haupenthal, Reinhard (2005a), *Johann Martin Schleyer (1831–1912), Pfarrer von Litzelstetten (1875–1885)*, Schliengen: Edition Iltis.

Haupenthal, Reinhard (2005b), *Über die Startbedingungen zweier Plansprachen: Schleyers Volapük (1879/80) und Zamenhofs Esperanto (1887)*, Schliengen: Edition Iltis.

Hayek, Friedrich von (1997), *Socialism and War: essays, documents, reviews*, ed. Bruce Caldwell, Chicago: University of Chicago Press.

Hayek, Friedrich von (2007 [1944]), *The Road to Serfdom*, Chicago: University of Chicago Press (original published London: Routledge and Kegan Paul).

Heidegger, Martin (1959 [1935]), *An Introduction to Metaphysics*, trans. Ralph Manheim, New Haven: Yale University Press (trans. of *Einführung in die Metaphysik*, Tübingen: Max Niemeyer).

Hempel, Carl Gustav (1965), *Aspects of Scientific Explanation, and Other Essays in the Philosophy of Science*, New York: Free Press.

Hiz, Henry and Pierre Swiggers (1990), 'Bloomfield the logical positivist', *Semiotica* 79, 257–270.

Hockett, Charles Francis, ed. (1970), *A Leonard Bloomfield Anthology*, Chicago: University of Chicago Press.

Hookway, Christopher (1985), *Peirce*, London: Routledge and Kegan Paul.

Hotopf, William H. N. (1965), *Language, Thought and Comprehension: a case study of the writings of I. A. Richards*, London: Routledge and Kegan Paul.

Huck, Geoffrey J. and John A. Goldsmith (1995), *Ideology and Linguistic Theory*, London: Routledge.

Humboldt, Wilhelm von (1836), *Über die Verschiedenheit des menschlichen Sprachbaues und ihren Einfluss auf die geistige Entwicklung des Menschengeschlechts*, Berlin: Dümmler.

Hymes, Dell and John Fought (1981 [1975]), *American Structuralism*, The Hague: Mouton.

IALA (1945), *General Report 1945*, New York: IALA.

Innis, Robert E. (1982), *Karl Bühler, semiotic foundations of language theory*, New York: Plenum Press.

Jespersen, Otto (1894), *Progress in Language*, London: Sonnenschein.

Jespersen, Otto (1910 [1909]), 'Linguistic principles necessary for the construction of an international auxiliary language, with an appendix on the criticism of Esperanto', in Couturat *et al.* (1910), pp. 27–41.

Jespersen, Otto (1922), *Language, its Nature, Development and Origin*, London: Allen & Unwin.

Jespersen, Otto (1928), *International Language*, London: Allen and Unwin.

Jespersen, Otto (1960 [1920]), 'The classification of languages', in Jespersen (1960), pp. 693–704 (original in *Scientia* 28, 109–120).

Jespersen, Otto (1960 [1921]), 'History of our language', in Jespersen (1960), pp. 743–753 (original in *Two Papers on International Language in English and Ido*, London: International Language Society).

Jespersen, Otto (1960 [1941]), 'Efficiency in linguistic change', in Jespersen (1960), pp. 381–466 (original published Copenhagen: Ejnar Munksgaard).

Jespersen, Otto (1960), *The Selected Writings of Otto Jespersen*, London: Allen and Unwin.

Johnsen, Julia E., ed. (1944), *Basic English*, New York: H. W. Wilson.

Jones, Emily Elizabeth Constance (1910), 'Mr. Russell's objections to Frege's analysis of propositions', *Mind* 19:75, 379–386.

Jones, Emily Elizabeth Constance (1910–1911), 'A new law of thought', *Proceedings of the Aristotelian Society* 11, 166–186.

Joseph, John E. (1995), 'Natural grammar, arbitrary lexicon: an enduring parallel in the history of linguistic thought', *Language and Communication* 15, 213–225.

Joseph, John E. (1996), 'The immediate sources of the "Sapir-Whorf Hypothesis"', *Historiographia Linguistica* 23, 365–404.

Joseph, John E. (1999), 'Basic English and the debabelization of China', in *Intercultural Encounters: studies in English literatures*, ed. Heinz Antor and Kevin L. Cope, Heidelberg: C. Winter, pp. 51–71.

Joseph, John E. (2000), *Limiting the Arbitrary: linguistic naturalism and its opposites in Plato's Cratylus and modern theories of language*, Amsterdam: John Benjamins.

Joseph, John E. (2001), 'Orwell on language and politics', in *Landmarks in Linguistic Thought II: the Western tradition in the twentieth century*, ed. John E. Joseph, Nigel Love and Talbot J. Taylor, London: Routledge, pp. 29–42.

Joseph, John E. (2012), *Saussure*, Oxford: Oxford University Press.

Joseph, John E. and Frederick J. Newmeyer (2012), '"All languages are equally complex": the rise and fall of a consensus', *Historiographia Linguistica* 39:2/3, 341–368.

Kallen, Horace (1940 [1939]), 'The meanings of "unity" among the sciences', *Educational Administration and Supervision* 26:2, 81–97.

Kallen, Horace (1946a), 'Reply', *Philosophy and Phenomenological Research* 6, 515–526.

Kallen, Horace (1946b), 'Postscript: Otto Neurath, 1882–1945', *Philosophy and Phenomenological Research* 6, 529–533.

Kamprath, Christine, Eric Adolphson, Teruko Mitamura and Eric Nyberg (1998), 'Controlled language for multilingual document production: experience with Caterpillar Technical English', in *Proceedings of the Second International Workshop on Controlled Language Applications*, ed. Teruko Mitamura, Pittsburgh: Language Technologies Institute, pp. 1–12.

Kant, Immanuel (1998 [1781]), *Critique of Pure Reason*, ed. and trans. Paul Guyer and Allen W. Wood, Cambridge: Cambridge University Press.

Kenny, Anthony, ed. and trans. (1970), *Descartes: philosophical letters*, Oxford: Oxford University Press.

Kerckhoffs, Auguste (1885), *Cours Complet de Volapük*, Paris: Libraire H. Le Soudier.

Knowlson, James (1975), *Universal Language Schemes in England and France, 1600–1800*, Toronto: University of Toronto Press.

Koerner, E. F. Konrad (1970), 'Bloomfieldian linguistics and the problem of "meaning"', *Jahrbuch für Amerikastudien* 15, 162–183.

Koerner, E. F. Konrad, ed. (1989a), *Practicing Linguistic Historiography*, Amsterdam: John Benjamins.

Koerner, E. F. Konrad (1989b), 'Friedrich Schlegel and the emergence of historical-comparative grammar', in Koerner (1989a), pp. 269–290.

Koerner, E. F. Konrad (1989c), 'August Schleicher and linguistic science in the second half of the nineteenth century', in Koerner (1989a), pp. 325–375.

Koerner, E. F. Konrad (2000), 'Towards a full pedigree of the Sapir-Whorf Hypothesis: from Locke to Lucy', *Explorations in Linguistic Relativity*, ed. Martin Pütz and Marjolijn Verspoor, Amsterdam: Benjamins, pp. 1–24.

Kotzin, Boris (1915 [1913]), *Geschichte und Theorie des Ido*, trans. Wilhelm Winsch and Hans Reuß, Dresden: Ader and Borel (trans. of *Historio kaj Teorio de Ido*, Moscow: Lebrejo 'Esperanto').

Krajewski, Markus (2006), *Restlosigkeit, Weltprojekte um 1900*, Frankfurt am Main: Fischer Taschenbuch Verlag.

Kripke, Saul (1980 [1972]), *Naming and Necessity*, Oxford: Blackwell.

Kuhn, Thomas S. (1962), *The Structure of Scientific Revolutions*, Chicago: University of Chicago Press.

Künzli, Andreas (2001), 'René de Saussure (1868–1943) – Tragika sed grava esperantologo kaj interlingvisto el Svislando', in *Studoj pri Interlingvistiko, Festlibro Omaĝe al la 50-jariĝo de Detlev Blanke*, ed. Sabine Fiedler and Liu Haitao, Prague: Kava-Pech, pp. 524–546.

Lakoff, George and Mark Johnson (1980), *Metaphors We Live By*, Chicago: University of Chicago Press.

Lalande, André (1988 [1902–1923]), *Vocabulaire Technique et Critique de la Philosophie*, 2 vols, Paris: Presses Universitaires de France.

Large, J. Andrew (1985), *The Artificial Language Movement*, Oxford: Blackwell.

Lauwerys, Joseph Albert (1977), 'Basic English – its position and plans', in Florence and Anderson (1977), pp. 161–168.

Lewis, Sinclair (1922), *Babbit*, New York: Harcourt, Brace and Co.

Lins, Ulrich (1988), *Die gefährliche Sprache: die Verfolgung der Esperantisten unter Hitler und Stalin*, Gerlingen: Bleicher Verlag.

Locke, John (1975 [1690]), *An Essay Concerning Human Understanding*, Oxford: Oxford University Press.

Lockhart, Leonora Wilhelmina (1928), 'Word formation', *Psyche* 9:2, 8–12.

Lockhart, Leonora Wilhelmina (1931a), *Word Economy*, London: Kegan Paul.

Lockhart, Leonora Wilhelmina (1931b), 'Critical discussion', *Psyche* 11:3, 81–88.

Lorenz, Richard (1910 [1909]), 'The Délégation pour l'adoption d'une langue auxiliaire internationale', in Couturat *et al.* (1910), pp. 11–26.

Lyon, David (1994), *The Electronic Eye: the rise of surveillance society*, Minneapolis: Minneapolis University Press.

Lyons, Francis S. L. (1963), *Internationalism in Europe 1815–1914*, Leyden: A. W. Sythoff.

Lyons, John (1963), *Structural Semantics: an analysis of part of the vocabulary of Plato*, Oxford: Blackwell.

Maat, Jaap (1999), Review of *The Search for the Perfect Language*, Eco (1995 [1993]), *Semiotica* 126:1/4, 121–142.

Maat, Jaap (2004), *Philosophical Languages in the Seventeenth Century: Dalgarno, Wilkins, Leibniz*, Dordrecht: Kluwer.

Maat, Jaap and David Cram (2000), 'Universal language schemes in the seventeenth century', in *History of the Language Sciences*, vol. 1, ed. Sylvain Auroux, E. F. K.

Koerner, Hans-Josef Niederehe and K. Versteegh, Berlin: Walter de Gruyter, pp. 1030–1043.

Malinowski, Bronisław (1935), *Coral Gardens and their Magic*, London: Allen and Unwin.

Malinowski, Bronisław (1989 [1923]), 'The problem of meaning in primitive languages', in Ogden and Richards (1989 [1923]), pp. 296–336.

Mandelbaum, David G. (1949), *Selected Writings of Edward Sapir in Language, Culture and Personality*, Berkeley: University of California Press.

Mannoury, Gerrit (1934), 'Die signifischen Grundlagen der Mathematik', *Erkenntnis* 4, 288–309.

Mannoury, Gerrit (1937), 'Psikologia analizo de la matematika pensmaniero', *Synthese* 2:1, 407–418.

Mannoury, Gerrit (1987 [1938]), 'Significs', trans. Hans Kraal, in McGuinness (1987), pp. 162–164 (trans. of a lecture in *Einheitswissenschaft* 6).

Matthews, Peter Hugoe (2001), *A Short History of Structural Linguistics*, Cambridge: Cambridge University Press.

McElvenny, James (2017), 'Linguistic aesthetics from the nineteenth to the twentieth century: the case of Otto Jespersen's "progress in language"', *History of Humanities* 2:2, 417–442.

McGuinness, Brian, ed. (1979), *Wittgenstein and the Vienna Circle: conversations*, Oxford: Blackwell.

McGuinness, Brian, ed. (1987), *Unified Science: the Vienna Circle monograph series originally edited by Otto Neurath, now in an English edition*, Dordrecht: D. Reidel.

Meinong, Alexius (1904), *Untersuchungen zur Gegenstandstheorie und Psychologie*, Leipzig: J. A. Barth.

Meinong, Alexius (1910 [1902]), *Über Annahmen*, Leipzig: J. A. Barth.

Meyer, Gustav (1976 [1891]), 'Weltsprache und Weltsprachen', in Haupenthal (1976), pp. 27–45 (original in *Schlesische Zeitung*, 12 and 14 July 1891).

Milkov, Nikolay (2003), 'Susan Stebbing's criticism of Wittgenstein's Tractatus', in Stadler (2003), pp. 351–363.

Moch, Gaston (1897), *La Question de la Langue Internationale et sa Solution par l'Esperanto*, Paris: V. Giard et E. Brière.

Monk, Ray (1990), *Ludwig Wittgenstein: the duty of genius*, London: Jonathan Cape.

Monk, Ray (1996), *Bertrand Russell: the spirit of solitude*, London: Jonathan Cape.

Monk, Ray (1997), 'Was Russell an analytic philosopher', in *The Rise of Analytic Philosophy*, ed. Hans-Johann Glock, Oxford: Blackwell, pp. 35–50.

Monk, Ray (2000), *Bertrand Russell, 1921–1970: the ghost of madness*, London: Jonathan Cape.

Moore, George Edward (1993 [1903]), *Principia Ethica*, Cambridge: Cambridge University Press.

More, Adelyne [pseudonym of C. K. Ogden] (1916), *Uncontrolled Breeding, or Fecundity versus Civilization: a contribution to the study of over-population as the cause of war and the chief obstacle to the emancipation of women*, London: Allen and Unwin.

More, Adelyne [pseudonym of C. K. Ogden] (1928), 'Bentham on the verb', *Psyche* 8:4, 19–39.

More, Adelyne [pseudonym of C. K. Ogden] (1929), 'The theory of fictions', *Psyche* 10:1, 31–38.

Morpurgo Davies, Anna (1975), 'Language classification in the nineteenth century', in *Current Trends in Linguistics: historiography of linguistics*, ed. Thomas A. Sebeok, The Hague: Mouton, pp. 607–716.

Morpurgo Davies, Anna (1998), *History of Linguistics*, vol. 4: *Nineteenth-century Linguistics*, London: Longman.

Morris, Charles (1938), *Foundations of the Theory of Signs*, Chicago: University of Chicago Press.

Morris, Charles (1946), *Signs, Language and Behavior*, New York: Prentice Hall.

Mulder, Henk L. (1968), 'Wissenschaftliche Weltauffassung – der Wiener Kreis', *Journal of the History of Philosophy* 6:4, 386–390.

Müller, Karl H. (1991), 'Neurath's theory of pictorial-statistical representation', in *Rediscovering the Forgotten Vienna Circle: Austrian studies on Otto Neurath and the Vienna Circle*, ed. Thomas E. Uebel, Dordrecht: Kluwer, pp. 223–251.

Myers, Adolph (1938), *Basic and the Teaching of English in India*, Bombay: The Times of India Press.

Nemeth, Elisabeth and Friedrich Stadler (1996), *Encyclopedia and Utopia. The life and work of Otto Neurath (1882–1945)*, Vienna: Springer.

Nerlich, Brigitte (1992), *Semantic Theories in Europe, 1830–1930: from etymology to contextuality*, Amsterdam: John Benjamins.

Nerrière, Jean-Paul (2006), *Parlez Globish! Don't speak English*, Paris: Eyrolles.

Neurath, Marie (2009), 'Wiener Methode and Isotype: my apprenticeship and partnership with Otto Neurath', in Marie Neurath and Kinross (2009), pp. 9–76.

Neurath, Marie and Robert S. Cohen, eds. (1973), *Empiricism and Sociology*, Dordrecht: Reidel.

Neurath, Marie and Robin Kinross (2009), *The Transformer: principles of making Isotype charts*, London: Hyphen Press.

Neurath, Otto (1906–1907 [1906]), 'Zur Anschauunge der Antike über Handel, Gewerbe und Landwirtschaft', *Jahrbücher für Nationalökonomie und Statistik*, 3rd series, 32, 577–606, and 34, 145–205.

Neurath, Otto (1930–1931), 'Chronik', *Erkenntnis* 1, 72–79.

Neurath, Otto (1936), *Isotype: international picture language*, London: Kegan Paul.

Neurath, Otto (1937), *Basic by Isotype*, London: Kegan Paul.

Neurath, Otto (1938), 'Unified science as encyclopedic integration' (= *International Encyclopedia of Unified Science*, vol. 1, no. 1), Chicago: University of Chicago Press.

Neurath, Otto (1939), *Modern Man in the Making*, New York: Knopf.

Neurath, Otto (1973 [1942]), 'International planning for freedom', in Neurath and Cohen (1973), pp. 442–440 (original in *The New Commonwealth*, April 1942, 281–292; July 1942, 23–28).

Neurath, Otto (1981 [1928]), Review of *Der logische Aufbau der Welt* and *Scheinprobleme in der Philosophie*, in *Gesammelte philosophische und methodologische Schriften*, ed. Rudolf Haller and Heiner Rutter, Vienna: Hölder-Pichler-Tempsky, pp. 295–297 (original in *Der Kampf* 21, 624–626).

Neurath, Otto (1983 [1930–1931]), 'Ways of the scientific world-conception', trans. Robert S. Cohen, in Cohen and Neurath (1983), pp. 32–47 (trans. of 'Wege der wissenschaftlichen Weltauffassung', *Erkenntnis* 1, 106–125).

Neurath, Otto (1983 [1931]), 'Physicalism: the philosophy of the Viennese Circle', in Cohen and Neurath (1983), pp. 48–51 (original in *The Monist* 41, 618–623).

Neurath, Otto (1983 [1932]), 'Protocol statements', trans. Robert S. Cohen, in Cohen and Neurath (1983), pp. 91–99 (trans. of 'Protokollsätze', *Erkenntnis* 3, 204–214).

Neurath, Otto (1983 [1935]a), 'The unity of science as a task', trans. Robert S. Cohen and Marie Neurath, in Cohen and Neurath (1983), pp. 115–120 (trans. of 'Einheit der Wissenschaft als Aufgabe', *Erkenntnis* 5, 16–22).

Neurath, Otto (1983 [1935]b), 'Pseudorationalism of falsification', trans. Robert S. Cohen and Marie Neurath, in Cohen and Neurath (1983), pp. 121–131 (trans. of 'Pseudorationalismus der Falsifikation', *Erkenntnis* 5, 353–365).

Neurath, Otto (1983 [1946]), 'The orchestration of the science by the encyclopedism of logical empiricism', in Cohen and Neurath (1983), pp. 230–242 (original in *Philosophy and Phenomenological Research* 6, 496–508).

Neurath, Otto (1987 [1933]), 'Unified science and psychology', trans. Brian McGuinness, in McGuinness (1987), pp. 1–23 (trans. of *Einheitswissenschaft und Psychologie*, Vienna: Gerold and Co.).

Neurath, Otto (1987 [1938]), 'The new encyclopedia', trans. Hans Kraal, in McGuinness (1987), pp. 132–141 (trans. of a lecture printed in *Einheitswissenschaft* 6).

Neurath, Otto (1991 [1925]), 'Gesellschafts- und Wirtschaftsmuseum in Wien', in Haller and Kinross (1991), pp. 1–17 (original in *Österreichische Gemeindezeitung* 2:16, 1–155).

Neurath, Otto (1991 [1926]), 'Die Tätigkeit des Gesellschafts- und Wirtschaftsmuseums in Wien', in Haller and Kinross (1991), pp. 34–39 (original in *Österreichische Gemeinde-Zeitung* 3:10, 324–327).

Neurath, Otto (1991 [1933]), 'Bildstatistik nach Wiener Methode in der Schule', in Haller and Kinross (1991), pp. 265–336 (original *Bildstatistik nach Wiener Methode in der Schule*, Vienna: Deutscher Verlag für Jugend und Volk).

Neurath, Otto (1991 [1935]), 'Isotype und die Graphik', trans. Rudolf Haller, in Haller und Kinross (1991), pp. 342–354 (trans. of 'Isotype en de graphiek', *De Delver* 9:2, 17–29).

Neurath, Otto (1996), 'Visual education: humanisation versus popularisation', in Nemeth and Stadler (1996), pp. 245–335.

Neurath, Otto (2010), *From Hieroglyphics to Isotype: a visual autobiography*, London: Hyphen Press.

Newmeyer, Frederick J. (1986 [1980]), *Linguistic Theory in America: the first quarter-century of transformational generative grammar*, New York: Academic Press.

Nolan, Rita (1990), 'Anticipatory themes in the writings of Lady Welby', in Schmitz (1990), pp. 83–101.

Ogden, Charles Kay (1926), *The Meaning of Psychology*, London: Kegan Paul.

Ogden, Charles Kay (1927a), 'Editorial', *Psyche* 27, 1–2.

Ogden, Charles Kay (1927b), 'Orthology (editorial)', *Psyche* 8:1, 1–7.

Ogden, Charles Kay (1928a), 'Editorial', *Psyche* 8:4, 1–2.

Ogden, Charles Kay (1928b), 'Forensic orthology. Back to Bentham', *Psyche* 8:4, 3–18.

Ogden, Charles Kay (1928c), 'Debabelization (editorial)', *Psyche* 9:1, 1–3.

Ogden, Charles Kay (1929a), 'The universal language (editorial)', *Psyche* 9:3, 1–9.

Ogden, Charles Kay (1929b), 'Work in progress (editorial)', *Psyche* 10:1, 1–30.

Ogden, Charles Kay (1929c), 'Editorial', *Psyche* 10:2, 1–38.

Ogden, Charles Kay (1930), 'Penultima (editorial)', *Psyche* 10:3, 1–29.

Ogden, Charles Kay (1931), *Debabelization*, London: Kegan Paul.

Ogden, Charles Kay (1932a), *The ABC of Basic English*, London: Kegan Paul.

Ogden, Charles Kay (1932b), *The Basic Words: a detailed account of their uses*, London: Kegan Paul.

Ogden, Charles Kay (1932c), *The Basic Dictionary*, London: Kegan Paul.

Ogden, Charles Kay (1932d), *Bentham's Theory of Fictions*, London: Kegan Paul.

Ogden, Charles Kay (1933 [1930]), *Basic English: a general introduction with rules and grammar*, London: Kegan Paul.

Ogden, Charles Kay (1934a), *The System of Basic English*, New York: Harcourt, Brace and Co.

Ogden, Charles Kay (1934b), 'The Magic of Words', *Psyche* 14, 9–87.

Ogden, Charles Kay (1935), *Basic English versus the Artificial Languages*, London: Kegan Paul.

Ogden, Charles Kay (1936), 'Basic English and grammatical reform', *Psyche* 16, 51–75.

Ogden, Charles Kay (1938–1952), 'Word Magic', *Psyche* 18, 19–126.

Ogden, Charles Kay (1943), 'Can Basic English be a world language?', *Picture Post* 21:4, 23–25.

Ogden, Charles Kay (1952), 'Editorial', *Psyche* 18, 5–18.

Ogden, Charles Kay (1968), *Basic English: international second language*, ed. E. C. Graham, New York: Harcourt, Brace and World.

Ogden, Charles Kay (1993 [1932]), *Jeremy Bentham: 1832–2032*, Bristol: Thoemmes Press (original published London: Kegan Paul).

Ogden, Charles Kay (1994 [1911]), 'The progress of significs', in Gordon (1994), vol. 1, pp. 1–48.

Ogden, Charles Kay and Ivor Armstrong Richards (1989 [1923]), *The Meaning of Meaning*, San Diego: Harcourt Brace Jovanovich (original published London: Kegan Paul).

Orwell, George (1968 [1941]), 'Wells, Hitler and the world state', in Orwell (1968), vol. 2, pp. 166–171.

Orwell, George (1968 [1946]), 'Politics and the English language', in Orwell (1968), vol. 4, pp. 127–140.

Orwell, George (1968), *The Collected Essays, Journalism and Letters of George Orwell*, ed. Sonia Brownell Orwell and Ian Angus, 4 vols, London: Secker and Warburg.

Orwell, George (1989 [1949]), *Nineteen Eighty-Four*, London: Penguin (original published London: Secker and Warburg).

Ostwald, Wilhelm (1915), 'Weltdeutsch', *Monistische Sonntagspredigten* 36, 545–58.

Padley, George Arthur (1976), *Grammatical Theory in Western Europe, 1500–1700: the Latin tradition*, Cambridge: Cambridge University Press.

Padley, George Arthur (1985), *Grammatical Theory in Western Europe, 1500–1700: trends in vernacular grammar*, Cambridge: Cambridge University Press.

Partee, Barbara (2011), 'Formal semantics: origins, issues, early impact', *The Baltic International Yearbook of Cognition, Logic and Communication* 6, 1–52.

Paulhan, Frédéric (1927), 'La double fonction du langage', *Revue Philosophique* 104, 22–73.

Paulhan, Frédéric (1930 [1887]), *The Laws of Feeling*, trans. C. K. Ogden, London: Kegan Paul (trans. of *Les Phénomènes Affectifs, et les Lois de leur Apparition*, Paris: Ancienne Librairie Germer Baillière et Cie).

Peano, Giuseppe (1903), 'De Latino sine Flexione', *Revue des Mathématiques* 8:3, 74–83.

Pei, Mario (1968 [1958]), *One Language for the World*, New York: Devin-Adair.

Peirce, Charles Sanders (1977 [1903]), Double review of *What is Meaning?*, Welby (1983 [1903]), and *Principles of Mathematics*, Russell (1903), in Hardwick (1977), pp. 157–159 (original in *The Nation* 77, 308–309).

Peirce, Charles Sanders (1984 [1867]), 'On a new list of categories', *Writings of Charles S. Peirce*, vol. 2, ed. Edward C. Moore *et al.*, Bloomington: Indiana University Press, pp. 49–59 (original in *Proceedings of the American Academy of Arts and Sciences* 7, 287–298).

Petrilli, Susan (1988), 'Victoria Lady Welby and significs: an interview with H. Walter Schmitz', in *The Semiotic Web 1988*, ed. Thomas A Sebeok and Jean Umiker-Sebeok, The Hague: Mouton de Gruyter, pp. 79–92.

Petrilli, Susan (1999), 'The biological basis of Victoria Welby's significs', *Semiotica* 127:1/4, 23–66.

Petrilli, Susan (2009), *Signifying and Understanding: reading the works of Victoria Welby and the Signific Movement*, Berlin: De Gruyter Mouton.

Phillipson, Robert (1992), *Linguistic Imperialism*, Oxford: Oxford University Press.

Pietarinen, Ahti-Veikko (2009), 'Significs and the origins of analytic philosophy', *Journal of the History of Ideas* 70:3, 467–490.

Popper, Karl (1945), *The Open Society and its Enemies*, vol. 1, London: Routledge and Kegan Paul.

Popper, Karl (1959 [1934]), *The Logic of Scientific Discovery*, trans. Karl Popper, Julius Freed and Lars Freed, London: Hutchison (trans. of *Die Logik der Forschung*, Vienna: Springer).

Quine, Willard van Orman (1953 [1951]), 'Two dogmas of empiricism', in *From a Logical Point of View*, ed. Quine, Cambridge, MA: Harvard University Press, pp. 20–46 (original in *The Philosophical Review* 60, 20–43).

Ramsey, Frank P. (1923), Review of *Tractatus Logico-Philosophicus*, Wittgenstein (1922), *Mind* 32:128, 465–478.

Ramsey, Frank P. (1924), Review of *The Meaning of Meaning*, Ogden and Richards (1989 [1923]), *Mind* 33:129, 108–109.

Reisch, George A. (1997), 'Economist, epistemologist … and censor? On Otto Neurath's Index Verborum Prohibitorum', *Perspectives on Science* 5:3 (electronic resource: no page numbers).

Reisch, George (2005), *How the Cold War Transformed Philosophy of Science: to the icy slopes of logic*, Cambridge: Cambridge University Press.

Richards, Ivor Armstrong (1926 [1924]), *Principles of Literary Criticism*, London: Kegan Paul.

Richards, Ivor Armstrong (1926), *Science and Poetry*, London: Kegan Paul.

Richards, Ivor Armstrong (1930), *Practical Criticism*, London: Kegan Paul.

Richards, Ivor Armstrong (1932), *Mencius on the Mind*, Richmond: Curzon Press.

Richards, Ivor Armstrong (1935), *Basic in Teaching: east and west*, London: Kegan Paul.

Richards, Ivor Armstrong (1936), *The Philosophy of Rhetoric*, Oxford: Oxford University Press.

Richards, Ivor Armstrong (1943), *Basic English and its Uses*, London: Kegan Paul.

Richards, Ivor Armstrong (1948), 'Emotive meaning again', *The Philosophical Review* 57, 145–157.

Richards, Ivor Armstrong (1973 [1938]), *Interpretation in Teaching*, London: Routledge and Kegan Paul.

Richards, Ivor Armstrong (1977), 'Co-author of the "Meaning of Meaning"', in Florence and Anderson (1977), pp. 96–109.

Richardson, Alan W. (1998), *Carnap's Construction of the World: the* Aufbau *and the emergence of logical empiricism*, Cambridge: Cambridge University Press.

Riemer, Nick (2006), 'Reductive paraphrase and meaning: a critique of Wierzbickian semantics', *Linguistics and Philosophy* 29, 347–379.

Riemer, Nick, ed. (2016), *The Routledge Handbook of Semantics*, Oxford: Routledge.

Rosenberger, Woldemar (1902), *Wörterbuch der Neutralsprache (Idiom Neutral)*, Leipzig: E. Haberland.

Russell, Bertrand (1903), *Principles of Mathematics*, Cambridge: Cambridge University Press.

Russell, Bertrand (1905), 'On denoting', *Mind* 14, 479–493.

Russell, Bertrand (1906–1907), 'On the nature of truth', *Proceedings of the Aristotelian Society* 7, 28–49.

Russell, Bertrand (1910–1911), 'Knowledge by acquaintance and knowledge by description', *Proceedings of the Aristotelian Society* 11, 108–128.

Russell, Bertrand (1914), 'On the nature of acquaintance, part II', *The Monist* 24, 161–187.

Russell, Bertrand (1918–1919), 'The philosophy of logical atomism', *The Monist* 28, 495–527; 29, 32–63, 190–222, 345–80.

Russell, Bertrand (1919), 'On propositions: what they are and how they mean', *Proceedings of the Aristotelian Society*, Supplementary Volume 2, 1–43.

Russell, Bertrand (1921), *Analysis of Mind*, London: Allen and Unwin.

Russell, Bertrand (1923), 'On vagueness', *The Australasian Journal of Psychology and Philosophy* 1, 84–92.

Russell, Bertrand (1924), 'Logical atomism', in *Contemporary British Philosophy*, vol. 1, ed. J. H. Muirhead, London: Allen and Unwin, pp. 357–383.

Russell, Bertrand (1925), *What I Believe*, New York: Dutton.

Russell, Bertrand (1926 [1914]), *Our Knowledge of the External World*, London: Allen and Unwin.

Russell, Bertrand (1935), *Religion and Science*, New York: Henry Holt and Company.

Russell, Bertrand (1937 [1900]), *A Critical Exposition of The Philosophy of Leibniz*, London: Allen and Unwin.

Russell, Bertrand (1940), *An Inquiry into Meaning and Truth*, London: Allen and Unwin.

Russell, Bertrand (1959 [1957]), 'Mr Strawson on referring', in Russell (1959), pp. 238–245 (original in *Mind* 66:263, 385–389).

Russell, Bertrand (1959), *My Philosophical Development*, London: Allen and Unwin.

Russell, Bertrand (1967–1969), *The Autobiography of Bertrand Russell*, 3 vols, Boston: Little Brown.

Russell, Bertrand (1988 [1923]), 'The mastery of words', Review of *The Meaning of Meaning*, Ogden and Richards (1989 [1923]), in Slater and Frohmann (1988), pp. 135–137 (original in *The Nation and Athenaeum* 33, 87–88).

Russell, Bertrand (1988 [1926]), Review of *The Meaning of Meaning*, Ogden and Richards (1989 [1923]), in Slater and Frohmann (1988), pp. 138–144 (original in *The Dial* 81, 114–121).

Russell, Dora (1977), 'My friend Ogden', in Florence and Anderson (1977), pp. 82–95.

Russo, Paul (1989), *I. A. Richards: his life and work*, Baltimore: Johns Hopkins University Press.

Salzmann, Oswald (1913), *Das vereinfachte Deutsch: die Sprache aller Völker*, Leipzig: self-published.

Sapir, Edward (1925), 'Memorandum on the problem of an international auxiliary language', *Romanic Review* 16, 244–256.

Sapir, Edward (1929), 'Foundations of language', *International Auxiliary Language Association in the United States, Inc.: Annual Meeting, May 19, 1930*, New York: IALA, pp. 16–18.

Sapir, Edward (1930), *Totality*, Baltimore: Linguistic Society of America/Waverly Press.

Sapir, Edward (1931), 'Wanted: a world language', *American Mercury* 22, 202–209.

Sapir, Edward (1933), 'The case for a constructed international language (résumé)', *Actes du Deuxième Congrès International de Linguistes, Genève, 25–29 Aout 1931*, Paris: Libraire d'Amérique et d'Orient.

Sapir, Edward (1949 [1944]), 'Grading: a study in semantics', in Mandelbaum (1949), pp. 122–149.

Sapir, Edward and Morris Swadesh (1932), *The Expression of the Ending-point Relation in English, French, and German*, Baltimore: Linguistic Society of America/Waverly Press.

Saussure, Ferdinand de (1983 [1916]), *Course in General Linguistics*, trans. Roy Harris, London: Duckworth (trans. of *Cours de Linguistique Générale*, Paris: Payout).

Scheurmann, Erich (1920), *Der Papalagi: die Reden des Südseehäuptlings Tuiavii aus Tiavea*, Buchenbach: Felsenverlag.

Schiller, Ferdinand Canning Scott, Bertrand Russell and Harold Henry Joachim (1920), 'The meaning of "meaning": a symposium', *Mind*, 29:116, 385–414.

Schilpp, Paul Arthur, ed. (1962), *The Philosophy of Rudolf Carnap*, La Salle: Open Court.

Schlegel, August Wilhelm von (1818), *Observations sur la Langue et la Littérature Provençales*, Paris: Librairie grecque-latine-allemande.

Schlegel, Friedrich von (1808), *Ueber die Sprache und Weisheit der Indier*, Heidelberg: Mohr und Zimmer.

Schleicher, August (1860), *Die deutsche Sprache*, Stuttgart: Cotta.

Schleicher, August (1865), *Über die Bedeutung der Sprache für die Naturgeschichte des Menschen*, Weimar: H. Böhlau.

Schleyer, Johann Martin (1888), *Grosses Wörterbuch der Universalsprache Volapük*, Konstanz am Bodensee: Schleyers Zentralbüro der Weltsprache.

Schleyer, Johann Martin (1982 [1880]), *Volapük: die Weltsprache*, Hildesheim: Georg Olms.

Schleyer, Johann Martin (2001 [1900]), *Über die Pfuschersprache des Pseudo-Esperanto*, Schliegen: Edition Iltis.

Schmidt, Bernd (1984), *Malinowskis Pragmasemantik*, Heidelberg: Carl Winter Universitätsverlag.

Schmidt, Johann (1998 [1963]), *Geschichte der Universalsprache Volapük*, Saarbrücken: Edition Iltis.

Schmitz, H. Walter (1983), 'Victoria Lady Welby und die Folgen', *Zeitschrift für Semiotik* 5, 123–138.

Schmitz, H. Walter (1985a), *Significs and Language*, Amsterdam: John Benjamins.

Schmitz, H. Walter (1985b), 'Tönnies' Zeichentheorie zwischen Signifik und Wiener Kreis', *Zeitschrift für Soziologie* 14, 373–385.

Schmitz, H. Walter, ed. (1990), *Papers Presented on the Occasion of the 150th Anniversary of the Birth of Victoria Lady Welby (1837–1912)*, Amsterdam: John Benjamins.

Schmitz, H. Walter (1995), 'Anmerkungen zum Welby-Russell-Briefwechsel', in *History and Rationality*, ed. Klaus D. Dutz and Kjell-Ake Forsgren, Münster: Nodus, pp. 293–305.

Schumann, Wolfgang (1973), 'Memories of Otto Neurath', in Neurath und Cohen (1973), pp. 15–18.

Seiler, Martin (1991), 'Heinrich Gomperz (1873–1942): Philosophie und Semiotik', in *Philosophie und Semiotik*, ed. Ludwig Nagel, Elisabeth List, Jeff Bernard and Gloria Withalm, Vienna: Österreichische Gesellschaft für Philosophie, pp. 101–124.

Seiler, Martin (1994), 'Espitemologie, Sprachanalyse und Semiotik bei Heinrich Gomperz', *Heinrich Gomperz, Karl Popper und die österreichische Philosophie*, ed. Martin Seiler and Friedrich Stadler, Amsterdam: Rodopi, pp. 31–46.

Semon, Richard (1909), *Die mnemischen Empfindungen in ihren Beziehung zu den Originalempfindungen*, Leipzig: Wilhelm Engelmann.

Semon, Richard (1921 [1904]), *The Mneme*, London: Allen and Unwin (trans. of *Die Mneme als erhaltendes Prinzip im Wechsel des organischen Geschehens*, Leipzig: Wilhelm Engelmann).

Semple, Janet (1993), *Bentham's Prison: a study of the panopticon penitentiary*, Oxford: Oxford University Press.

Seuren, Pieter A. M. (1998), *Western Linguistics: an historical introduction*, Oxford: Blackwell.

Shelden, Michael (1991), *Orwell: the authorised biography*, London: Heinemann.

Shenton, Herbert N. (1930), 'Can social engineers improve the international language situation?', *Psyche* 11:1, 6–20.

Shenton, Herbert N. (1933), *Cosmopolitan Conversations: the language problems of international conferences*, New York: Columbia University Press.

Silverstein, Michael (2001 [1977]), 'The limits of awareness', in *Linguistic Anthropology: a reader*, ed. Alessandro Duranti, Oxford: Blackwell, pp. 382–401 (transcript of a lecture originally given in 1977).

Skinner, Burrhus Frederic (1957), *Verbal Behavior*, Englewood Cliffs: Prentice Hall.

Slater, John G. and Bernd Frohmann, eds. (1988), *Collected Papers of Bertrand Russell*, vol. 9, London: Allen and Unwin.

Slaughter, Mary M. (1982), *Universal Languages and Scientific Taxonomy in the Seventeenth Century*, Cambridge: Cambridge University Press.

Soames, Scott (2003), *Philosophical Analysis in the Twentieth Century*, Princeton: Princeton University Press.

Sperber, Hans (1914), *Über den Affekt als Ursache der Sprachveränderung – Versuch einer dynamologischen Betrachtung des Sprachlebens*, Halle an der Saale: Niemeyer.

Stadler, Friedrich (1997), *Studien zum Wiener Kreis. Ursprung, Entwicklung und Wirkung des Logischen Empirismus im Kontext*, Frankfurt am Main: Suhrkamp.

Stadler, Friedrich (1982), *Vom Positivismus zur 'wissenschaftlichen Weltauffassung': am Beispiel der Wirkungsgeschichte von Ernst Mach in Österreich von 1895 bis 1934*, Vienna: Locker.

Stadler, Friedrich, ed. (2003), *Vienna Circle and Logical Empiricism: re-evaluation and future perspectives*, Secaucus: Kluwer Academic Publishers.

Stebbing, L. Susan (1933), 'Logical positivism and analysis', *Proceedings of the British Academy of Sciences* 19, 53–87.

Stern, Gustaf (1931), *Meaning and Change of Meaning*, Gotheburg: Elanders.

Stevenson, Charles L. (1944), *Ethics and Language*, New Haven: Yale University Press.

Stojan, Petr E. (1929), *Bibliografio de Internacia Lingvo*, Geneva: Bibliografio Servo de Universala Esperanto-Asocio.

Strawson, Peter F. (1950), 'On referring', *Mind* 59, 320–344.

Strub, Harry (1989), 'The theory of panoptical control: Bentham's Panopticon and Orwell's *Nineteen Eighty-Four*', *The Journal of the History of the Behavioural Sciences* 25, 40–59.

Swadesh, Morris (1944), 'Scientific linguistics and Basic English', in Johnsen (1944), pp. 194–206.

Swadesh, Morris (1955), 'Towards greater accuracy in lexicostatistic dating', *International Journal of American Linguistics* 21, 121–137.

Swadesh, Morris (1972), *The Origin and Diversification of Language*, London: Routledge.

Swadesh, Morris and Alice Vanderbilt Morris, under direction of Edward Sapir (1934), *Preliminary Survey of the Relation Complexes of Starting-point, Passage-point, and Ending-point in Latin, Italian, Spanish, French, English, German, Russian; Esperanto, Novial, and Occidental*, manuscript, New York.

Szczesny, Gerhard (1969 [1966]), *The Case against Bertolt Brecht*, trans. Alexander Gode,

New York: F. Ungar (trans. of *Das Leben des Galilei und der Fall Bertolt Brecht*, Frankfurt am Main: Ullstein).

Tarski, Alfred (1956 [1933]), 'The concept of truth in formalised languages', *Logic, Semantics, Metamathematics: papers from 1923 to 1938*, trans. J. H. Woodger, Oxford: Oxford University Press, pp. 152–278 (trans. of various earlier versions, the earliest in Polish dating from 1933).

Thorndike, Edward L. and Laura H. V. Kennon (1927), *Progress in Learning an Auxiliary Language*, New York: IALA.

Tomalin, Marcus (2004), 'Leonard Bloomfield: linguistics and mathematics', *Historiographia Linguistica* 31:1, 105–136.

Tomalin, Marcus (2006), *Linguistics and the Formal Sciences: the origins of generative grammar*, Cambridge: Cambridge University Press.

Tonkin, Humphrey (1988), Review of *The Artificial Language Movement*, Large (1985), *Language in Society* 17:2, 282–287.

Tönnies, Ferdinand (1899–1900), 'Philosophical terminology (I–III)', *Mind* 8/9:31–33, 289–332, 467–491, 46–61.

Trabant, Jürgen (2012), *Weltansichten: Wilhelm von Humboldts Sprachprojekt*, München: Beck.

Uebel, Thomas (2007), *Empiricism at the Crossroads. The Vienna Circle's Protocol Sentence Debate*, Chicago: Open Court.

Uebel, Thomas (2008), 'On the production, history, and aspects of the reception of the Vienna Circle's manifesto ', *Perspectives on Science* 16:1, 70–102.

Ullmann, Stephen (1962), *Semantics: an introduction to the science of meaning*, Oxford: Blackwell.

Vaihinger, Hans (1924 [1911]), *The Philosophy of As-If*, trans. Charles Kay Ogden, London: Kegan Paul (trans. of *Die Philosophie des Als-Ob*, Leipzig: Felix Meiner).

Verbeke, Charles A. (1973), 'Caterpillar Fundamental English: a basic approach for multination technical communication in an industry', *Training and Development Journal* 27:2, 36–40.

Verein Ernst Mach (2006 [1929]), 'Wissenschaftliche Weltauffassung: der Wiener Kreis', in *Wiener Kreis*, ed. Michael Stöltzner and Thomas E. Uebel, Hamburg: Felix Meiner, pp. 1–29 (original published Vienna: Artur Wolf).

Voice of America (2009), *Special English Word Book*, Washington: Voice of America.

Wainger, Bertrand M. (1930), 'Henry Sweet – Shaw's Pymalion', *Studies in Philology* 27:4, 558–572.

Waismann, Friedrich (1979), *Wittgenstein and the Vienna Circle: conversations*, Oxford: Blackwell.

Walker, Leslie J. (1910), *Theories of Knowledge: absolutism, pragmatism, realism*, London: Longmans, Green and Co.

Walpole, H. (1937), 'The theory of definition and its application to vocabulary limitation', *The Modern Language Journal* 21, 398–402.

Wegener, Philip (1991 [1885]), *Untersuchungen über die Grundfragen des Sprachlebens*, Amsterdam: John Benjamins (original published Halle an der Saale: Niemeyer).

Welby, Victoria Lady (1983 [1903]), *What is Meaning?* Amsterdam: John Benjamins (original published London: Macmillan and Co.).

Welby, Victoria Lady (1985 [1893]), 'Meaning and metaphor', in Schmitz (1985a), reproduced with original pagination (original in *The Monist* 3:4, 510–525).

Welby, Victoria Lady (1985 [1896]), 'Sense, meaning and interpretation', in Schmitz (1985a), reproduced with original pagination (original in two parts: *Mind* 5:17, 24–37 and 5:18, 186–202).

Welby, Victoria Lady (1985 [1911]), *Significs and Language: the articulate form of our expressive and interpretative resources*, Amsterdam: John Benjamins (original published London: Macmillan).

Welby, Victoria Lady, George Frederick Stout and James Mark Baldwin (1902), 'Significs', in *Dictionary of Philosophy and Psychology in Three Volumes*, vol. 2, ed. J. M. Baldwin, New York: Macmillan, p. 529.

Wells, Herbert George (1933), *The Shape of Things to Come*, London: Hutchinson.

West, Michael (1944 [1939]), 'Vocabulary limitation', in Johnsen (1944), pp. 148–152 (original in *Journal of Education* 71, 582–584).

Whately, Richard (1845), *Elements of Logic*, Boston: James Munroe and Company.

White, Morton G. (1950), 'The analytic and synthetic: an untenable dualism', in *John Dewey: philosopher of science and freedom*, ed. Sidney Hook, New York: Barnes and Noble, pp. 316–333.

Whitehead, Alfred North and Bertrand Russell (1950 [1910–1913]), *Principia Mathematica*, 3 vols, Cambridge: Cambridge University Press.

Whorf, Benjamin Lee (1956), *Language, Thought and Reality: selected writings of Benjamin Lee Whorf*, Cambridge, MA: MIT Press.

Wierzbicka, Anna (1980), *Lingua Mentalis: the semantics of natural language*, Sydney: Academic Press.

Wierzbicka, Anna (1987), *English Speech Act Verbs: a semantic dictionary*, Sydney: Academic Press.

Wierzbicka, Anna (1988), *The Semantics of Grammar*, Amsterdam: John Benjamins.

Wierzbicka, Anna (1992), 'The search for universal semantic primitives', in *Thirty Years of Linguistic Evolution*, ed. Martin Pütz, Amsterdam: John Benjamins, pp. 215–242.

Wierzbicka, Anna (1996), *Semantics: primes and universals*, Oxford: Oxford University Press.

Wierzbicka, Anna (2011), 'Common language of all people: the innate language of thought', *Problems of Information Transmission* 47:4, 378–397.

Wierzbicka, Anna (2014), *Imprisoned in English: the hazards of English as a default language*, Oxford: Oxford University Press.

Wilkins, John (1968 [1668]), *An Essay Towards a Real Character and a Philosophical Language*, Menston: Scolar Press.

Willems, Klaas (2012), 'Intuition, introspection and observation in linguistic enquiry', *Language Sciences* 34, 665–681.

Wisdom, John (1930), 'Analysis and interpretation', *Psyche* 11:2, 11–31.

Wisdom, John (1931), *Interpretation and Analysis*, London: Kegan Paul.

Wittgenstein, Ludwig (1922), *Tractatus Logico-Philosophicus*, London: Routledge and Kegan Paul.

Wittgenstein, Ludwig (1953), *Philosophical Investigations*, Oxford: Blackwell.

Wittgenstein, Ludwig (1958), *The Blue and Brown Books*, Oxford: Blackwell.

Wolf, George (1988), 'C. K. Ogden', in *Linguistic Thought in England, 1914–1945*, ed. Roy Harris, London: Duckworth, pp. 85–105.

Wright, Georg Henrik von, ed. (1973), *Letters to C. K. Ogden, with Comments on the English Translation of the Tractatus Logico-Philosophicus*, Oxford: Blackwell.

Zamenhof, Ludwig Lazarus (1889 [1887]), *Dr Esperanto's International Language: introduction and complete grammar*, trans. Richard H. Geoghegan, Warsaw: self-published (trans. of Международный языкъ: Предисловie: Полный учебникъ por Rusoj, Warsaw: self-published).

Zamenhof, Ludwig Lazarus (1905), *Fundamento de Esperanto*, Paris: Hachette.

Zamenhof, Ludwig Lazarus (1911), 'International language', in *Papers on Inter-racial Problems*, ed. Gustav Spiller, London: P. S. King and Son, pp. 425–432.

Zamenhof, Ludwig Lazarus (1929 [1896]), Letter from Zamenhof to Nikolaj Afrikanoviĉ Borovko, in Zamenhof (1929), pp. 417–422.

Zamenhof, Ludwig Lazarus (1929), *Originala Verkaro*, Leipzig: Ferdinand Hirt und Sohn.

EU Authorised Representative:

Easy Access System Europe Mustamäe tee 50, 10621 Tallinn, Estonia

gpsr.requests@easproject.com

Printed and bound by CPI Group (UK) Ltd, Croydon, CR0 4YY

26/08/2025

01943803-0001